ARCHAEOLOGY
OF THE DREAMTIME

The Story of Prehistoric Australia and Its People

REVISED EDITION

JOSEPHINE FLOOD

Yale University Press   New Haven and London

Josephine Flood was born in Yorkshire and came to Australia in 1963 having completed her B.A. at Cambridge. She began lecturing in archaeology at the Australian National University soon after her arrival and has since gained her M.A. and Ph.D. from the university.

Dr Flood has participated extensively in field work in most States in Australia, her most recent research being on rock art and archaeology in the Northern Territory. She has published widely on Australian prehistory and is the author of two other books: *Four Miles High* (the story of two women's mountaineering expeditions to the Himalayas of India and Nepal, 1966) and *The Moth Hunters* (the first account of Aboriginal prehistory in the Australian Alps, 1980).

Dr Flood works as an Assistant Director in the field of Aboriginal heritage with the Australian Heritage Commission in Canberra.

This book is dedicated to Philip and Tim Scarr, in gratitude

First published in Australia in 1989 by Collins Publishers.

Published in the United States of America in 1990
by Yale University Press.

Printed in the United States of America.

Library of Congress catalog card number: 90-70927
International standard book number: 0–300–04924–2

1   3   5   7   9   10   8   6   4   2

CONTENTS

LISTS OF ILLUSTRATIONS

LIST OF COLOUR PLATES

All scales are in centimetres unless otherwise stated.
1. *Sthenurus* jawbone *in situ*, Cloggs Cave, Victoria
2. Waisted axe from New Guinea
3. Erosion at Lake Mungo, New South Wales
4. Koonalda Cave, South Australia
5. Bone bead from Devil's Lair, Western Australia
6. Kartan tools, South Australia
7. Barbed spear from Wyrie Swamp, South Australia
8. Kutikina Cave, Tasmania
9. Burial from tomb 108, Roonka, South Australia
10. Ice age hand stencils, Wargata Mina Cave, Tasmania
11. Fly River turtle painting, Little Nourlangie Rock, Northern Territory
12. Bogong moths at Mount Gingera, Australian Capital Territory
13. Fish traps at Brewarrina, New South Wales

LIST OF BLACK AND WHITE PLATES

1. Cloggs Cave, Buchan, Victoria
2. Mangrove log raft, Western Australia
3. Mungo III burial during excavation, New South Wales
4. Kow Swamp skull 5, Victoria
5. Kow Swamp skeleton 14 during excavation, Victoria
6. Necklace from Lake Nitchie, New South Wales
7. Robust skull from Cossack, Western Australia
8. Gracile skull from Lake Mungo, New South Wales
9. Malangangerr rockshelter, Kakadu National Park, Northern Territory
10. Excavation at Kenniff Cave, Queensland
11. Fernhill Tree Gully, Lake George, New South Wales

LIST OF FIGURES

PREFACE

This is a book about the archaeology of prehistoric Australia. It examines both what we know about Aboriginal prehistory and how we know it, with the emphasis on the tangible remains left by Australians of the distant past.

There are only two sources of knowledge about the really distant human past of Australia: archaeological evidence and Aboriginal oral traditions passed down as stories about the Dreamtime. The Dreamtime is the era of creation, the time of the great Spirit Ancestors, who have profoundly influenced the traditional pattern of life as Aborigines know it today. The myths tell the story of human origins in Australia, of which much has been substantiated by scientific investigation. Oral traditions about events that took place many thousands of years ago have endured: the eruption of volcanoes, the rising of the seas and the change from lush vegetation to desert in the heart of Australia.

The human story has been unfolding for over 40 000 years in Australia, and for 99.5 per cent of Australia's human history it is Aborigines who have been on the stage. Yet their past has been woefully neglected. A number of books have described Aboriginal life as it was at the time of first European settlement, but only three general books have been written about Australian prehistory: John Mulvaney's *Prehistory of Australia* and Geoffrey Blainey's *Triumph of the Nomads*, both published in 1975, and Peter White and Jim O'Connell's *A Prehistory of Australia, New Guinea and Sahul*, a textbook published by Academic Press in 1982. The reasons for adding another work to these distinguished predecessors are threefold. Firstly, a great deal of archaeological work has been done in recent years and many exciting new discoveries are presented to the public here for the first time. Secondly, the focus of this work is rather different, since it concentrates on the distant rather than the recent Aboriginal past and hence on archaeological rather than historical evidence. The story, therefore, covers events long before the period of European settlement. And lastly, this book also encompasses topics not dealt with by the other prehistories, such as Aboriginal oral traditions.

For the first 30 000 years of Australian prehistory, from 40 000 to 10 000 years ago, archaeological evidence is our only source of information, so this is examined in some detail. The last six chapters cover the last 10 000 years of prehistoric culture, from the rising of the sea at the end of the ice age until the dramatic impact of European colonization. There is so much information available on this more recent period that the approach is, of necessity, more selective.

Within the chronological framework adopted, the organization is by topic and by region, because there are significant regional differences.

Archaeology of the Dreamtime has been written for the general reader, for Aborigines interested in learning more of their own heritage, and for secondary and tertiary students. Every effort has been made to avoid jargon and unnecessary technical terms, but at the same time to maintain scientific integrity.

There are no easy answers to questions such as 'When did people first come to Australia?' 'Where did they come from?' 'Why did the giant marsupials become extinct?' or 'Why did the Tasmanians stop eating fish?'. In these cases the evidence and theories are presented and then the readers are left to make up their own minds. The Further Reading and Notes also give the opportunity to pursue particular topics or the prehistory of a particular region in greater depth. A list of radiocarbon dates for major archaeological sites is also included.

I would like to express my appreciation to those who have directly helped in the production of this book. The encouragement and support of my three children have been invaluable. Adrian, Michael and Nadine have all helped as critical sounding boards. Helen Campbell has also helped in this and many other ways. For maps and drawings I am indebted to Irene Jarvin, and for secretarial assistance to Margaret Stewart, Margaret Benson, Helen Deane, Julianne O'Connell, Joanne Campbell and Pam Dickhart. The manuscript was improved by the comments of Alex Barlow, Sandra Bowdler, Rhys Jones and Nigel Wace who read the whole, and of Jim Bowler, John Chappell, Charles Dortch and Jeannette Hope, who read certain parts. I am especially grateful to Sandra Bowdler for her detailed, constructive suggestions. Any errors are of course my own responsibility.

Illustration is a necessary and important part of any book on archaeology and I am grateful to all who have provided photographs or drawings – individual acknowledgements are given in the captions – but I should record the generous response from all those archaeologists whose assistance was sought.

Editing was carried out by Meryl Potter, whom I thank for her patience and outstanding skill. Thanks also go to Elizabeth Bradhurst and Patrick Coyle of Collins for their constant support and enthusiasm.

The Australian Heritage Commission and, in particular, Chairmen David Yencken, Kenneth Wiltshire and Pat Galvin and Directors Max Bourke and

Colin Griffiths, have been generous with support. Finally, I would like to acknowledge my great debt to John Mulvaney, Jack Golson and Rhys Jones, who have been a continuing source of advice, information and encouragement since I first turned to Australian prehistory.

This book was first published in 1983, but some updating and revisions have been incorporated in this new edition. In particular, chapter 9, *An ice age walk to Tasmania*, has been completely re-written to take account of the many new exciting archaeological discoveries there over the last five years. I am grateful to Richard Cosgrove and Steve Brown for the new information they provided for this chapter, to Jane Newbery for the new figure 9.1 and revisions to figure 2.3, and to Alan Thorne for useful discussions leading to up-dating of Part II on Human Origins.

Josephine Flood
Canberra, 1989

PART I

INTRODUCTION

CHAPTER ONE

DOCUMENTS OF STONE AND BONE

Archaeology is the study of human cultures in the past. In Australia this means that most archaeologists study the material evidence of past Aboriginal activity, although a growing number of historical archaeologists concentrate on the traces of early European settlement. The human story in Australia is generally divided into two periods, prehistoric and historic, prehistory being the period before the use of written records. Because there are no written records about prehistoric Aboriginal Australia, knowledge of the distant past comes from archaeological evidence and Aboriginal oral traditions handed down from generation to generation.

While Aborigines have sometimes said that they see no need for archaeology for they already know what happened in the past, they also acknowledge the value of scientific evidence showing the tremendous length, continuity and complexity of Aboriginal culture in Australia. If the time scale of human occupation of Australia were represented by one hour on a clock, Aboriginal society would occupy over fifty-nine and a half minutes, European society less than half a minute. Yet most Australian history books devote barely a chapter to the Aboriginal past.

What archaeologists try to do is to discover the patterns of past culture history, past life-styles, and the processes of culture change. Culture is the distinctive and complex system developed by a group of human beings to adapt to their environment. It includes ways of getting food, social organization, religion, artefacts, dwellings and the like. And because the environment is always changing, in small or large ways, so too culture is continually adapting and changing.

Australian Aboriginal traditional culture is no exception, but because the changes are less obvious than those in many other parts of the world, even as late as the 1920s Aborigines were categorized as 'unchanging man in an unchanging environment'. The first real archaeological excavation in Australia was not carried out till 1929,[1] and the first university post in Australian archaeology not established until the 1960s.[2] Since then there has been an amazing acceleration in archaeological studies and it has now been well established that Aboriginal culture has changed and evolved over more than 40 000 years. Moreover, Aboriginal society has the longest continuous cultural history in the world, its roots being back in the ice age of Pleistocene (the period from about 2 million years ago to 10 000 years ago), when the Australian continent was both larger and greener than today.

Australian Aborigines have been called by world-renowned anthropologist Claude Levi-Strauss, 'intellectual aristocrats' among early peoples. Outstanding features of traditional Aboriginal society are highly sophisticated religion, art and social organization, an egalitarian system of justice and decision-making, complex far-flung trading networks, and an ability to adapt and survive in some of the world's harshest environments.

Traditional Aboriginal society as it existed 200 years ago has been recorded by anthropologists, who study living human societies. Their data can then be used by archaeologists to provide analogies in the interpretation of prehistoric culture. Such ethnographic analogies are particularly useful in Australia because of the long continuity of Aboriginal culture, although they must always be used with caution, since amid the vast prehistoric continuities there are also fundamental changes.

It is fortunate that there is such a rich ethnography (writings about local indigenous people) about traditional Aboriginal society, for the archaeological record is largely restricted to stones and bones. These data, the results of field survey and excavation, serve as the documents from which we piece together the jigsaw of prehistory. Stone tools are the most lasting items, surviving in the soil under almost all conditions, but organic substances, such as bone, wood and shell, tend to perish after a few hundred years under normal Australian conditions. In a few remarkable exceptions conditions have remained constantly wet or dry over many millennia. The water-logged peat bog of Wyrie Swamp preserved wooden boomerangs for 10 000 years, bones of giant kangaroos dead for more than 20 000 years have been found in constantly dry desert sand, and bone tools of a similar antiquity have been found at Devil's Lair in Western Australia and other limestone caves.

Although the material traces of the distant past are usually fragmentary and confined to only the most lasting materials, archaeologists, in their detective hunt to piece together the events of the past, are aided by scholars from other disciplines.

Geologists, by studying the sediments and landforms associated with ancient campsites, contribute to discovering past environments and climate. Palynologists, from their analysis of pollen grains and charcoal contained in cores drilled out of lake beds, can establish what prehistoric vegetation was like and how much burning took place. Palaeontologists and palaeobotanists identify respectively the animal bones and plant remains from prehistoric sites, produc-

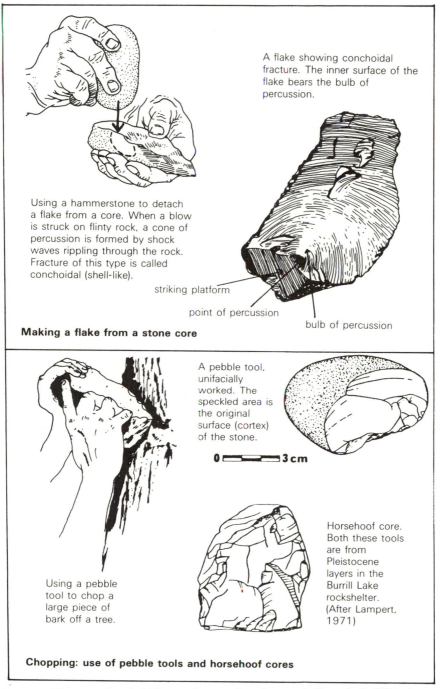

A flake showing conchoidal fracture. The inner surface of the flake bears the bulb of percussion.

Using a hammerstone to detach a flake from a core. When a blow is struck on flinty rock, a cone of percussion is formed by shock waves rippling through the rock. Fracture of this type is called conchoidal (shell-like).

striking platform

point of percussion

bulb of percussion

Making a flake from a stone core

A pebble tool, unifacially worked. The speckled area is the original surface (cortex) of the stone.

0 ▬▬▬▬ 3 cm

Using a pebble tool to chop a large piece of bark off a tree.

Horsehoof core. Both these tools are from Pleistocene layers in the Burrill Lake rockshelter. (After Lampert, 1971)

Chopping: use of pebble tools and horsehoof cores

Figure 1.1 *This page and overleaf. The manufacture and use of stone tools* (drawn by R. O'Brien)
A   Making a flake from a stone core
B   Chopping; the use of pebble tools and horsehoof cores
C   Wood-working with scrapers
D   Chopping with ground-edge axes

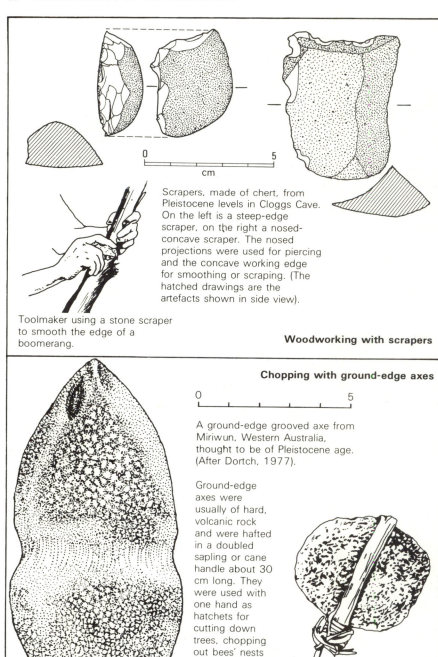

0 — 5
cm

Scrapers, made of chert, from
Pleistocene levels in Cloggs Cave.
On the left is a steep-edge
scraper, on the right a nosed-
concave scraper. The nosed
projections were used for piercing
and the concave working edge
for smoothing or scraping. (The
hatched drawings are the
artefacts shown in side view).

Toolmaker using a stone scraper
to smooth the edge of a
boomerang.

Woodworking with scrapers

Chopping with ground-edge axes

0 ———————————— 5

A ground-edge grooved axe from
Miriwun, Western Australia,
thought to be of Pleistocene age.
(After Dortch, 1977).

Ground-edge
axes were
usually of hard,
volcanic rock
and were hafted
in a doubled
sapling or cane
handle about 30
cm long. They
were used with
one hand as
hatchets for
cutting down
trees, chopping
out bees' nests
or shaping a
shield or canoe.

ing important information not only about past fauna, vegetation and environment but also about prehistoric human diet.

Human remains are the province of the physical anthropologist, who finds out about the appearance of prehistoric people and their physical links with other human groups. By a careful study of the form of human skulls – the most durable part of a skeleton – the age and sex of the dead person can be determined, together with their physical affinities with other human populations. Finally, physicists and chemists have developed methods of dating organic materials, such as charcoal and shell, from prehistoric sites.

The archaeologist's particular role is to study artefacts, the material traces of past behaviour. An artefact is 'anything which exhibits any physical attributes that can be assumed to be the result of human activity'.[3] Artefacts thus include stone or bone tools, butchered animal bones, and rock engravings. There is both continuity and change in Australia's prehistoric tool kit (figure 1.1). Stone tools have been in use from the beginnings of humankind in Australia until the twentieth century. Some, such as adzes and scrapers, were tools to make tools, so they tended to be in use continent-wide and to change little over the millennia. Other more specialized types, such as stone spear points, were in fashion more briefly and regionally, so they can be used as cultural markers, diagnostic of a particular time and place in the prehistoric world.

In general in Australia there had been a progression from large, heavy stone tools to lighter, smaller ones, and from simple hand-held, general purpose tools to more specialized forms, including composite ones.[4] Composite tools involve mounting or hafting tools on a handle for greater leverage. In nineteenth century Aboriginal Australia most stone tools were hafted, but the widespread adoption of hafting had been a relatively recent occurrence in Australian prehistory.

While a remarkable amount of information may be derived even from a single isolated artefact found lying on the ground, the most valuable find is a site with a number of artefacts in their cultural context. A site is any place containing traces of past human activity: it may be a scatter of a few stone artefacts on the ground surface, a mound of shells, or 'midden', the remains perhaps of a single meal, or a cave containing debris from thousands of years of human occupation.

The archaeologist carefully records the location of all artefacts in a site. If the site is stratified, with more than one layer of occupation debris, an excavation may be carried out, and the precise position of each artefact recorded. It can thus be determined which artefacts are associated with each other and to which layer or archaeological horizon they belong. When a site has been excavated, it should be possible to say which artefacts belong together and which are the younger ones.[5]

The relative age of artefacts is established by the 'law of superposition', the principle that the lowest occupation debris in a site is older than that accumulated on top of it. The absolute age can be established by radiocarbon dating, if there are sufficient organic remains present such as charcoal or shell. Radiocarbon dating is based on the fact that the percentage of the radiocarbon isotope carbon 14 (C-14) in living organisms is equal to that in the atmosphere. When the organism dies, its C-14 begins to disintegrate at a known rate (one half every 5570 years). The age of an organic object can thus be calculated by measuring the amount of C-14 left in any gram of organic material and comparing this with what is normally present in a modern sample or standard. Since the initial quantity of C-14 in a sample is low, samples more than about 40 000 years old hold too little for dating, although efforts are now being made, with some success, to extend the limit of detectability back to 70 000 years and beyond.

Radiocarbon dating does not give a precise date as to when the death of an animal or shell occurred or exactly when a tree was cut down and used as firewood, producing the charcoal that is the most common material to be dated by this method. Thus radiocarbon years do not precisely equal calendar or solar years. When a date is received from a radiocarbon dating laboratory, it will bear a statistical plus or minus factor and will be expressed in years BP, which means Before the Present – the Present being 1950, when this dating method was first developed. For example, in the date 4000 ± 200 BP the 200 years represents one standard deviation and means that there are two chances out of three that the reading is between 4200 and 3800 years BP. However, there is a further complication: radiocarbon dates do not calibrate exactly with dates obtained from tree ring dating, because the amount of C-14 in the atmosphere has fluctuated over time. Since radiocarbon dates can only be corrected over the last 8000 years by comparison with tree rings, no C-14 dates in Australia have been calibrated, which means that they will generally be a few hundred years too young. In any case, all C-14 dates are approximate, but without them Australian prehistory would be virtually undated.

Dating is only one of the archaeologist's tools in unravelling the past and reconstructing prehistoric lifeways. Analysis of artefacts can tell us a great deal about past cultural systems, prehistoric people's level of technological skill, diet, settlement patterns, seasonal movement, trading partners, cultural groupings, and even religious and social systems. And by studying remains from different periods, the archaeologist can also uncover cultural changes through time, such as changes in diet or artefact types. The next step is to explain why such changes took place and what they meant, in other words the process or mechanisms by which cultures change.

Archaeology is both a science and an art, utilizing scientific data and methods to produce the art of prehistory. Fieldwork, such as a survey for prehistoric surface sites or excavation of a stratified cave deposit, is only the beginning. Then comes analysis of the data, placing of the artefacts and site records in the appropriate museum, and finally publication of the archaeologist's findings and their significance in the general context of Australian prehistory.

To give an idea of the whole process, the rest of this chapter is devoted to description of the discovery, excavation and study of one ice age cave. In the whole of mainland south-eastern Australia, only one cave has been found so far with Pleistocene human occupation and good preservation of bone. This is Cloggs Cave in eastern Victoria.[6]

People sometimes ask, 'how do you find sites?' The answer is that fieldwork usually starts in libraries, reading what has already been written about the region in question: not only the ethnography, but also accounts of the area by geologists, foresters, historians, bushwalkers and cavers. The next step is to seek from local people information about where caves or rockshelters are located or where some stone tools have been ploughed up. In the case of Cloggs Cave, a combination of these approaches plus a little luck led me to the site.

I had chosen the south-eastern highlands for a regional archaeological study, for there is a fatal fascination and challenge about an area completely blank on the archaeological map. The likelihood of finding any early human occupation in the Snowy Mountains area seemed remote, and everyone said that I would find nothing. Fortunately, they were wrong. Not only did I find a great deal of evidence concerning the last few thousand years of highland prehistory but I also discovered one major ice age site.

I was looking for a cave in, or as close as possible to, the Snowy Mountains to find out how early the highlands were occupied. I therefore drew on a map a series of concentric circles from the top of Mt Kosciusko, Australia's highest mountain with a height of 2228 metres, and explored every likely cave within each ring. This is not as difficult as it may sound, for most states now have guidebooks that list and describe caves of interest to speleologists. These are usually confined to limestone caves and do not include sandstone and granite rockshelters, but it was limestone caves in which I was particularly interested, because they have the best preservation conditions for bone tools and faunal remains.

It emerged that there are few caves or rockshelters suitable for human occupation in the south-eastern highlands, and those I tried, such as Yarrangobilly, proved apparently barren. However, in the outermost concentric circle lay Buchan, a region of over 200 limestone caves in eastern Victoria. Buchan lies at the foot of the Victorian Alps, 76 metres above sea level and 37 kilometres inland from the present coast. Through consultation with the Victorian Speleological Association I was able to eliminate many of the 200 caves as being too wet, steep or rocky for human occupation. Then, reduced to a 'short list', I began visiting the possible candidates one by one.

I was driving down the Buchan to Orbost road on my way to another cave when I noticed a dark cleft in a cliff near the top of a hill (plate 1). This

Plate 1. *Cloggs Cave, Buchan, Victoria. The small black overhang on the right protects the rockshelter and the high cleft leads into the inner chamber*

meant that it was likely to be a dry cave, instead of having a river running through like so many others, so I abandoned my previous plans and headed across the paddocks up to the cliff, even ignoring what looked suspiciously like a bull!

Cloggs Cave, for such it was, proved to be just what I had been looking for. Outside the cave entrance was a rockshelter with the roof blackened from the smoke of many campfires. A short rocky passage led into a dimly lit inner cavern, with high cathedral-like roof. I had feared there would be a rock-strewn floor; instead the earth floor was soft and dry, perfect for prehistoric and indeed modern campers. The back of the cave is higher than the entrance, which means that cold air drains out but warm air remains inside, simply rising to the back of the cave where there is a narrow passage but no exit. In fact, in every way it was a perfect prehistoric residence. Even had there been no traces of prehistoric occupation, I would have done a test excavation, but there were some small artefacts and mussel shells on the surface of the rockshelter floor.

The first step in organizing the excavation was to obtain permission to excavate from both the landowner and the State authority with statutory responsibility for Aboriginal sites. Then a team of student diggers was arranged and equipment was borrowed from the Australian Institute of Aboriginal Studies, who were generously financing the research. At last, all was ready and we set off for what was to prove the first of three seasons of excavation at the site.

The Cloggs Cave project began with making detailed maps of the site, with both plan and profile views. When a full record had been made of the site before excavation, digging commenced both in the rockshelter and the inner chamber of the cave.

The digging was a slow, painstaking process. No tools larger than a trowel were used, and everything was screened through fine mesh sieves. At times dental tools and soft paint brushes were used to prize or gently brush the covering off artefacts and bones so that they could be identified, photographed and fully recorded in position before removal. Small areas were dug at any one time and the deposit sieved, so that if any small artefacts were found during the screening rather than during the digging, their original position could be established reasonably accurately.

There are varying views on how much of a site should be dug. In the past it was the custom to excavate the whole, or at least most, of a site. This total approach has the advantage that one can see how various parts of the site were used for activities such as tool-manufacturing, sleeping, or cooking. It has been done very effectively in some overseas sites, especially in France, but there most of the caves were completely dug out in this total approach in the nineteenth century.

In Australia, prehistory is still in its infancy, little is known of the vast continent, and there are far more known sites than archaeologists available. It is, therefore, more practical to carry out a large number of small-scale digs in order to gain a preliminary idea of Australia's archaeological resources, rather than to spend twenty years on a single site. The main reason for doing small test excavations is that, by only digging a small pit in a site, the rest of the site is left for the future, when scientific methods will have advanced so that even more information is gained from the site than at present.

Why then dig at all? There are several good reasons. One is the need to answer specific questions about people in the past, to test carefully formulated hypotheses about prehistoric life. These may be fairly general questions, such as 'How long have people lived here?' 'What did they eat?' 'What were their tools like?' Or they may be very specific. Such research is an important scientific pursuit in its own right. And before we can protect the prehistoric past, we must know what is there and how important it is. This necessitates survey and sometimes excavation. For example, Cloggs Cave lies in an area containing minerals and good quality limestone that is being extensively quarried for building material. If its archaeological importance had not been established, it might have been inadvertently destroyed.

The increase in knowledge that each excavation brings (and even finding nothing can tell you something!) helps to predict the location of other important sites. When enough research has been done in a region, it becomes possible to predict with reasonable accuracy how many and what types of site will be present in other unsurveyed parts of the region. Finally, much of the archaeology being done nowadays is salvage archaeology: excavation of sites that will be destroyed because they stand in the way of developments such as mines, reservoirs, pipelines or housing projects.

The size of an excavation depends on many factors. The minimum size pit that it is practicable to work in is 1 metre square, and if the deposit is deep, a larger pit will be needed. The usual technique in excavating a rockshelter is to put a trench at least 1 metre wide from the back wall right out beyond the edge of the shelter down the slope below, which often contains occupational debris. In this way the excavation may pick up traces of perhaps a sleeping area against the rock wall, then perhaps a stone-tool manufacturing area sheltered from the elements, cooking hearths near the front of the overhang, and occupational debris such as food refuse thrown or fallen down onto the slope.

The Cloggs Cave rockshelter divided naturally into two zones: the area under the smoke-blackened overhang and the area outside the entrance to the inner chamber. A small excavation was carried out in both these zones. The overhang area proved to be a chipping floor. Thousands of small stone chips and flakes showed that this had been a tool manufacturing area. Only a few definite implements were present and they were all small tools including backed blades and small flattish scrapers. Radiocarbon dates from the basal layers of this occupation showed that it belonged to the last 1000 years.

Outside the cave entrance, a similar small tool industry gave way lower down to something quite different. The floor was a jumbled mass of huge limestone blocks interspersed with earth, dust and rubble. It was not a promising deposit and the diggers' enthusiasm was flagging when we came across the first large pebble tool, with an encrustation of carbonate testifying that it had been in the ground for much longer than the fresh-looking small tools above. Our efforts redoubled, and eventually this area of 5 square metres outside the cave entrance yielded three pebble-tools and eight steep-edged scrapers, all of them carbonate encrusted.

Meanwhile excavation had also commenced in the inner chamber, where a pit of 4 square metres was opened up against the far wall of the lower cave. There were no artefacts on the surface and the top 20 centimetres of dusty earth yielded only two small tools. This might have discouraged some, but I was convinced that if Pleistocene people used any caves in south-eastern Australia for shelter, they would have used Cloggs, for who could resist such an ideal piece of prehistoric real estate? I was right, for below the sterile surface layer we came across an occupation layer of consolidated ash and charcoal from ancient hearths. This layer eventually proved to be 8000 years old. And it was only the youngest occupation! When the sterile surface layer from the area between the pit and the entrance was removed, we found that the hearth level continued right across this lower part of the cave floor. (This area has now been covered up again with plastic sheeting and the surface earth replaced, to await possible future excavation.)

The hearth layer consisted of a series of fireplaces containing ash, charcoal and burnt bones, surrounded by hearth stones, river pebbles blackened and cracked by heating. These probably result from the use of 'ground ovens', which were recorded by such observers as Richard Helms as being in use in south-eastern Australia in the nineteenth century. According to Helms, a fire was made in which stones were heated, then game was placed on top of the heated stones, covered first with bark and green bushes, and then with hot ashes, and left to cook.

The burnt bones in the hearth layer may be merely the result of lighting fires on top of cave earth already containing a lot of bone. They cannot, therefore, be assumed to be human food debris. In fact, in this situation it is virtually impossible to distinguish between the remains of human meals, animal predation, and natural death in the cave. However, at least we know which species were present in the late Pleistocene period. The fauna included possums, gliders, koalas, bandicoots, kangaroos, rock and swamp wallabies, rats, marsupial mice, wombats and a wide range of birds. No fish bones or shellfish remains were present, so if these foods were exploited, they were not brought back to the cave for cooking.

There were a few stone artefacts in the hearth layer and, as digging progressed downward, more artefacts and a great deal of bone were recovered. Indeed, parts of the deposit could be described as a bone bed. The bones found close to the rock wall were more numerous and larger than those in the centre of the cave. Two cubic metres of deposit from a square adjacent to the rock wall yielded 11 368 grams of bone, of which 10 906 grams, or almost 90 per cent, were from small mammals. Yet the same volume of deposit in a square further away from the wall produced only 4487 grams, of which 2244 grams, or only 50 per cent, were from small mammals. Why the difference? If the same sort of animal bones were found in both areas but just in different quantities, it would seem that the bone had simply fallen or been swept against the cave walls. However, the much larger proportion of small creatures found near the cave wall made me examine the wall closely. I found projecting ledges where birds could sit. What seems to have happened is that owls brought their prey to the cave, sat on the ledges, ate their catch, and then regurgitated the remains of their dinner on to the floor below. Bones derived from the regurgitated pellets of owls show the following characteristics: the bones are generally unbroken and whole skulls may be present; the animals represented are small (the largest is about the size of a bandicoot); the largest-sized animals are represented by juveniles. The small mammal bones found close to the walls of

Cloggs Cave show all these characteristics, so they are almost certainly derived from owl predation.

The mass of bone was analysed by palaeontologist Jeannette Hope, and the species were identified from their jaws, and the minimum number of each species present in each level of each square of excavation was established. This

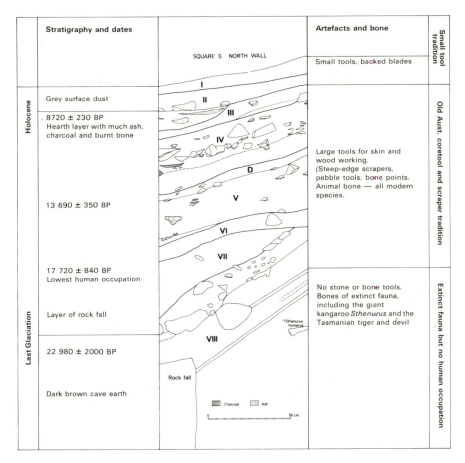

Figure 1.2 *The stratification and evidence from Cloggs Cave, Victoria*

was done by counting for each species the number of left and right mandibles and left and right maxillae, and then taking the number of jaws in the largest of these four categories as the minimum number for the species. Twenty-nine species of mammals were found in Cloggs Cave, representing a minimum of 1350 individual animals.

A column sample was also taken from the cave. This involved taking a 50 × 50 centimetre pillar of the deposit layer by layer, putting the deposit of each layer into a plastic bag and taking them back to the laboratory for detailed analysis. Analysis included 'flotation', a process in which each bag of the column sample was immersed in water, causing bone, seeds or any other organic matter to float up to the surface. Using this technique, we were able to recover enough charcoal to obtain a whole series of dates for the deposit. We also found organic matter, such as 12 000-year-old leaves and coprolites, fossilized faeces of animals. Further analysis of the contents of the coprolites told us what grasses animals were eating 20 000 years ago.

As we dug on downwards, it became clear that the occupation was very old. The colour of the bones changed from white at the top to dark orange at the bottom. The bones of locally extinct species also began to appear, such as *Pseudomys higginsi*, the long-tailed rat which now frequents rainforests in Tasmania. At a depth of 2 metres no more artefacts were found, but below the lowest traces of human occupation was the jaw of a giant extinct kangaroo, *Sthenurus orientalis* (colour plate 1). Also from this lowest layer came teeth of the Tasmanian tiger and the Tasmanian devil. Some of the associated bone bore teethmarks, which indicated that the cave may have been a lair of one of these carnivorous predators 20 000 years ago.

Huge limestone blocks which could not be removed had fallen from the roof so further digging was prevented. However, the cave floor could not have been very far below the lowest excavated level, because near the bottom of the pit we kept encountering stalagmites, the limestone formations that grow up from a cave floor as the result of water dripping from the roof.

Excavations at Cloggs Cave allow us to reconstruct its prehistory with a reasonable degree of certainty (figure 1.2). Before humans first occupied the cave, it was at times a lair of the Tasmanian devil and tiger, at other times a home for rock wallabies. Outside the cave, the landscape was similar to today's, with grassland and dry sclerophyll woodland bordering the river, but the climate was considerably colder and rather wetter than at present. Giant marsupials, such as the large kangaroo, still inhabited the area but gradually died out as the climate became more arid.

Then, some 17 000 years ago, humans began to use the cave. At first they used simple flakes and pebble tools of local quartz, but gradually their toolkit expanded to include scrapers of chert and jasper. They only visited the cave occasionally, and in the meantime it provided a home for owls. The cave was fairly dry, but drips from the limestone roof slowly built up stalagmites, and from time to time small stalactites fell from the ceiling into the soft earth floor. Occasionally a large stone block also crashed down.

Use of the cave increased between about 13 000 and 9000 years ago, as it became warmer at the end of the glacial phase. During the daytime the rockshelter was used; the rock ledges provided warm sitting places and a good vantage point out over the valley. At night, fires were lit on the cave floor from *Eucalyptus* wood. The group gathered round, heating hearth stones and cooking food items collected during the day, whittling with scrapers to make wooden spears and boomerangs, and rubbing hides with smooth river pebbles until they were pliable enough to sew together as cloaks. With sharp quartz flakes the possum or kangaroo skins were trimmed to size, holes were pierced with a bone point, its tip ground and polished to needle-like sharpness, and kangaroo tail sinews were chewed till supple enough to be used as thread.

About 8500 years ago, the climate became so warm that the inner chamber of Cloggs Cave was permanently vacated. Only the rockshelter was used as a camping place by later hunter-gatherers. Over the last thousand years occasional groups camped there, manufacturing small, backed blades and quartz flakes and eating fresh-water mussels from the river. Then came European settlement. Aborigines and Europeans co-existed in the Buchan Valley from the 1830s to 1860s, and the hunter-gatherers learned the use of clay pipes and steel axes. Then came measles and other epidemics and the group died out, leaving the cave to the bats, and later to the bushwalkers and speleologists. Now it has been placed on the Register of the National Estate by the Australian Heritage Commission, and the archaeological remains are protected against vandals by a steel grille, through which it is possible to peer, but not to disturb the site.

The significance of Cloggs Cave is the long sequence of artefacts and fauna that it revealed, which enabled reconstruction of the cultural and environmental history of the region over 20 000 years. Radiocarbon dates provide a firm chronological framework for changes in tool technology and fauna, and in particular for the presence of extinct megafauna. There are very few indisputable dates for megafauna in Australia, so the Cloggs Cave evidence is of particular importance. So too is the evidence that megafauna and humans were *not* associated, in view of the controversy about man's part in the extinction of the megafauna (see chapter 12).

Artefacts at Cloggs Cave are not numerous, but the few found are important (see figure 1.1). The first evidence that bone tools went back into the ice age was found there, and this has since been confirmed by evidence from Devil's Lair and a few other sites. The Cloggs Cave Pleistocene toolkit also bears a close resemblance to that from the 8000-year-old levels at Rocky Cape Cave in northern Tasmania. This similarity strongly supports the derivation of Tasmanian culture from the mainland in the Pleistocene by means of the land bridge that then spanned Bass Strait. Cloggs Cave is still the only ice age site in the south-eastern corner of mainland Australia in which bone and bone tools are preserved and it provides a valuable reference point with which to compare the new finds described from other Pleistocene sites.

CHAPTER TWO

THE FIRST BOAT PEOPLE

The truth is, of course, that my own people, the Riratjingu, are descended from the great
Djankawu who came from the island of Baralku far across the sea. Our spirits return to Baralku
when we die. Djankawu came in his canoe with his two sisters, following the morning star
which guided them to the shores of Yelangbara on the eastern coast of Arnhem Land. They
walked far across the country following the rain clouds. When they wanted water they plunged
their digging stick into the ground and fresh water flowed. From them we learnt the names of
all the creatures on the land and they taught us all our Law.

That is just a little bit of the truth. Aboriginal people in other parts of Australia have
different origins and will tell you their own stories of how the mountains came to be, and the
rivers, and how the tribes grew and followed the way of life of their Spirit Ancestors.

The huge Wandjina, makers of thunder, rain and lightning, soared over the sea to Western
Australia. Their faces stare at us from the cave walls of the Kimberley Ranges and the spears
that fought their giant battles are still in the sands on the coast north of Derby. The giant
Rainbow Serpent emerged from beneath the earth and as she moved, winding from side to
side, she forced her way though the soil and rocks, making the great rivers flow in her path,
and carving through mountains she made the gorges of northern Australia. From the Rainbow
Serpent sprang many tribes, and tales about her are told all over Arnhem Land – over to
Western Australia, in central Australia and even to New South Wales. Our paintings on rocks
illustrate this true story about one of our Ancestors . . .

In Queensland Giroo Gurrll, part man and part eel, rose out of the water near
Hinchinbrook Island and named the animals, birds and all the places there, while the great
Ancestor Chivaree the Seagull paddled his canoe from the Torres Islands down the western
coast of Cape York to Sandy Beach where his canoe turned into stone.[1]

Many Aboriginal myths about origins, like this one recounted by Wandjuk
Marika, agree with scientific evidence that the Aborigines came to Australia
from across the sea. There are innumerable stories about the beginning of
Creation in the Dreamtime, but in northern Australia one of the major themes
concerns the arrival of the Great Earth Mother, symbol of fertility and creator
of life. Amongst the Kakadu people of the Alligator Rivers region the great
ancestress was called Imberombera. Imberombera came from across the sea and
arrived on the coast of Arnhem Land. Her womb was filled with children and
from her head were suspended woven dilly bags in which she carried yams,
bulbs and tubers. She travelled far and wide, she formed the hills, creeks,

plants and animals and left behind her many spirit children, giving a different language to each group.

The Gunwinggu people of Arnhem Land tell a similar story about the Mother, Waramurungundji, who came across the sea from the north-west, the direction of Indonesia, to land on the north Australian coast at the beginning of Creation. Not only did these Dreamtime ancestors come from across the sea, but they also came by canoe.

Some Aborigines have always believed that their ancestors came from across the sea in canoes in the Dreamtime, and now scientists have come to the same conclusion from archaeological and other evidence. In the same way that archaeology has revealed material traces of the oral traditions enshrined in Homer's Iliad and Odyssey or the Old Testament stories of the Bible, it has uncovered evidence for some of the historic events remembered in the rich body of Aboriginal myths.

The human history of Australia encompasses the time since the first migrant stepped ashore – which we now know from archaeological evidence was well in excess of 40 000 years ago. To begin at the beginning of prehistory (the whole period before 1788), there is no possibility that human evolution occurred in Australia independently of the rest of the world, for the ape-like ancestors from which *Homo sapiens* – the modern human race – developed in Africa have never been present in Australia. Where, then, did the Australian Abori-

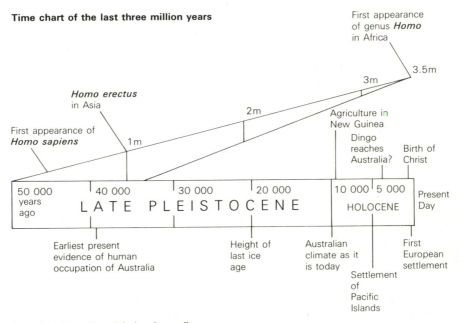

Figure 2.1 *Time chart of the last three million years*

ginal race originate? The first migrants could not have walked to Australia but must have come across the sea. Since people have been in South-East Asia for more than a million years, it would theoretically have been possible for Australia to have been colonized any time during this period (figure 2.1). There was, however, one serious barrier to cross – water.

At no time during the last three million years has there been a complete land bridge between the Asian and Australian continents. And before then the gulf was even wider. We know from geological evidence that until some fifty million years ago, Australia was part of the great southern continent of Antarctica, well removed from the Asian mainland. It had by then evolved a marsupial fauna. About thirty-five million years ago, the Australian continent drifted northwards, acting as a Noah's Ark for the marsupials. Australia was isolated until about twenty-five to fifteen million years ago, when it approached the southern fringes of the island chain of the East Indies. Austra-

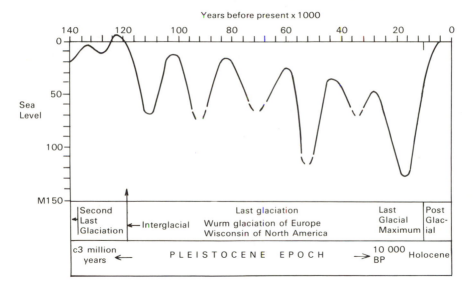

Figure 2.2 *Changes in sea level over the last 140 000 years. During the last interglacial some 120 000 years ago (a period of warm climate and consequent high sea level between glaciations) the sea stood 5 to 8 metres higher than its present level. Thereafter, until about 10 000 years ago, sea level has always been lower than today. The two major lowerings (to about 120 to 150 metres below present level) occurred around 52 000 and 18 000 years ago. (After Chappell and Thom 1977; Chappell 1983)*

lia is still in fact a continental raft drifting northwards, but it will take some time to reach Asia at the current rate of less than 5 centimetres a year.

The lack of Asian animals in Australia is evidence that for many millions of years there has been a significant sea barrier between Asia and Australia, which prevented them spreading southward. For the last two million years (the Pleistocene or ice age), the sea gap isolating Australia from Asia is thought never to have been less than 50 kilometres wide.

The world's sea level has fluctuated dramatically during the last million years as the result of a series of glacial periods. During these glaciations, the mean annual temperature dropped by as much as 6 to 10 degrees Celsius, much of the world's water was frozen into ice sheets at the poles, and vast glaciers made large areas of the northern hemisphere uninhabitable. The huge amounts of water locked up in ice sheets caused a drop in sea level of as much as 150 metres (figure 2.2).[2] This turned the two and a half million square kilometres

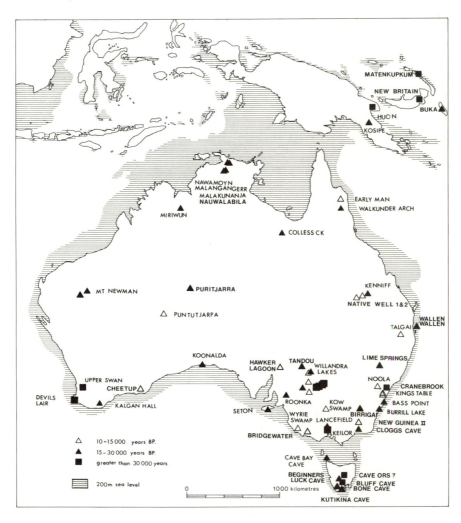

Figure 2.3 *Pleistocene sites in Australia and New Guinea*

of continental shelf around Australia into dry land and added on to South-East Asia an area the size of the Indian sub-continent.

When the drop in sea level was only 65 metres, the continent of 'Greater Australia' stretched from the equator to latitude 45° south and included not only Papua New Guinea and Tasmania but also the present Gulf of Carpentaria, Arafura Sea and north-west shelf (figure 2.3). It was possible to walk from Burma to Bali, from New Guinea to northern Australia, and from southern Australia to Tasmania, but the gap between the Australian continent and Asia remained a substantial water barrier.

The Australian continental shelf is known as Sahul Land, that fringing Asia, as Sunda Land. Sunda Land includes islands on the continental shelf of Asia, such as Java, Sumatra and Kalimantan. The edge of the Sunda shelf marks the south-eastern boundary of the oriental faunal region. The Sahul shelf marks the boundary of the Australian faunal region. In between lies a zone of thousands of islands, usually termed Wallacea, after the nineteenth century geographer Alfred Russel Wallace. Wallacea is not a distinct faunal zone but includes many different regional sets of fauna.[3]

Wallacea is also a geologically unstable area, which means that land bridges or stepping-stone islands that once existed may have disappeared. The distribution of fossil land mammals, including the extinct elephant-like *Stegodon*, on islands such as the Philippines, Sulawesi, Flores and Timor, suggests that water barriers between Sunda Land and these islands were much less at some time in the distant past than they are now. Opinion is divided on the question of whether there was early human occupation of some of the islands of Wallacea.[4]

Beyond the islands of Wallacea there was still a wide stretch of sea to cross to Australia. Humans managed to cross this in early prehistoric times, but the only other mammals, apart from birds and bats, that made the crossing were rats, mice and dingoes. Evidence suggests that dingoes were brought to Australia by humans, but the Asian ancestors of Australian rodents arrived unaided, probably carried across on logs or 'rafts' of vegetation more than two million years ago.[5]

ROUTES TO AUSTRALIA

We tend to imagine that the first migrants would have taken the shortest and most logical route from Asia to Australia. But we must constantly remind ourselves that the shape of the continent was different then and that these people had no maps, did not know that Australia existed, and even after arrival would have had no idea that they had reached a continent rather than another small island. It is likely that there was nothing deliberate or planned about the first settlement of Australia. Planned long-distance voyages, such as those that colonized the Pacific Islands, are probably a phenomenon of only the last few thousand years.

The routes by which the first migrants may have arrived in Australia have been examined in great detail by distinguished American anthropologist Professor Joseph Birdsell (figure 2.4).[6] Although the landfalls in Australia must

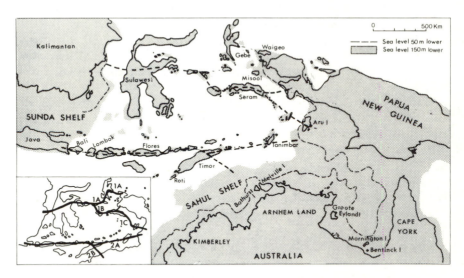

Figure 2.4 *The region between the Sunda and Sahul shelves and possible routes to Australia*
Route 1 *From the Sunda shelf, via Kalimantan to Sulawesi, and thence by a series of islands to Western New Guinea (Irian Jaya) arriving at either (A) Waigeo in the Bird's Head region by ten stages, one of 93 kilometres; or (B) south-east of Misool by eight stages, the longest of 69 kilometres; or (C) near the Aru Islands to the south, by eighteen stages, including one of 103 kilometres.*

Route 2 *From Indonesia through Lombok and Flores to Timor, then either (A) from Timor to Tanimbar and Sahul shelf near the Aru Islands, by seventeen stages, including three of more than 60 kilometres; or (B) from Timor directly across to the Sahul shelf at Fantome Bay in the Kimberley district of northern Australia, by eight stages, all less than 30 kilometres except for the last one of 87 kilometres. (After Birdsell 1977)*

have been chance events, assessing the comparative likelihood of each possible route gives the archaeologists clues as to which are the islands most worth searching for evidence of early human occupation.

Birdsell analysed the distance to be travelled, whether the island destination is visible from the point of departure, and the general size of the target island. His conclusions are that at the time of *lowest* sea level, the shortest route across the ocean-deep of Wallacea still involved eight sea voyages. There are two routes most likely to have been used by human migrants. The first, via a series of the islands from Sulawesi to the Sahul shelf near north-western New Guinea, was in eight stages, none greater than 70 kilometres. The second is a shorter route through Timor. This also has eight stages, all less than 30 kilometres, except for the last crossing of 87 kilometres from Timor to the Kimberley coast.

At other times during the last glacial period, when sea level was perhaps only 50 metres below the modern level, both these routes would have been more difficult. The most likely route at times of a more moderate lowering in sea level is through Java and Timor to the Aru Islands between New Guinea and Arnhem Land. This route did not increase much in difficulty with the more modest drop in sea level: the greatest distance to be traversed increased only from 98 to 103 kilometres.

In so far as sea level and minimum sea distance are the most critical factors, it seems likely that migrations occurred from the Sunda shelf by way of Timor to the Kimberley region of north-western Australia, or via New Guinea or the Aru Islands on to the central or north-eastern coast of northern Australia.

Distant smoke from natural bush fires on the Sahul shelf should have been visible from some Indonesian islands, providing an incentive for deliberate voyages to Australia. The vegetation on the shelf at the time is likely to have been semi-arid savanna woodland, which is prone to fires caused by lightning. Even small fires in this type of vegetation produce billows of smoke rising to 1000 metres or more above sea level, and smoke from large bush fires commonly reaches 5000 metres. Smoke plumes 1000 metres high could have been seen by people standing at sea level up to 110 kilometres away.[7] When the sea was at its lowest level, smoke could have been visible ahead on any route to Australia. And at any time during the ice age the smoke and glare of bush fires on the Australian shore should occasionally have been visible on such Indonesian islands as Timor, Roti, Tanimbar, Seram and Gebe.

The founding population might have been only a few castaways making landfall on the Sahul shelf from time to time.[8] Such landfalls would have become much less likely, although still just possible, when sea level rose to its present height at the end of the last glacial period. Given the sea barriers already described, the number of migrants must in any case have been relatively small, whether they arrived as castaways or by boat.

WATERCRAFT

In order to make successful landfalls across more than 50 kilometres of open sea, the colonists would have needed buoyant and sturdy watercraft. No archaeological evidence of Pleistocene watercraft has been found or is likely to be found in Australia, since such perishable artefacts are most unlikely to survive and most Pleistocene coastal sites have now been submerged by present sea level.

None of the watercraft known from prehistoric Australia seems a likely candidate for Pleistocene voyages. The Tasmanian Aborigines used either simple driftwood logs for crossing rivers or watercraft made from three bundles of paperbark or stringybark lashed together. These craft were generally not taken more than 5 to 8 kilometres off the coast, as the bark became waterlogged after a few hours.[9]

The bark canoes used in southern mainland Australia were more rigid but likewise unsuitable for long sea voyages. In northern Australia the sewn-bark canoe was used; it was much more seaworthy. Some of these canoes were as much as 5.5 metres long and 0.5 metre wide and could carry six to eight people. A sewn canoe is recorded as having made a 32 kilometre open sea voyage off Arnhem Land from the Sir Edward Pellew Islands to Macarthur River, but generally trips of over 10 kilometres were rare. Evidence of such canoes has been found only in the Australian tropics and, on the analogy of other items found only in the tropics, they may have been a relatively late introduction to Australia.

Plate 2. *Mangrove log raft, Western Australia. A'Worora youth paddles this raft on George Water, Glenelg River district.* (Photo by H. Basedow 1916, in the Basedow Collection, National Museum of Australia, Canberra)

It is possible that the earliest colonists were tide-riders, using rafts like the *kalum*, a light, triangular, mangrove-wood raft of double construction, used until recently by four tribal groups on the north-western coast of Australia (plate 2). This raft was paddled and was normally used over a distance of 8 to 16 kilometres along this coast, one of the most dangerous and inhospitable in the world. Its tides are among the world's highest, fluctuating 9 metres, and its currents attain a speed of 10 knots, swirling among numerous islands and coral reefs.

The Kaiadilt of Bentinck Island in the Gulf of Carpentaria used similar rafts made of mangrove or driftwood to exploit the rich sea food around their low, barren islands. Their log rafts did tend to become waterlogged, they did not undertake long sea voyages, and the death rate on even medium-length voyages was extremely high. For example, two recorded sea voyages of about 13 kilometres each made by the Kaiadilt on rafts resulted in an average death rate of 50 per cent.[10]

The tide-riders of northern Australia may be the best model for Pleistocene voyagers from the Sunda to Sahul shelf. The colonists no doubt used the north-west monsoon winds to carry them eastwards across the island stepping stones of South-East Asia. Bamboo may have been used for their rafts or canoes. Bamboo shafts are coated in silica and thus are impervious to water and extremely buoyant. Bamboo would have been present in areas of high rainfall, certainly all along the northern migration route, and at least as far as Java on the southern route. Since bamboo was not available in Australia, it would have been hard or even impossible for them to sail north again. In other words, even accomplished sailors might have been trapped in Australia by the lack of bamboo. Cordage would have been required to lash the bamboo tubes together, but ropes could easily have been made from the rich vegetable and animal resources of South-East Asia.

As well as appropriate raw materials, such sea voyages require a high level of technology to fabricate a suitably sturdy craft. Recent archaeological discoveries in Australia and New Guinea indicate that there was the necessary technical skill; for example, it is known that ground stone axes were in use at least 20000 years ago. Fire would probably have been taken on deliberate voyages to keep the voyagers warm and to cook fish. A clay hearth could be made in the bottom of the boat; this was the custom among Tasmanian Aborigines.

MIGRANTS AND ENVIRONMENT

The expansion of the habitable area of land at times of very low sea level no doubt caused expansion of population, but when the sea rose again, the habitable area would have shrunk within a few thousand years. The loss of hunting grounds may have been a factor in causing dispersal of population to previously uninhabited islands. Volcanic activity, for which the islands of South-East Asia are notorious, may have driven people further afield to find safer homelands.

There is growing evidence for an explosive spread of the modern human race, *Homo sapiens*, across South-East Asia and the western Pacific region in Upper Pleistocene times, around 40000 years ago. Recently, traces of this early occupation have been found in the limestone cave of Lang Rongrien in peninsular Thailand dated between 37 000 and 40 000 years ago. By 38 000 years ago people were occupying the cave of Leang Burung 2 in Sulawesi in Indonesia. Similarly, early remains, more than 30 000 years old, have been discovered on some of the large Melanesian islands of the western Pacific, in New Britain and in the 32 000 year old cave of Matenkupkum in New Ireland, east of New Guinea.

Over the centuries, island by island, small groups may have moved imperceptibly closer to Australia. The environment on the Sahul shelf encountered by early migrants was probably similar to that of the northern third of the Australian continent today. During the last ice age, rainfall was rather lower, evaporation was reduced and mean annual temperatures were several degrees lower than today. Increased aridity at this time of lower sea level would have caused a coastward migration of the vegetation of arid inland Australia. The resulting open woodland on the Sahul shelf would have been a suitable human habitat and facilitated movement for prehistoric people. There may also have been extensive swamps on the shelf. One aspect of the Australian environment to which newcomers would have had to adapt is the marked seasonality of climate in the north, with a long dry season in winter.

There would also have been very little stone for making tools, so these early migrants are likely to have left little or no trace of their passing. As the earliest inhabitants of Australia probably lived on or near the shoreline where they could obtain fish and shellfish, it is unlikely that we will find evidence of early sea-voyaging, because of submergence of the occupation sites where such evidence might be found.

NEW GUINEA

Throughout most of human history the island of New Guinea (comprising Papua New Guinea and Irian Jaya) formed part of the same land mass as Australia. This has been called 'Greater Australia'.[11] New Guinea also lay on the route from Asia to Australia. To a coastal, maritime-adapted people from tropical islands clad in rainforest, the coast of New Guinea would have offered a familiar environment. Exciting new evidence suggests that the human settlement of New Guinea may go back 40 000 to 50 000 years.

The Huon terraces are one of the best sets of relict Pleistocene coastlines anywhere in the world.[12] The terraces rise like a giant flight of steps out of the sea: each 'tread' is an ancient coral reef now raised up high above modern sea level. The massive earth movements, earthquakes and volcanic eruptions to which New Guinea is subject have raised the coral reef formed at the shoreline 120 000 years ago to 400 metres above sea level. On one of the lower terraces 80 metres above sea level, twenty-four weathered axes were found.[13] These 'waisted axes' (colour plate 2) are large, heavy stone tools with a flaked cutting edge. A notch flaked out of each side edge gives them a 'waist' or hour-glass shape. The notches are not just to provide a grip on hand-held stone tools, since some of them are too wide apart for a hand to stretch across. The notches were probably made to aid hafting – the attaching of a handle. Wear marks, obvious even to the naked eye, show that the groove must have been for a cane or vine binding. The function of these large, heavy, hafted stone axes is uncertain, but their discoverers, Les Groube and Jo Mangi, consider forest clearance the most likely. Even today in Papua New Guinea, bananas are cultivated in the middle of rainforests simply by axing back enough vegetation cover for sunlight to reach a banana clump.

One of these extremely weathered stone axes was found with some other stone tools under two metres of volcanic ash in a layer dated to about 40 000 years ago. It was sandwiched between ash layers firmly dated by the thermo-luminescence method to between 37 000 and 45 000 years. This makes it the earliest hafted stone axe in the world.

These waisted stone tools resemble the 26 000-year-old tools from Kosipe – the earliest site previously known in New Guinea. The discovery of Pleis-tocene occupation at Kosipe, a 26 000-year-old campsite,[14] was a surprise, for it lies in the south-east corner of New Guinea at least 1400 kilometres from the western ice age coastline and, even more surprising, in the highlands at 2000 metres above the present sea level. It seems clear that humans were paying at least seasonal visits to the highlands of south-east New Guinea 26 000 years ago, when the snowline was only about 1000 metres above the campsite and the temperature would have been about 6 degrees Celsius lower than at present.

The Kosipe artefacts, although few in number, are important, because they reflect the great antiquity of the concept of hafting, which involves binding a tool to a handle for greater efficiency and leverage, and of the concept of edge-grinding, in which the working edge of a tool is ground to a chisel-like form for better cutting properties (see figure 1.1). Until these discoveries at Kosipe, it was thought that the techniques of stone-grinding and of hafting were developed in Australia only during the post-glacial period. Kosipe revolu-tionized ideas about the early technological history of the Australian region and lent support to surprising discoveries made in mainland Australia (the subject of the following chapters).

The first Australians may have been the world's earliest ocean voyagers, or at least the first successful castaways. New finds in Australia suggest that people had reached the necessary technological level to cross substantial bodies of open sea and adapt to a new continent at least 40 000 years ago. The settling of Australia marked the first human expansion beyond the single land mass comprising Africa, Europe and Asia, for settlement of the Americas seems to have come rather later. This adaptation to a strange, new continent at such an early date must be counted as one of the major achievements in the world's human story.

CHAPTER THREE

LIFE AND DEATH AT LAKE MUNGO

The first migrants to the Australian continent encountered a favourable environment. Once they penetrated inland, most of the fauna would have been unfamiliar but would have presented little threat to the new arrivals. There are few carnivorous predators in Australian fauna. Those that existed then in mainland Australia were the native cat (*Dasyurus*), the Tasmanian 'tiger' or 'wolf', the Tasmanian 'devil' and the Tasmanian 'lion', a leopard-sized marsupial carnivore, which may have been a predator or may have eaten only carrion. There would also have been crocodiles in the tropical rivers and some poisonous snakes, fish and insects, but these would have been familiar dangers to migrants from Asia.

In addition, a number of giant animals and birds (megafauna), which are now extinct, existed over much of Australia until the last phase of the ice age, which ended some 10 000 years ago. These included huge flightless birds and giant animals, such as a donkey-sized wombat, kangaroos 3 metres tall, and the marsupial *Diprotodon*, which was the size of a rhinoceros. Some of these animals were relatively slow-moving herbivores and would have fallen easy prey to hunters. However, their extinction may have been caused by climatic change rather than by human overkill, or be a combination of both (see chapter 12).

The fauna, although largely unfamiliar, would have offered little danger to the human migrants, and the tropical environment in coastal and riverine northern Australia provided familiar fish, shellfish, birds and plant foods. The arid-adapted flora further south would have been quite new, together with the marked seasonality of rainfall. Australia is also the world's driest inhabited continent; on over 75 per cent of its surface rainfall is exceeded by potential annual evaporation. This was not always the case, for great changes in the Australian climate occurred during the ice age. One of the key areas where both climatic changes and early human occupation have been documented is the semi-arid belt fringing the desert core. Indeed, some of the earliest certain evidence at present of human occupation in Australia comes from this zone in the south-east of the continent, in the far west of southern New South Wales.

In 1968 Jim Bowler, a geomorphologist at the Australian National University, was studying the nature of sediments to establish the pattern of climatic change over the last 100 000 years. His work was focused on the Willandra Lakes in western New South Wales, a series of interconnected lake basins that carried the waters of a tributary of the Lachlan River towards the Murray (figure 3.1). These 'lakes' have been dry for the last 15 000 years, but once they had a surface area of more than 1000 square kilometres of fresh water.

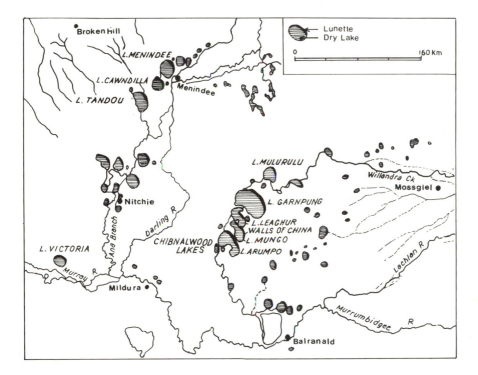

Figure 3.1 *The Willandra Lakes region, western New South Wales*

During the Pleistocene there were long periods when western New South Wales and Australia as a whole had much more standing water than occurs today. For about 30 000 years the Willandra Lakes were full of water, mainly because of the much lower evaporation rate caused by lower temperatures. The present barren landscape of the Willandra Lakes would have been very different 30 000 years ago, with lakes full of fresh water and teeming with large fish. The now dry bed of Lake Mungo would have been 20 kilometres long and 10 wide, with a depth of some 15 metres. On its eastern side sand dunes provided sheltered campsites by the lake shore.

Most research in the fossil lake system was concentrated on Lake Mungo, which has suffered extensive erosion of its lunette, the crescent-shaped dune formed on the lake shore, exposing 600 hectares of its core and partially exposing much of the rest (colour plate 3). The Mungo lunette is 25 kilometres long and was, before deflation, up to 40 metres high. It is visible from several kilometres distant as a long low white hill among the flat brown plains. Erosion has sculpted the lunette into such spectacular shapes that it was named 'the Walls of China' in the 1860s, possibly by Chinese who were working on the local sheep stations.

The earliest sediments in the area, called the Golgol sediments, were laid down possibly about 120 000 years ago, when the lake was full. No evidence of human presence has ever been found in the Golgol sediments, and it seems that people did not begin to camp at Lake Mungo until the latest full-water phase. During the mainly lake-full stage, from about 45 000 to 26 000 years ago, sand was blown up from lakeside beaches to form a lunette on the eastern lee shore. This dune consists of the Zanci, Mungo and Golgol units, named after local pastoral properties (colour plate 3). Over the next 10 000 years the lakes gradually dried up, and the increasingly arid environment is reflected in the Upper Mungo and Zanci sediments. The study of these deposits downwind of the lakes has allowed reconstruction of the past climate and environment not only of the semi-arid Willandra area but also of the whole of inland Australia[1] (figure 3.2).

HUMAN REMAINS

Among the stark residuals and shifting sands of the massive eroding dunes, Jim Bowler came across the first exciting hint of early human presence at Mungo. He found some stone artefacts and mussel shells bearing an encrustation of carbonate and eroding out from a small midden in the upper part of the Mungo sediment. The presence of these large fresh-water mussel shells in the dune and their association with the artefacts is difficult to explain except by invoking human transport. Radiocarbon dating of these shells gave an age of 32 750 ± 1250 BP.

Bowler later noticed some burnt, carbonate-encrusted bones protruding from a low hummock on the dunes, which clearly belonged to the Mungo sediments. He marked the site and left it intact for future archaeological excavation. A group from the Australian National University inspected the site in March 1969 and immediately suggested that the bones were human.

The bones were contained in a quarter of a metre square calcrete block, which was only 15 centimetres thick and was fragmenting; many wind-eroded, broken pieces were scattered around. The features of the site were plotted,

photographed, and fully recorded, the loose bones were numbered and collected. Then the central carbonate block was undercut and removed to take
the whole block back to the laboratory for closer analysis. The most secure
container available was Professor John Mulvaney's suitcase, which he nobly
emptied out to transport the precious finds safely back to Canberra.

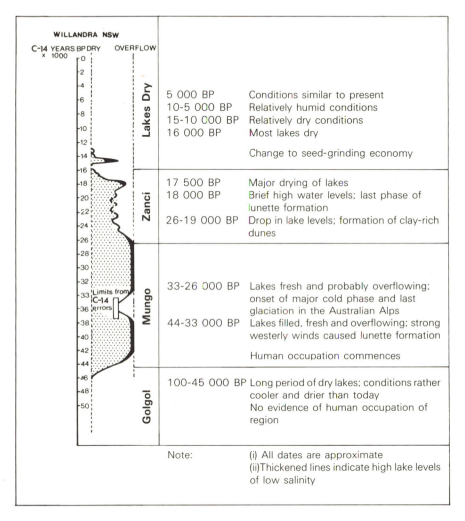

Figure 3.2 *Climate and lake levels at the Willandra Lakes* (Based on Bowler *et al.* 1976)

The archaeologists returned to the site fully prepared for a major excavation
just one week later, only to find that a freak rainstorm had totally changed the
scene. If they had left the Mungo skeleton there, it might have been washed

away. But the storm had revealed hitherto hidden stone tools in the same area, and two hundred carbonate-encrusted stone tools were collected.

Also exposed were fifteen patches of black deposit. They were roughly circular or oval in shape, 60 to 90 centimetres in diameter, and 5 to 10 centimetres deep. The black deposits contained charcoal, burnt animal and fish bones, fresh-water mussel shells, emu egg shells, and in four places stone artefacts. The black deposits seem to have been hearths and their contents,

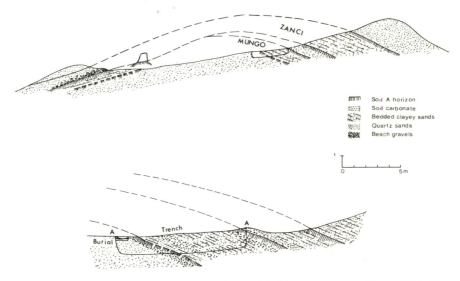

Figure 3.3 *Section through the eroding lunette at the sites of the Mungo cremation and Mungo III burial* (After Bowler and Thorne 1976)

the discarded remains of human meals and tools associated with food collection and preparation. The human bones had lain about 15 metres away from the nearest hearth, and the whole area appears to have been a campsite on the lake shore. Here the ancient inhabitants camped, and roasted and ate their food. They used stone tools and burnt their dead on the sandy dune and beach a few yards from the shingle of the high fresh-water lake shore.

The people also collected raw material for tool-making and ochre pigment, consolidated earth made up of clay and hydrated oxide of iron. The ochre did not occur in the Mungo area but must have been brought from at least ten kilometres away.

Back in the laboratory, physical anthropologist Alan Thorne had begun the painstaking removal of the concrete-hard carbonate crust from 'Mungo Man', as the bones had been named. Reconstruction of the skull was a massive task, since it was broken into 175 small fragments. When Mungo Man finally emerged from this process, 'he' proved to be a 'she'. Mungo I, as she is officially called, was a young adult female of slender build and small stature;

she was 148 centimetres tall (four feet ten inches). Her head is very round in shape and her eyebrow ridges are small compared with the heavy, beetling brows of some archaic Australian skulls. Nonetheless, she is one of the oldest human beings so far discovered in Australia.[2] Radiocarbon dating of the bone confirmed the age of the remains, which had been worked out from its position in the Mungo sediments (figure 3.3), as approximately 26 000 years old (26 250 ± 1120 BP).

How she died we do not know, but careful analysis of the surface and fractures of the bones tells us that the corpse was first cremated, then the burnt skeleton was thoroughly smashed, and finally the ash and smashed bones were gathered together and deposited in a small depression beneath or adjacent to the cooled funeral pyre. This method of disposal of the dead was still in use among Australian Aborigines in the eighteenth and nineteenth centuries in some parts of eastern Australia and Tasmania.

The Mungo I site has provided the oldest evidence of ritual cremation in the world. It is interesting that it is a woman who was cremated. Although no conclusions can be drawn from a sample of one, it at least shows that 26 000 years ago women were considered worthy of complex burial rites. What emotions inspired those rites – love, fear, or religious awe – we will never know, but all show a concern for the deceased which is the essence of humanity.

The burial also affords us a tantalizing glimpse of life in the Pleistocene. The presence of pellets of red ochre suggest the use of this pigment for ritual, art or decoration, and another nearby site has shown that ochre was used in funerary rites 30 000 years ago. This is the site of another burial, but this time of a male, who was not cremated but placed in a grave with his body thickly coated with red ochre. This Mungo III burial was discovered 500 metres east of the Mungo I cremation site (figure 3.3). (The name Mungo II was reserved for some very fragmentary, burnt human remains at the Mungo I site.)

In 1974 Jim Bowler was examining an eroded area of the Mungo stratigraphic deposit[3] when the slanting rays of the late afternoon sun highlighted a small white object protruding 2 centimetres above the surface. It was part of a human skull. Heavy rain had made it erode out of the lunette, and rapid excavation was essential because of the great fragility of the bones and the possibility of further rainstorms. Again, archaeologists from the Australian National University rushed to Mungo, and there was elation when excavation gradually revealed not just fragments of bone or a skull, but a whole skeleton (plate 3). Finds of complete skeletons are extremely rare, and archaeologist Wilfred Shawcross recalls the excitement of the find. 'Two to three people worked flat out for two days. All the time you felt it couldn't go on; but it did. A neck appeared, then a rib. Normally you are lucky to get a skull; in Africa they are lucky to get a jaw. But this was a whole skeleton.'[4]

Excavation revealed that a tall man had been laid in a shallow grave on his side with his hands clasped. The bones and surrounding sand were stained pink; the pink colour, derived from ochre powder that had been scattered over the corpse, clearly defined the size and shape of the grave. The age of the burial has now been determined as about 30 000 years, and it lies within the Mungo sediments (figure 3.3). In physical form Mungo Man is similar to Mungo Woman: fine-featured and gracile (lightly built), with no archaic characteristics, such as very thick bone or steeply sloping forehead. Surprisingly, these ice age Mungo people are far more gracile than the twentieth century Aboriginal inhabitants of the region, the Bagundji.

The significance of this ochred burial is that it shows that such rituals go back at least as far in Australia as in other parts of the world such as France, where ochred burials have been found in Grimaldi Cave at a similar time. In fact, at Mungo red pigment was in use even earlier, for lumps of ochre and stone artefacts were found deep below the ashes of a fire lit 32 000 years ago. As the ochre did not occur naturally at Mungo, it must have been deliberately carried there from some distance away. Similar lumps of pigment, some of them showing signs of use, have been found in Pleistocene levels in other widely separated sites, such as Kenniff Cave in Queensland, Cloggs Cave in Victoria, Miriwun in Western Australia, and several Arnhem Land rockshelters. Ochre has no utilitarian functions, such as medicinal use; it is simply a pigment used (at least in the recent past) to decorate rock walls, artefacts, dancers' bodies in ceremonies, and corpses during some burial rites. Its use in burial ritual is the only use documented so far in ice age sites, but then as now ochre was probably also used for other purposes.

Many campsites, hearths and middens (prehistoric refuse heaps) have now been excavated in the Willandra Lakes region and more than a hundred radiocarbon dates obtained. Many of these dated occupation sites are between ten and thirty thousand years old, but a considerable number also belong to the last five thousand years. No trace of human presence has been found in the Golgol sediments, so it looks as if humans only came to camp by these inland lakes when they last filled with water 45 000 years ago. From then until about 25 000 years ago, occupation was intensive and the rich resources of the fresh-water environment were fully exploited.

Continuing work in the Willandra Lakes region has added considerably to these discoveries. The area has been the focus of a study involving archaeologists, geomorphologists, palaeontologists and others.

Cooking methods in Aboriginal society seem to have persisted unchanged over 30 000 years. Two types of Aboriginal fireplace occur in the Willandra Lakes region: 'hearths' and 'ovens'. Hearths are small areas of blackened earth resulting from an open fire. They were probably used for roasting small animals and do not contain cooking stones. Ovens consist of a shallow depression or pit containing a band of ash and charcoal and cooking stones or lumps of baked clay. The use of such ovens in the region was described by the explorer

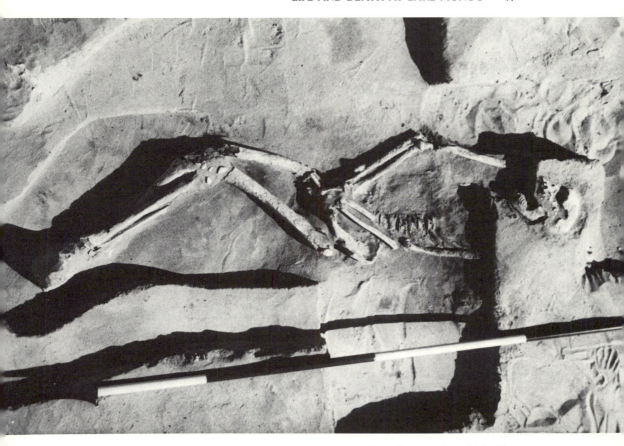

Plate 3. *Mungo III burial during excavation. Red ochre was scattered over this corpse during his burial. (The scale is marked in 20 centimetre sections.)* (A. Thorne)

Edward Eyre in his *Journals of Expeditions of Discovery* published in 1845 (vol. 2 p. 289):

> The native oven is made by digging a circular hole in the ground, of a size corresponding to the quantity of food to be cooked. It is then lined with stones in the bottom [or clay balls where stones are unavailable], and a strong fire made over them so as to heat them thoroughly, and dry the hole. As soon as the stones are judged to be sufficiently hot, the fire is removed, and a few of the stones taken, and put inside the animal to be roasted if it be a large one. A few leaves or a handful of grass, are then sprinkled over the stones in the bottom of the oven, on which the animal is deposited, generally whole, with hot stones . . . laid on top of it. It is covered with grass, or leaves, and then thickly coated over with earth, which effectually prevents the heat from escaping.

A remarkable find at Lake Mungo, 5 kilometres north-east of the Mungo I and III sites, was a group of five fireplaces 26 000 or more years old. The oldest fireplace was a typical Aboriginal oven – a shallow depression filled with ash and charcoal, with several lumps of baked clay on top. This oven was dated to 30 780 ± 520 BP.

A surprise furnished by these fireplaces was the evidence they gave concerning palaeomagnetism: the phenomenon of fossil magnetism of archaeological material such as baked earth and clay from ancient fireplaces. The first Australian evidence for deviations in the earth's magnetic field was found in the early 1970s by Michael Barbetti.[5] His research revealed that 30 000 years ago magnetic north had swung right round 120 degrees to the south-east. This magnetic 'reversal' or 'excursion' lasted for about 2500 years, after which the direction of magnetization reverted to normal again. This major magnetic reversal is now known as the Mungo excursion, and is one of the youngest and best-documented examples of such changes in polar magnetic direction. When such reversals in magnetism are found in other archaeological sites, they can be dated by comparison with the Mungo and other reversals. A series of thermoluminescence dates have been done on baked clay in Aboriginal fireplaces at Mungo by Professor Mortlock, Dr Bell and others of the Australian National University. The TL dates are generally consistent with the radiocarbon dates.

TECHNOLOGY

The artefacts recovered from the Willandra Lakes area give us some idea of the technological level that these Mungo people had attained. Very few bone tools have been found, but it is difficult to know whether this is because they were not present, or because they have rotted away. Since the alkaline soils have preserved both large and small animal bones, it is unlikely that bone tools were numerous.

Only three bone tools have been found in the first decade of archaeological work at the Willandra Lakes. These are three pointed bone implements, all less than 10 centimetres long. Two were found at the Mungo I site, on the Walls of China, and one on the Lake Mulurulu lunette. One has been worked to a sharp point at both ends. It is possible that this bi-point was used as a lure to catch the large Murray cod, bones of which were found at the same Mungo I site. In the nineteenth century, Aborigines often caught Murray cod by attaching a fishing line to the middle of a bi-pointed bone and then pulling it rapidly through the water so that the bone looked like a small darting fish. These bone lures, or fish gorges, were called 'muduk' by Aborigines of the River Murray and this name has been adopted by some archaeologists for bone points. However, it is not certain that all, or even any, of the prehistoric bone bi-points and uni-points were used as lures. Bone points in historic times were used as spear tips, as awls for piercing holes in animal skins being sewn together into cloaks, as nose pegs, as pins for fastening cloaks, and possibly as netting needles in the manufacture of fishing nets.

Stone tools were far more plentiful than bone ones in the Willandra Lakes region. Most are made from silcrete, a hard, fine-grained stone available locally. The major tool types are choppers and flakes (figure 3.4). Choppers are large heavy tools made from lumps of rock, and they have a flaked cutting edge. They are used for heavy wood-working, such as chopping down trees. A flake is a piece of stone formed when a lump of rock is struck with a hammerstone (see figure 1.1). The force of the percussion blow detaches a flake of stone that has sharp edges and can be used to cut or scrape flesh, sinew

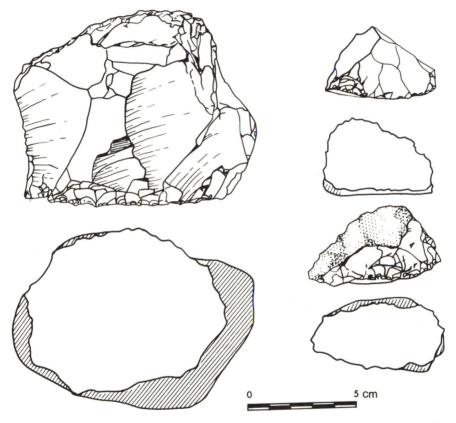

Figure 3.4 *Stone tools from Lake Mungo. The Australian core tool and scraper tradition is exemplified by such tools (made of silcrete) horsehoof core on the left and steep-edged scrapers on the right. Below each tool is shown its plan view from the base; the hatched areas indicating overhanging edges.*

or fur. Sturdy, steep-edged flakes were also used for wood-working, such as scraping, sawing, incising and chiselling.

These smaller tools are traditionally called scrapers, although they were not necessarily used for scraping. They may be made on a flake or on a core – a lump of rock from which flakes have been struck. Some rather specialized scrapers found at Mungo have deeply notched, concave working edges suitable for use as spokeshaves for smoothing wooden shafts such as spear shafts. The large tools made from lumps or nodules of rock are generally termed core tools. Some of them have a flat base, an overhanging, step-flaked edge and a high, domed shape like a horse's hoof, hence they have been called horsehoof cores.

The toolkit from the Mungo cremation site has been described as 'the Australian core tool and scraper tradition'. This term has now been adopted Australia-wide for the early Australian stone industry. Its main characteristics are the presence of large core tools, steep-edged, chunky, high-backed scrapers and concave, notched and 'nosed' working edges. Flatter, convex-edged and round scrapers also occur, which may have been used to make skins pliable for use as cloaks.

These tools were used for the manufacture and maintenance of wooden tools rather than to extract food from the environment. Parallel industries are found on Pleistocene sites throughout Australia and Tasmania. Where river or beach cobbles are available, they tend to be used to make chopping tools, termed pebble tools, but they have the same function as the Mungo-type horsehoof cores. Similar industries have also been found at a similar date in South-East Asia, in Sulawesi, and at sites such as Tabon Cave in the Philippines and Niah Cave in Borneo. This early core tool and scraper technology may have provided the toolkit of the earliest migrants into Australia.

Over the millennia at Mungo new tools were invented to suit new uses in response to environmental change. The drying-up of the Willandra Lakes was accompanied by a change from a reliance on fresh-water resources to an economy based on the exploitation of wild grass seed. The small, hard grass seeds were crushed to make flour by means of large, flat grindstones or mortars. Considerable human activity continued in the region after the lakes had dried, but it was not related to lake exploitation.

ECONOMIC LIFE

The Willandra Lakes have provided evidence for the Pleistocene exploitation of a fresh-water environment. Mussel shells on Lake Outer Arumpo lunette were dated to about 35 000 years ago. This midden (Top Hut III) was discovered by Isabel McBryde in 1975, exposed in a gully wall. Buried under 5 metres of lake shore sediments, the midden consists of mussel shells, ash and charcoal. These are probably the remains of a single meal eaten by a small group. The shell is dated to about 35 500 years ago.[6]

Valuable insights into the prehistoric economy have been gained by careful analysis of the well-preserved shell, fish bones and other organic remains by a whole band of researchers working over the last decade. As well as 'base' camps containing remains of many different creatures, 'dinnertime' camps have been found containing the remains of a single meal. One such site, on the Lake

Tandou lunette, has only remains of 500 yabbies, a small fresh-water crayfish. This dinnertime camp is dated to 25 000 years ago. Another Tandou site has been identified by Jeanette Hope as a frog kill site!

The number, size and species of fish remains in sites have been identified by comparing their otoliths, or ear bones, with those of modern fish in the same region.[7] Seventy per cent of fish caught in the Pleistocene Willendra Lakes were golden perch (*Plectroplites ambiguus*). Remarkably, they tended to be a similar size, which suggests that they may have been caught by netting techniques. Fishing with fixed gill nets is a highly selective process: it tends to catch fish of the same species and age. The size uniformity was probably also the result of setting nets at the time of a spring spawning run, when the fish migrate up the rivers in large numbers. Golden perch are difficult to catch by other means, such as spearing, lines or poisoning, and if such methods had been employed, there would be a far greater age range among the fish remains. In the last century on the Darling River, Aborigines used to set nets 100 metres long about 20 metres offshore to catch golden perch. These nets were made from bulrush fibre (*Typha*) and had wide mesh in which to catch the fishes' gills. Other fishing methods were probably used for larger fish. Some bones have been found in middens of huge Murray cod (*Maccullochella macquariensis*), which were estimated to weigh as much as 15 kilograms. These were probably speared or caught with line and lure.

The diet of the hunter-gatherers at Lake Mungo was varied and rich in protein. As well as fish and mussels, they ate the rat kangaroo, the western native cat, the brown-haired wallaby, the hairy-nosed wombat, and various other small animals and birds. Remains of these creatures have been found in ancient fireplaces, together with numerous broken emu shells. Since emu eggs hatch in spring, their presence indicates that people were camping at Lake Mungo in late spring. In the heat of summer they would have stayed close to the plentiful fresh-water and shellfish of the lakes. In the cooler winter they probably spread out away from the lakes onto the arid plains and hunted land animals, thus conserving the lake's food supplies for the harsh summers. Such a pattern of exploitation and seasonal movement is characteristic of Aborigines in arid regions and was observed in the Willandra Lakes region in the nineteenth century.

Very few bones of extinct animals have been found in the Mungo region, and none in association with remains of human occupation. The few bones of the giant kangaroo, *Procoptodon*, found so far do not suggest big game hunting.

Life for the small group of hunter-gatherers at Lake Mungo seems to have continued with little change, at least in the basic way of life and technology, until the drastic drying of the lakes about 15 000 years ago. Water became saline, and the fish and shellfish disappeared. New food sources were needed, and the people, infinitely resourceful, adapted to the new arid conditions by moving to the large rivers and collecting, grinding and baking the seeds of wild grass to make a sort of bread. This use of grass-seed as food was a great technological step forward.

INTELLECTUAL LIFE

The Mungo evidence documents the most distant dispersal in the world of *Homo sapiens sapiens* and his achievement in adapting so successfully to a fresh-water but semi-arid environment. The site also provides early evidence of intellectual life. The deliberate transport and use of coloured pigment more than 32 000 years ago parallels its contemporary use in Grimaldi Cave on the Riviera in France, indicating early development of an aesthetic sense. This was to flower later into the rich decorative and ritual art for which Aboriginal Australia is renowned.

The elaborate cremation of a young woman 26 000 years ago is the earliest evidence for this rite in the world and shows not only complex ritual concepts and respect for the dead, but also respect for women. Women have always held an important place in Aboriginal society as gatherers of most of the staple food for the community. At Mungo, shellfish are clearly one of the most important foods, and gathering shellfish is traditionally women's work.

The archaeological evidence from the Willandra Lakes also reveals great cultural continuity in Aboriginal society from the Pleistocene to the present day. The ritual, symbolic and aesthetic concepts of modern Aboriginal society have their roots in the remote past. Not only is this complex culture found on the shores of Lake Mungo important in understanding the development of *Homo sapiens* in world prehistory, but it endows Aboriginal society with the dignity and respect it has often been denied.

PART II

HUMAN ORIGINS

CHAPTER FOUR

THE ROBUST AND
THE GRACILE

The question of the origin of Australian Aborigines has long fascinated scholars. Ever since their distinctive appearance was described by early European voyagers in the seventeenth century and given the name 'Australoid', many theories explaining Aboriginal origins have been put forward. Rather than repeating this speculation here, the fossil evidence is examined, first from Australia and then from South-East Asia (see figure 2.3).

TALGAI

The first Australian Pleistocene human skull was found in southern Queensland in 1886. This is the Talgai skull, which was found by a contractor, William Naish, when it was exposed in the banks of a billabong after an exceptional flood in the Darling Downs. Naish gave the skull to the Clark family, who kept it for the next thirty years in their homestead at East Talgai. In 1914 it came to the attention of the Australian geologist Sir Edgeworth David, of Sydney University. He was shown the precise find-spot of the skull by Naish, then aged 76 and crippled with rheumatism, who was carried to the site.

The Talgai skull was purchased by Sydney University. When found, it was covered by a massive encrustation of calcium carbonate, but once this was chipped away an archaic, robust type of skull was revealed. All Australian skulls so far found belong to the youngest form of the human race, *Homo sapiens sapiens*, but the fossil skulls tend to divide into two groups: robust and gracile. The robust are more archaic in appearance, being large and thick-boned, whereas the gracile are lightly built, thin-boned and more like contemporary Aborigines. Everywhere in the world the robust, rugged thick-boned type of physique is earlier than the lightly built form.

In 1948 the late Professor Macintosh, of Sydney University, became interested in the Talgai skull and embarked on what was to become a twenty-year-long detective hunt to find its precise original location and age.[1] He

55

examined all the written records and then began the search for a local contact who could guide him to the spot. Despite false trails, destroyed evidence, and conflicting testimony, at last in 1967 he found one of the men who had carried Naish to the site in 1914: 70-year-old Charles Fraser of Pratten. The long search for a first-hand witness to Naish's identification of the site was over. The site to which Charles Fraser guided Macintosh and geologist the late Edmund Gill, accorded very well with the descriptions of David and Naish.

Analysis of the Talgai skull has shown that it belonged to a boy of about 15, who died as the result of a massive blow on the side of the head. The skull had been 'rolled', that is, transported by water along a water-course. The generally accepted dating of the skull is now between 9000 and 11 000 years.

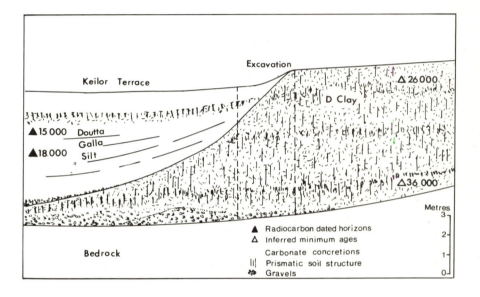

Figure 4.1 *Diagrammatic cross section through the Keilor site, Victoria* (After Bowler 1976)

COHUNA

The next significant skull to be found was the Cohuna cranium, unearthed in 1925 by a plough on the north-west edge of Kow Swamp, south-east of the town of Cohuna, which lies 16 kilometres south of the Murray River (figure 4.2). Like the Talgai skull, it seemed to have been transported by water to its find spot from elsewhere. No means were available to find the age of the skull. The teeth and palate, whilst typically Aboriginal, are much larger than the Australian average. The outstanding feature of Cohuna is great size. In robustness it far exceeds both the average Aboriginal cranium and Talgai.[2]

KEILOR

In 1940 another major fossil find in Victoria was made at Keilor. This skull was discovered by an alert quarry worker, James White, who unearthed it whilst digging into soft terrace silts being removed to make fine mouldings. Swinging his pick while standing on the quarry floor he felt it enter something hard. He dug out the object, washed it in the river, and found he had put a neat hole into a fossil skull!

The site, which lies near the junction of Dry Creek and the Maribyrnong River 2.5 kilometres north of Keilor and 16 kilometres north of Melbourne, was then investigated by a number of workers. Among them was Edmund Gill,

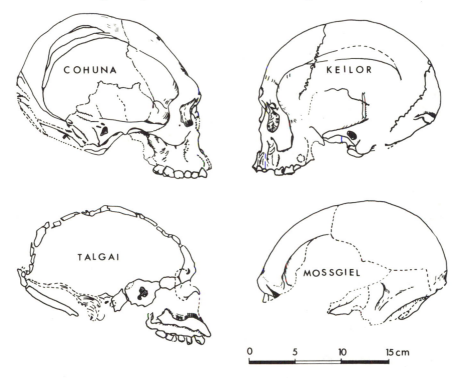

Figure 4.2 *Comparison of the gracile Keilor skull with more robust skulls from Cohuna, Talgai and Mossgiel. The forehead of the Cohuna skull has probably been flattened by artificial deformation.* (After Macintosh 1965)

then curator of palaeontology at the National Museum of Victoria. He showed that the cranium was contemporary with faunal remains embedded in the Keilor terrace.

The skull was encrusted with a 2 millimetre thick layer of carbonate, but, when this was removed, a yellow loess-like silt was found trapped inside the cranium. This was identical to the upper part of the silt comprising the Keilor terrace (figure 4.1). Moreover, the carbonate encrustation on the skull could only be accounted for if the skull came from a zone of secondary carbonate deposition in the silt.

The cranium did not belong to a burial intruding into this layer from above but showed evidence of wear, indicating that it was a 'rolled skull', which must have been water-rolled into position from a distance upstream, at a time roughly contemporary with the deposition of the sediments. The chemical composition of the skull and other faunal remains from the terrace were found to be similar, which suggested that the skull was *in situ*.

Recent radiocarbon dates obtained from a small sample from the femur and skull itself have provided an age of about 13 000 years.[3] The skull is characterized by a full and rounded forehead and lack of the prominent eyebrow ridges and projecting jaw of Talgai and Cohuna.

Many excavations have been conducted in the Keilor terraces, but particular mention should be made of the work of Alexander Gallus, a Hungarian archaeologist now based in Melbourne, who has concentrated on the oldest deposits.[4] In the base of the D clay he has uncovered separately both the remains of extinct megafauna and some undoubted stone tools. Many pieces of stone and bone claimed to be tools by Gallus have been rejected by other archaeologists. Indeed, after a conference in 1971, a large group of scientists visited Keilor, filled with scepticism after seeing Gallus's 'tools', only for Jim Bowler to find an indisputable flake implement firmly embedded in the D clay. There is thus at least some evidence of human activity in the oldest deposits at Keilor. Many radiocarbon dates have been obtained on charcoal particles and burnt earth, and 'a conservative age estimate of the lower levels of the D clay would place it at 36 000 BP whilst an age of 45 000 BP is indeed possible'.[5] Gallus's claims of an antiquity of not less than 75 000 to 100 000 years for the earliest chopper industry remain to be substantiated.

It was generally thought in the mid 1960s that the Talgai and similar fossil skulls represented an archaic form of *Homo sapiens*, bearing some resemblance to the fossil skulls of Java, whereas Keilor was a younger, more evolved form. However, discoveries at Mungo and Kow Swamp soon overturned this simple theory and considerably complicated the picture.

THE ENIGMA OF KOW SWAMP

The remarkable discoveries at Kow Swamp stemmed from an outstanding piece of detective work by physical anthropologist Alan Thorne. In August 1967, he was examining the human skeletal collections held in the National Museum of Victoria in Melbourne, when he came across a museum drawer containing a partial skeleton of remarkably archaic appearance. The bones were heavily mineralized and carbonate-encrusted, and the skull was reminiscent of the

Cohuna cranium. From a police report of the location of the find, he traced the skeleton back to the exact find spot, which was not far from where the Cohuna skull was found. Excavation began in 1968 and revealed part of the same skeleton still *in situ*, including the other half of one of the bones in the museum drawer.

The skeleton was called Kow Swamp 1, since it lay on the shore of Kow Swamp in northern Victoria. Within a few months of the excavation of Kow Swamp 1, additional burial areas were found around the swamp by an in-

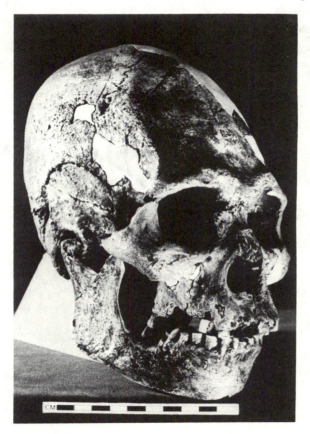

Plate 4. *Kow Swamp skull 5, Victoria, showing the massive and archaic features of this group of robust, early Australians. The burial is about 13 000 years old.* (D. Markovic, courtesy A. Thorne)

terested local resident, Gordon Spark. By 1972, the remains of at least forty individuals had been excavated.

Most of the human remains were located along the eastern shore of Kow Swamp in a narrow belt of lake silt, partially overlain by a low crescentic sand dune. Radiocarbon dates, obtained from bone and charcoal samples associated

Plate 5. *Kow Swamp skeleton 14, during excavation. Quartz stone artefacts and fresh-water mussel shells were included in the grave fill.* (A. Thorne)

with the burials, showed that the burials span a period of at least 6000 years, from about 15 000 to 9000 BP.[6] The graves had been dug into relatively soft silt and sand. Carbonate mineralization of the skeletons after burial had enhanced their preservation, leading to an encrustation up to 1 centimetre thick. Although many burials had been disturbed by earth-moving when an irrigation channel was constructed through part of the site, these disturbed skeletons could be reassembled fairly easily, because differential mineralization had rendered the bones of each individual a slightly different colour.

Twelve undisturbed graves were excavated, in which the bodies were oriented in a variety of positions. Three were laid out horizontally and fully extended, two on their backs, and one on its left side. Others were in a crouched position, including one facing forward and downward, with the knees drawn up under the chest and hands placed in front of the face (plate 5). Tightly flexed burials, with the knees brought up to the chest, were also present; the body laid on the left side or on its back. At least one instance of cremation was also found. As in more recent traditional societies, a great variety of burial styles were practised.

The skeletons found at Kow Swamp included men, women, juveniles and infants. This burial complex at present is the largest single population of the late Pleistocene epoch found in one locality anywhere in the world. Kow Swamp is thus of great importance not only for Australian but also for world prehistory.

The enigma of Kow Swamp is that the skulls, although younger than Keilor and only half the age of Mungo I and III described in the last chapter, appear much more archaic (plate 4). The people buried at Kow Swamp had large, long heads with exceptionally thick bone, up to 1.3 centimetres thick. Their faces were large, wide and projecting, with prominent brow ridges, and flat, receding foreheads. Seen from above, the skulls show pronounced inward curvature behind the eye sockets, which makes the skull look rather like a flask. The jaws and teeth are massive, but archaic features are restricted to the front of the mandibles.

Teeth are not generally well preserved at Kow Swamp, and few teeth survive with their enamel crowns intact. In addition to damage from post-mortem erosion of teeth and disturbance to the site, all adult individuals have suffered pronounced tooth wear. The use of grinding stones to grind up seeds and hard fruits was probably responsible for producing gritty foods, which led to pronounced wear on the molars. Only one individual is of advanced age, yet almost every adult's first molars show such a high degree of wear that the roots have been exposed and worn down halfway to their ends. This led to the chronic periodontal disease evident in many individuals.

The rugged, heavy, archaic-looking Kow Swamp remains suggest a population physically similar to those of Cohuna and Talgai, contrasting the more modern-looking, gracile Keilor and Mungo I and III people. In particular the gracile group lack the marked eyebrow ridges, flat receding foreheads, thick bone, and massive jaws of the robust Kow Swamp skulls (figure 4.2).

Grave goods were found with several of the Kow Swamp burials. These were ochre, shells, marsupial teeth and quartz artefacts, and one body was laid to rest on a bed of mussel shells. As at Mungo 20 000 years earlier, ochre was powdered over a corpse, which shows the long continuity of such customs.

The presence of grave goods may mean simply that the corpses were being buried with the normal equipment of everyday life, but there are indications that special non-utilitarian regalia were also sometimes included. One body buried at Kow Swamp some 12 000 years ago wore a band of kangaroo incisor teeth round the head. Traces of resin on the teeth showed that they had been stuck together in a band. Similar headbands of kangaroo teeth, plant fibre and resin were worn by Central Desert Aborigines, both men and women, in the nineteenth century.

One of the most spectacular finds of this kind was the huge pierced tooth necklace slung from the neck of the man buried in the lunette of the relict Lake Nitchie in western New South Wales (plate 6).[7] No fewer than 178 pierced teeth of the Tasmanian devil made up the necklace. The teeth must derive from a minimum of forty-seven individual animals, which are now extinct on the Australian mainland. Indeed, if such necklaces were common, it is not surprising that Tasmanian devils became extinct. Each tooth is pierced by a hole that was ground and gouged, involving a tremendous amount of labour. This necklace is unique both in present Aboriginal culture and in prehistoric Australia.

The Nitchie burial has other important features. The skeleton was compressed downwards into a shaft-like pit, there were ochre pellets in the grave,

Plate 6. *Necklace from the Lake Nitchie burial, New South Wales. The Lake Nitchie man wore a unique necklace of 178 pierced Tasmanian devil teeth, taken from at least 47 different animals. Each tooth is pierced by a hole that was ground and gouged out.* (The Australian Museum)

and the tall man lacked his two central upper front teeth. This indicates prehistoric tooth avulsion, the widespread practice in male initiation rites of knocking out one or two of the novice's upper incisors. If so, this ritual practice goes back at least some 6500 to 7000 years, the age of the Lake Nitchie burial. In fact the radiocarbon date for Nitchie man is surprisingly young, for he has a skull very similar to Kow Swamp man. And he is remarkably tall, measuring 1875 millimetres, or six feet one and a half inches.

COSSACK SKULL

A skull with even more extreme 'robust' characteristics was found near Cossack in the north-west of Western Australia, almost 5000 kilometres from Lake Nitchie and Kow Swamp. The remains lay at the base of an eroding coastal

1. Sthenurus *jawbone in situ Cloggs Cave, Victoria. The remains of this species of kangaroo lay at a depth of 2 metres in a layer older than 21 000 years.*

CM

dune, which on geomorphological grounds cannot be more than 6500 years old, when the sea reached its present level and formed the dunes. The skull was that of a man about 40 years old, of a large powerful build (plate 7).[8] The cranial bones are very thick, and the forehead has a marked backward slope. In fact, Cossack man has the most sloping forehead and is the most long-headed (dolichocephalic) Aborigine yet found in past or present Australia. He also had his right upper front tooth missing long before death, probably indicating its removal in initiation rites.

Cossack is similar to Kow Swamp man but differs markedly from recent male Aborigines in Western Australia. The importance of this find is that it demonstrates that the robust type of Aboriginal physique was not confined to

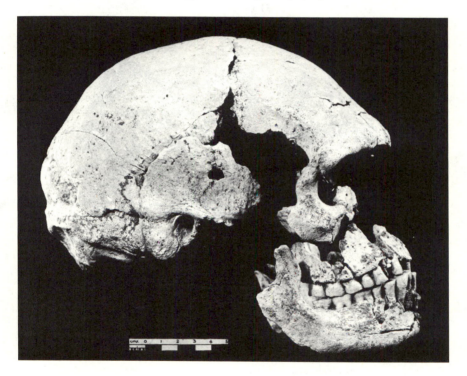

Plate 7. *Robust skull from Cossack, Western Australia* (L. Freedman and M. Lofgren, with permission from Academic Press, London)

the east but was widespread in the continent, and that it lasted into postglacial times. The age of less than 6500 years agrees well with the Lake Nitchie evidence.

The long sloping foreheads (known as extreme frontal recession) of skulls such as Cossack, Cohuna and Kow Swamp prompted the suggestion that the skulls might have been artificially flattened and deformed. Deformation by

2. *This waisted axe from Papua New Guinea was one of twenty-four flaked axes found on the 80-metre Huon terrace. It was discovered in a layer of volcanic ash dated to about 40 000 years old, and is the earliest stone axe adapted for hafting yet found in the world.* (By courtesy of L. Groube)

bindings or by strapping boards to children's heads has occurred in various parts of the world, for example among the Maya of Mexico and in some of the Melanesian islands north of Australia, but it was rare in Aboriginal Australia.

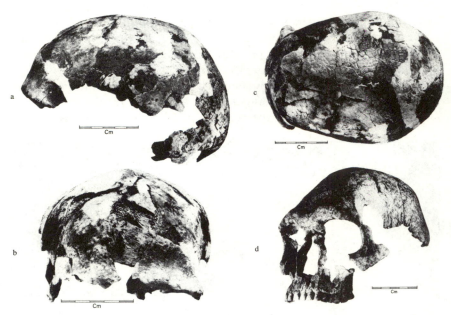

Plate 8. *Gracile skull from Lake Mungo, New South Wales, compared with Kow Swamp I Three views of Lake Mungo I cranium A: left lateral; B: frontal; C: vertical; D: Kow Swamp I. The thin bone, rounded forehead and lack of brow ridges of Mungo I are characteristic of gracile early Australians.* (Photo by D. Markovic; reproduced from A. Thorne 1971 with permission from editors of *Mankind*)

Among Australian Aborigines only three groups are recorded as practising intentional head deformation, and there are no artificially flattened skulls in museum collections. These are groups from northern Victoria, Cape York and Mabuiag in Torres Strait. There is no record of what type of deformation was used in Victoria, but the other two societies practised infant head-pressing rather than binding. In Cape York an observer in 1852 recorded that 'Pressure is made by the mother with her hands . . . one being applied to the forehead and the other to the occiput, both of which are thereby flattened, while the skull is rendered proportionally broader and longer than it would naturally have been.'[9]

By a comparison of deliberately deformed Arawe (of southern New Britain) male skulls with other Melanesian male skulls that were definitely not deformed, physical anthropologist Peter Brown was able to identify the changes produced by deformation (figure 4.3). He then compared a series of skulls from Victoria, including Kow Swamp and Cohuna. Brown's study sought to establish that Cohuna and some of the Kow Swamp and other robust skulls were artificially deformed. An alternative explanation, however, according to Alan Thorne for the peculiarities of some robust skulls such as Kow Swamp and Cossack is that they reflect the admixture of the robust and gracile populations. Similar high, flat, sloping foreheads are seen on some contemporary Aborigines living in Central Australia, who were certainly never subjected to head-binding or pressing.

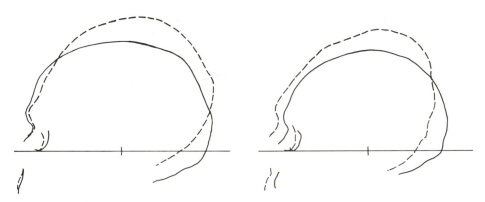

Figure 4.3 *The Kow Swamp 5 skull compared with modern artificially deformed and undeformed skulls. Left Midline cranial contours of Kow Swamp 5 (dashed line) and a modern Murray Valley male Aborigine. Right Midline cranial contours of an artificially deformed Arawe male (dashed line) and an undeformed male from northern New Britain. (After Brown 1981)*

COMPARATIVE ANALYSIS

Detailed comparisons have been made of the characteristics of the Mungo group, the Kow Swamp group, and modern Aborigines.[10] The modern material for comparison was a group of 167 Aboriginal crania in the National Museum in Victoria, all deriving from burials without significant antiquity in northern Victoria. It was found that some changes have occurred in the Aboriginal cranium over the last 10 000 years, particularly in the form of the face and forehead, associated with a general reduction in skull size. Thus, there are considerable differences between modern skulls and Pleistocene human remains. There are also differences among the fossil skulls, which divide into two groups. (It is necessary to differentiate between male and female skeletons when making comparisons. Sex can usually be determined from differences in the pelvic bones, the femur, or thigh bone, and from the greater size, ruggedness and muscle marking of the male skull.)

The main differences between the rugged, robust Kow Swamp–Cohuna–Mossgiel–Nitchie and lightly built Mungo–Keilor groups are in facial characteristics, bone thickness, and size. All the Australian Pleistocene human remains lie outside the range of present-day Aboriginal skeletal forms of the appropriate sex, but they fall into two contrasting groups, one more lightly built than any modern Australian Aborigines, the other more rugged and archaic-looking.

The problem is that the more massive, thick-boned and archaic-looking skulls belong to the Kow Swamp group, which are much younger than the gracile Mungo group. In other words the more advanced-looking remains are actually much older than those of more archaic appearance. Therefore, it seems that the terms 'robust' and 'gracile' are more appropriate to distinguish the two groups, than 'archaic' and 'advanced'. This problem of the co-existence of two different human groups in early Australia is the subject of the next chapter. Some physical anthropologists such as Peter Brown and Philip Hapgood[11] have argued that the robust and the gracile are two ends of a continuum, and that the differences are not so great as presented by Alan Thorne and Steve Webb. Whilst the debate will no doubt continue, current evidence is more readily explainable by Thorne's two people theory, and this also fits well with evidence from other parts of the world of the co-existence during the late Pleistocene of different types of *Homo sapiens*.

CHAPTER FIVE

THE ORIGIN OF THE FIRST AUSTRALIANS

Some discoveries complicate the puzzle of the past, others help to clarify the picture. Fortunately a new arrival on the scene, Willandra Lakes hominid 50, (W.L.H. 50), is one of the latter, clarifying both the physical development of the Australian type and relationships with possible Asian ancestors.

Willandra Lakes hominid 50 is the fiftieth set of human remains found in the Willandra region – and the most significant. The skull and some arm, hand and foot bones were found on the surface near Lake Garnpung, which lies close to Mungo. The bones may have eroded out of the Mungo sediments, but they were not *in situ* and it is uncertain to which sedimentary layer they belong. Their age is uncertain at present but Alan Thorne, who is studying the remains, has made public a general preliminary description of the find.[1]

There are two extraordinary things about W.L.H. 50: its condition and its form. Its condition is unique: all the normal phosphate in the bone has been replaced by silicates, in the same way that things become opalized, which suggests great antiquity. And W.L.H. 50 is massive: he is so robust, he makes Kow Swamp man look gracile! The cranium is extremely wide and approximately 210 millimetres long. The bone in the region of the temples is about 18 millimetres thick. Massive brow ridges form a continuous torus above the eyes, and the forehead is flat and receding. The back of the skull shows even more archaic characteristics. The neck muscle area is huge, the skull is extremely wide, the greatest width occurs very low in back view, and the difference between the width above and below the ears is much greater than in any modern people. Yet W.L.H. 50's brain was large, with a capacity of more than 1300 cubic centimetres, well within the modern range. The skull is flask-shaped, like the Kow Swamp skulls, in bird's eye view, but all the rugged features of Kow Swamp are much more pronounced in W.L.H. 50. Unfortunately the face, jaw and teeth of W.L.H. 50 have not survived, but enough is left of the rest of his skeleton to indicate that his body was equally massive; his elbow bone, for instance, is enormous.

Although, because his antiquity is unknown, it is premature to try to place

W.L.H. 50 on the world or even the Australian evolutionary ladder, his significance is immense. Firstly, it is now clear that the robust and gracile types co-existed for a long time in prehistoric Australia; there is no way that such a robust type as W.L.H. 50 could be descended from the gracile types of Mungo I and III and Keilor. It is not only the size and shape of the skulls that differ, the most striking difference is in the thickness of the bone: the contrast is as great as between bone china and earthenware, or egg shell and orange peel. Secondly, the extremely archaic features of hominid 50 make him an outstanding candidate for a representative of the earliest migrants to enter Australia – the very first Australians. Everywhere in the world the robust, rugged, thick-boned type of physique is earlier than the lightly built gracile form. The discovery of W.L.H. 50, therefore, puts Australia into step with trends in the rest of the world.

What is the explanation for the co-existence of these different groups in the same area of prehistoric Australia? There seem to be three possibilities. The first is that the two different groups entered Australia at very different times and later merged or hybridized to form the modern Aboriginal population. Rhys Jones explains the problem in terms of gradual inter-breeding. 'I think we are seeing the obvious, that the Kow Swamp people reflect a relict group of the original inhabitants of Australia, an archaic race of *Homo sapiens* who first colonised the continent at least 50 000 years ago. They occupied the well-watered regions and survived intact for tens of thousands of years. Australia was then occupied by a second group of modern *Homo sapiens*, the Mungo people. They came from south-east Asia and because of their superior technological powers . . . they were able to inhabit large areas of the continent. Eventually the two groups met, and intermarriage between them led to a new group, from which evolved the modern Aborigine.'[2]

The second possibility is that the two groups entered Australia at a similar time but from different places and, again, later hybridized to form the present population. Both these explanations involve the selective extinction or suppression of the extremes of Pleistocene physical characteristics when the two groups fused to form the modern Aboriginal population. Australian Aborigines are physically among the world's most variable people, and it may be that this great diversity was even greater in the past.

The third possibility is that a single, widely varied, founding population, ancestral to both Mungo and Kow Swamp, entered Australia a very long time ago, perhaps as much as 100 000 years, and underwent considerable change and diversification within Australia, leading to both the Mungo and Kow Swamp physiques, and some intermediate varieties. The theory of a single introduction of people to Australia has been proposed primarily by physical anthropologist A. A. Abbie, but he excluded the Tasmanian Aborigines in his analysis of Aboriginal origins, as he regarded them as being of Melanesian stock.[3]

Other theories have been proposed to explain the differing physical traits of Aboriginal groups noticed by the first European visitors to Australia. In particular a theory of three migrations was proposed by Joseph Birdsell in 1949, and this has been strongly espoused, with some modifications, ever since then by him and Norman Tindale. This theory is summarized below.

> The three types of population visualized as contributing to the modern populations of Australia, Tasmania and New Guinea commenced with an initial wave of Oceanic Negritos who saturated the regions to carrying capacity as determined by their technological adaptation . . .
>
> Subsequently in the model a second kind of population, called the Murrayian, reached Greater Australia and in the areas most favourable for their penetration, such as Australia proper, rolled back the original inhabitants, whose traces today survive only in a few marginal areas. The Murrayians themselves are best represented by the historic Aborigines of the Murray drainage system and the adjacent coastal regions.
>
> A third wave of peoples, called the Carpentarians from their preponderant position around the Gulf of that name in north Australia, arrived in the terminal portion of the last glaciation, and so were the last of the Pleistocene migrants to reach Greater Australia.[4]

This three-waves of colonists theory provides a convenient, but incorrect, explanation for differences observed in historic times between Aborigines of the north, the south, and Tasmania. The Tasmanians are taken to have been representatives of Oceanic Negritos, largely on account of their small stature and spirally curled hair. Other remnants of the Oceanic Negritos were said to be twelve Aboriginal tribes living in the rainforests of north-east Queensland. However, analysis of recent skeletal material from north Queensland did not produce any evidence of a Negritic component among the rainforest Aborigines. Moreover, recent genetic studies have shown that pygmy groups are not racially distinct but simply represent local modification in physique in relation to their neighbours.[5]

In Tasmania, skeletal remains (from West Point midden and Mt Cameron West)[6] show no differences between prehistoric Tasmanian Aborigines and contemporary mainlanders. It has also now become clear that Tasmania was populated in the ice age by means of the land bridge that joined the island to the mainland. This bridge was drowned some 8000 years ago by the post-glacial rise in sea-level. The differences between Tasmanian and mainland Aborigines observed in historic times are now generally thought to result from genetic change in an isolated population numbering only some 3000 people.

There is no evidence to support the identification of a Negrito element in Australia and, in any case, the earliest colonists of Australia were far more likely to have been of large and robust rather than slender, small build. Similarly, Birdsell's third type, the Carpentarians, are now generally thought to be the result of recent contact between Aborigines and non-Aborigines along the north coast of Australia rather than a separate wave of colonists. There has, therefore, been a general rejection of the three-wave theory.

GENETIC EVIDENCE

Genetic differences between different Aboriginal groups and between Australian Aborigines and overseas peoples have been examined by a number of researchers. The genetic traits compared include blood groups, hair form and colour, finger and palm print patterns (dermatoglyphs), and other genetic characteristics.

Aboriginal blood group genes were recorded and studied for many years by the late Roy Simmons and his colleagues of the Commonwealth Serum Laboratories. His conclusions were that Australian Aborigines are unique in certain genetic characteristics, such as the general lack of blood groups B and A_2, but research had been unable to provide any clues to the biological origin of the first Australians.[7] Further research has revealed no genetic connections between Australian Aborigines and distant groups such as the Veddoid populations of India or Sri Lanka or the Ainu of northern Japan.[8]

The problem is that most of the differences, such as hair form, blood groups and colouring, that distinguish between living human populations are not discernible on skeletons. But over the last fifteen years an exciting new approach has been used in the study of the origin of mankind. This is molecular biology – the study of the molecules of life from living species. Two species descended from a common ancestor start out with identical DNA (deoxyribonucleic acid), the carrier of the genetic code of life. As the generations go by, random changes accumulate. The longer two species have been separated, the greater the difference in their DNA. These differences are expressed as a percentage rate, for example haemoglobin might change 1 per cent after six million years. Understanding this process has led to the establishment of a 'molecular clock', which ticks off the years that elapse after two species have separated. The chronological framework is provided by conventional dating techniques of fossils, such as radiocarbon or potassium argon 'calendars'. For example, it is well established that the marsupials and mammals split between 125 and 100 million years ago. One fossil date is all that is needed to set the clock. This then provides a ratio of the time elapsed since various species shared a common ancestor, because DNA accumulates mutations at a relatively slow rate, and the same molecule changes at the same rate in all species.

Using this molecular clock, the remarkable discovery has been made that the genetic difference between humans and their closest relatives, the gorilla and the chimpanzee, is only 1 per cent. And they became separate species only four and a half million years ago.[9]

The history of our own species is encoded in the DNA in each of us. The genetic material of different human racial groups has been studied, and an evolutionary tree constructed from analysis of blood proteins and DNA in the chromosomes. This seems to show that the major racial grouping of mankind arose about 100 000 years ago with a three-way split into Africans, Caucasians and the Australian–Oriental lineage, which diverged about 40 000 years ago (figure 5.1). Nevertheless, whilst nuclear DNA can give a lot of information, the exact timing of the splits is uncertain.

A different human family tree seems to emerge from the study of mito-chondrial DNA, which is outside rather than inside the nucleus in every living

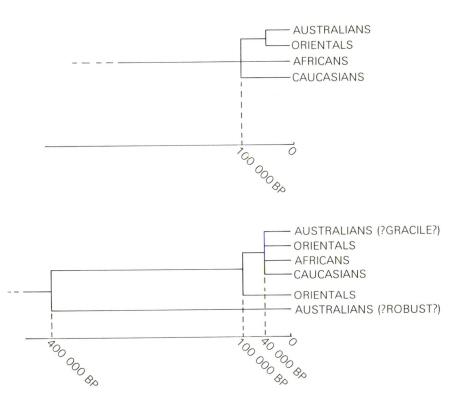

Figure 5.1 *The family tree of* Homo sapiens. Top *The picture provided by nuclear DNA, showing the human races originating about 100 000 years ago and diverging about 40 000 years ago.*
Bottom *Mitochondrial DNA would put the origin of* Homo sapiens *much further back, and suggests that Australian Aborigines are derived from mixing of two distinct lineages. The timing of the splits is uncertain due to the many assumptions involved, and may be wrong by several orders of magnitude. (Based on R. Cann's sample of 112 humans, including 12 Australian Aborigines, all from Western Australia. After Gribbin and Cherfas 1982.)*

cell.[10] Mitochondrial DNA is passed to the next generation only by the mother, so the genes are never subjected to shuffling and recombination, and it evolves ten times faster than DNA in the nucleus. It thus provides a new and independent molecular clock for the relatively recent past, although there are many assumptions involved in putting absolute dates onto forks in the family tree, and the timing may be incorrect by as many as ten orders of magnitude (i.e. 100 000 could be 1 000 000).

The family tree produced suggests that Australian Aborigines are a mixed and varied population, deriving from the hybridization of two lineages. The split and the mixing of the two lineages may have occured in Asia and South-East Asia, from where an already mixed population entered Australia at a much later time. The two distinct lineages seen in the mitochondrial DNA of Aborigines may well correlate with the two distinct physiques found in the fossil skeletons: the robust and the gracile, and indicate that the split between them goes back a long way.

Another, startling way of interpreting the data is that Australia is the cradle of the modern human race, which arose in Australia and spread about 40 000 years ago to cover the whole world. According to this theory,[11] *Homo sapiens*, free from competition, evolved from a small band of *Homo erectus* that somehow made its way into Australia about 400 000 years ago. Whilst an attractive theory, there has never been any hard (or even soft) evidence to support this concept, and the long sea voyages involved at such an early date argue strongly against an *Out of Australia* movement.

This type of analysis opens a new window on to the past in the quest for the origin of the Australians, although the researcher responsible for the mitochondrial DNA study, Rebecca Cann of the University of California, Berkeley, is much more cautious than the popular science writers who have publicized her work. In view of the documented variations between the rates of evolution of mitochondrial and nuclear DNA, it is difficult to place much reliance solely on genetic and molecular data in determining the origin of modern humans.

ASIAN ANCESTORS?

The search for the ancestors of Pleistocene Australians suffers from the scarcity of comparable human remains in Asia. Only a handful have been found, the dating is usually uncertain, and most come from only two areas: Java or China. Any attempt to work out a logical sequence of human evolution from these few data is like trying to complete a huge jigsaw from only a few pieces.

The 'gracile' Australian fossil group can be compared with several Asian hominids, all dating from the late Pleistocene. Some human remains recently found in southern China bear remarkable similarities to the Keilor skull. Comparisons between the human fossils of China and of Australia have shown a particularly close similarity between the gracile skulls of Keilor and Mungo and the skull from Liukiang in Guanxi Province in southern China. Gracile people were also in northern China in the upper cave at Zhoukoudian or Dragon Bone Hill (previously known as Chou-k'ou-tien), in the late Pleistocene, about 18 000 years ago. Likewise, in island South-East Asia gracile skulls have been discovered that are similar to the Mungo–Keilor type. The skull from Niah Cave in Sarawak, radiocarbon dated to about 40 000 years ago, is said to be a young adult of remarkable gracile form. Niah is generally said to be a juvenile but Joseph Birdsell, who recently examined casts of the skull in the British Museum, considers that it is a female aged between 20 and 30, who resembles in type Oceanic negritos and Tasmanians. Others compare Niah with Mungo skulls.

The 23 000-year-old Tabon Cave remains from Palawan in the Philippines are said to match only Aboriginal Australians. The forehead and mandible are distinctly Australoid, and gracile rather than heavy. The Australian appearance of the Wajak fossils from Java has likewise been noted, particularly Wajak I's similarity to the Keilor cranium. Thus late Pleistocene island South-East Asia has produced human fossils similar to the gracile form in Australia.

But where are robust Kow Swamp man's ancestors? The robust Australians show similarities in the form of the face and forehead to *Homo erectus* of Java. Alan Thorne believes that all the early hominids of Java belong to the genus *Homo erectus*,[12] and that they spread from Africa to Asia some one million years ago. The age of the earliest human remains so far found in Java is uncertain, but they are generally considered to be a little over a million years old.

Homo erectus was so-called because he walked nearly or completely upright rather than semi-erect, like the apes. He made more sophisticated tools and was larger brained than his predecessors, with a cranial capacity varying between 775 and 1300 cubic centimetres. Modern man's brain capacity averages 1300 cubic centimetres, whereas the earliest humans had brains less than half this size. *Homo erectus* had conspicuous brow ridges, a sloping forehead, projecting face, thick skull bones, and massive jaws and teeth, but he was not very tall, standing about 153 centimetres (five feet).

The most famous *Homo erectus* is the so-called *Sinanthropus* or Peking man, from Zhoukoudian Cave, 40 kilometres south-west of Beijing. The remains were excavated during the 1920s and 1930s, and fortunately casts were made from them, since they were lost during the Second World War when they were being taken to America for safe-keeping. The remains included fourteen skull caps, twelve lower jaws, and some other bones. These post-cranial bones are particularly valuable because usually only the toughest parts of a human skeleton – the lower jaw and skull cap which houses the brain – survive from the distant past. The average brain size of Peking man was 1075 cubic centimetres, and he is usually thought to date to between 300 000 and 500 000 years ago.[13]

Between *Homo erectus* and *Homo sapiens* on the evolutionary scale of Java there is Solo man. The Solo skulls have a cranial capacity of 1100 to 1200 cubic centimetres. Solo man is generally regarded as forming the central part of a continuous sequence from Javan *Homo erectus* to *Homo sapiens*. Most scholars class them as very early *Homo sapiens* and see them as a possible ancestor for the robust human type found in Aboriginal Australia.

The general features of most modern Aboriginal Australians and the robust Australian Pleistocene remains show close links with Indonesian finds.[14] The close similarity of Willandra Lakes hominid 50 (W.L.H. 50) to Solo man strengthens the Indonesian connection. And W.L.H. 50 seems to fall right into the middle of the Solo range in form. Solo man has similar 'beetling brows' and heavy muscle markings. In form, W.L.H. 50 bridges the gap between Solo man and Kow Swamp man, but it is still impossible to set up a precise chronological sequence because of uncertain dating. The age of Solo man is estimated to be between 100 000 and 300 000 years (on the basis of the associated sediments and fauna), and that of W.L.H. 50 is quite unknown at present.

It seems clear that the migrants who first landed on the Australian shore were among early, generalized representatives of modern man, *Homo sapiens*. There appears to be a general, continuous development from *Homo erectus* to *Homo sapiens* as represented by Australian Aborigines. The basic modern Aboriginal skeletal form is robust rather than gracile and so are the majority of Australian prehistoric remains. And the finding of the exceptionally robust and archaic W.L.H. 50 in the same region as the Mungo remains shows that the robust form is likely to be at least as old as and probably much older than the gracile.

The robust people were probably the first comers, and were followed later by lightly built gracile people. The gracile types were widely spread on the mainland of east Asia in the late Pleistocene and probably spread from there to Australia. The existence of the two distinct human forms, robust and gracile, in Australia means that, even if mixing through intermarriage occurred in Asia, relatively unmixed forms reached Australia. But it is uncertain whether there were two main migrations at times of low sea level, or a continuous trickle of people.

It is clear that Aboriginal roots go back a long way. We know that gracile people were camped by the shores of the Willandra Lakes more than 30 000 years ago, and it is now generally agreed that they were not the first migrants, but that they were preceded by more robust people. Since at least 50 kilometres of open sea had to be crossed, even at times of lowest sea level, it seems most probable that the gracile people entered Greater Australia at the time of very low sea level, about 50 000 to 55 000 years ago, and that the robust people came rather earlier, perhaps about 70 000. This is speculation and may well be disproved by new discoveries, but such a two migrations theory best fits the available evidence. If it is correct, it may well be that different sets of artefacts were used by the different waves of migrants. There are already tantalizing clues that this may be the case. The quest for the origins of the first Australians is one of the most difficult and challenging tasks for archaeologists and physical anthropologists, and each new discovery adds a piece to the jigsaw puzzle.

PART III

ICE AGE BEGINNINGS

CHAPTER SIX

THE PEOPLING OF AUSTRALIA

Much attention has been devoted to the question of when and how Aborigines first entered the Australian continent but very little has been paid to what happened after that. By the time Europeans reached Australia, there were several hundred thousand Aborigines in the continent, but how long did it take to build up to this number and when were the various environmental zones first occupied? Three attempts to answer these questions have been made. The first was by American anthropologist Joseph Birdsell, the second by Sandra Bowdler, and the third by David Horton (figure 6.1).

Birdsell's theory[1] involved numerous assumptions about generation length, rate of reproduction, and group size. The normal size of a colonizing group was taken as twenty-five persons, and it was proposed that new colonizing groups hived off when a population had reached 60 per cent of an area's carrying capacity. It was assumed that when Europeans first entered Australia the Aboriginal population was about 300 000 and that the continent was at maximum carrying capacity. However, the figure of 300 000 for the Aboriginal population of Australia at the time of European settlement is based on very slender evidence and is far too low. Nor can it be taken for granted that the continent was fully occupied during Pleistocene times; this may be a more recent phenomenon. Likewise, population density cannot be assumed to have remained unchanged from the Pleistocene, through a period of major climatic change, to modern times. It is, therefore, rather rash to use people/land ratios of modern Aboriginal groups in a model of ice age migrations.

Birdsell's theory, nevertheless, may give at least a rough idea of how long it took to populate the Australian continent. His computer model gave the answer of between 1350 and 2200 years. Not only did Birdsell argue for a fairly rapid 'filling-up' of Australia, but he also saw the inland regions as being populated more quickly than the coasts. The reasoning behind this argument is that the drier inland regions could support fewer people than the well-watered coastal zones, so the land's carrying capacity would be reached sooner, and people would move on in search of a new foraging area more often.

This theory is testable from both archaeological and environmental evidence and has been challenged on both grounds by Sandra Bowdler. She analysed the archaeological evidence and concluded that it did not support Birdsell's theory.[2] She proposed an alternative hypothesis, based on archaeological evidence, of a coastal colonization of Australia.

Bowdler's thesis is basically that the occupation of the continent was by people adapted to living on the coast who gradually moved along the coasts around the periphery of the continent. It is argued that their marine-based

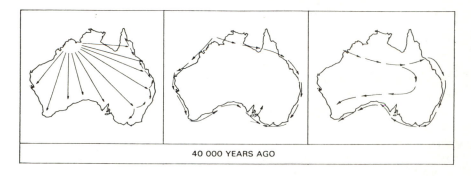

40 000 YEARS AGO

Figure 6.1 *Models for the peopling of Australia. The point of entry may have been Arnhem Land and/or the Kimberley region and/or Cape York. On the left is Birdsell's radiational model, in the centre, Bowdler's coastal colonization model, on the right, Horton's model.*

technology and economy, with a heavy reliance on scale fish, shellfish, and small mammals, underwent little change for many thousands of years, but gradually they did expand inland along major river and lake systems. It was not until much later, she suggests, that the dry heart of the continent was occupied, when people had developed techniques to hunt large kangaroos and began to use grindstones to exploit grass seeds as food.

Evidence in support of this coastal, gradual and conservative colonization, in contrast to Birdsell's rapid, radiational model, was the peripheral distribution of Pleistocene archaeological sites in Australia (see figure 2.3). Sites are either on or near the coast or lie up major river valleys and associated lake systems such as the Willandra Lakes in the Darling–Murray basin. A few sites are several hundred kilometres inland, but they may still have been reached by following large rivers up from the coast. For example, Kenniff Cave lies on the Great Dividing Range in southern Queensland, 500 kilometres inland from the present coastline, but it is near the headwaters of the Darling River system. A trek of some 1800 kilometres would have been required to reach Kenniff by way of the Murray and the Darling, but dispersal was probably over hundreds or thousands of years.

Bowdler's theory was attractive, but little archaeological work had been done in the centre of the continent which might support or refute it; excavation has been concentrated around the coast near the modern centres of population. When so much of Australia remained archaeologically unexplored, it was perhaps premature to try to establish the pattern of colonization. But hypotheses derived from these models can be tested by fieldwork. If colonization were coastal, the earliest sites should only be found near Pleistocene coasts or major river and lake systems; sites in desert and mountain environments should be post-glacial. If, on the other hand, colonization were radiational and continent-wide, some early sites should be found in inland areas, far from coasts, large rivers and associated lakes.

Horton's theory[3] is that people with an adaptable, all-purpose economy moved into Australia through well-watered regions on both sides of the Great Dividing Range and penetrated all but the arid core of the continent by 25 000 years ago. Then, when Australia began to dry up, Horton believes that the megafauna became extinct, and people retreated to the coastal regions, not moving back until the present climate was established about 12 000 years ago. Tindale[4] also believes that initial migration penetrated southwards on both sides of the Dividing Range, but present archaeological evidence does not support this or the rest of Horton's theory. No sites greater than 26 000 years old have been found far inland. Nor do inland areas appear to have been vacated between 15 000 and 25 000 BP. Indeed, occupation in the Willandra Lakes region was continuous in this time.

The discovery by Mike Smith[5] in 1986 of 22 000 year old occupation in the central desert has ended over a decade of speculation about the timing of human settlement in the core of the continent. Puritjarra rockshelter is west of Alice Springs, almost in the dead centre of Australia, and shows that the arid interior was settled by 22 000 years ago. Whilst it can still be argued that the initial peopling of the continent was coastal, it is now evident that for at least the last 20 000 years Aboriginal people have been ensconced in every type of environment, from the desert to the snows.

Not only were they living within sight of glaciers in Tasmania, but at the height of the last ice age occasional hunting parties were camping on the northern fringes of the Australian Alps. The small granite rockshelter of Birrigai[6] would then have been above the treeline, but was apparently used to provide a dry roof over the hunters' heads from 21 000 years ago onwards. Analysis of residues on the edges of the stone tools has revealed that these people were butchering game, processing plant food and using ochre. Human blood has been identified on the side of one quartz tool, in the exact position where the thumb would be whilst detaching flakes by the hammer and anvil technique; it seems that 16 000 years ago a stonemason hit his thumb!

One of the basic problems in the search for traces of the earliest colonists is that the earliest sites will now be underneath the sea. The earliest campsites were drowned by the rising post-glacial seas, and not until the people had gradually moved a hundred or more kilometres inland, to what is now the coastline of northern Australia, would any traces of these first migrants remain.

In Cape York, Arnhem Land, and the Kimberley, Pleistocene occupation has been found in rockshelters near rivers that flow across plains to the coast. All the early northern sites discovered so far lie at least 50 kilometres from the present coast and would have been much further from the shore at times of low sea level. Soundings in the sea have revealed the existence of river valleys, through which the present rivers would have flowed across the now submerged continental shelves, along which these early people would have moved.

The first landfalls could have been made anywhere across northern Australia from the Kimberleys in the west to Arnhem Land in the centre, to Cape York in the east. The oldest occupation yet found in the north is in Arnhem Land, but there has been very little excavation in the Kimberley or Cape York, so it is premature to draw any conclusions from this evidence as yet.

THE CAPE YORK CORRIDOR

Cape York has long been considered one of the most likely entry points for migrants arriving on the Pleistocene land bridge between Australia and New Guinea. Three excavated rockshelters in this remote and rugged part of the tropics have yielded deep occupation deposits. These all lie in the savanna woodland and sandstone ranges near Laura in the south-east of Cape York peninsula. Spectacular cliffs and gorges hide thousands of rockshelters, many with walls decorated with paintings or engravings. The sandstone plateaux known as Quinkan Country from a local Aboriginal name for supernatural beings, extend for some 15 000 square kilometres.

The first site to be excavated in Quinkan Country was Mushroom Rock Shelter.[7] It lies about 3 kilometres from Laura in flattish woodland not far from a permanent creek, an important feature in the long dry winters of Cape York, before the downpours of the summer monsoon. The mushroom-shaped rock provides shelter on all sides, with a maximum overhang of 5 metres. The rock walls and ceiling are covered in colourful paintings, including fresh-water crocodiles (which swim in the Laura River), human figures, Quinkan spirits and stencils of stone axes.

The occupation deposits, sheltered by the overhang on the west and east side of the rock, proved to be 6 metres deep, with stone artefacts to a depth of almost 4 metres. Several hundred flaked pieces of stone were found, and the tools at the bottom were considerably larger and heavier than those at the top. The lowest charcoal, at a depth of 2 metres, gave an age of 6870 ± 150 years. Since the human occupation continued down for another 2 metres, it was estimated that the shelter had been occupied for over 10 000 years.

Mushroom Rock gave a first, exciting indication of lengthy Aboriginal occupation of Cape York. The age estimate for the site was subsequently confirmed by excavation of the Early Man Shelter in 1974.[8] The Early Man Shelter was so-named by Percy Trezise, who has been involved in exploration and recording of rock art sites in north Queensland for many years. His interest in the Laura area was aroused in 1960, when road workers constructing the Cape York Development Road reported finding cave paintings in the cliffs south of Laura.

The discovery of these paintings (now known as the Split Rock Galleries) led Percy Trezise on an extensive programme of exploration. Amongst the hundreds of painted rockshelters he visited there were some that also bore engravings on their walls. Most of these engraved sites just have a few circular pits, mazes of lines, and motifs which appear to be tracks of emus or macropods (kangaroos or wallabies), but occasionally a rockshelter has its whole back wall covered with engravings. The Early Man Shelter is such a place, and the engravings are so heavily weathered and patinated that they seemed likely to be very old (plate 16). This proved to be the case. The base of the frieze of patinated engravings was covered by an occupation deposit containing 13 000-year-old charcoal. The engravings at the foot of the frieze must be, therefore, more than 13 000 years old. The same charcoal dates the approximate beginning of occupation of the shelter at 13 000 ± 170 BP.

Stone artefacts were found throughout the deposits and tended, like those at Mushroom Rock, to divide into two industries: an early large flake and core tool industry giving way to a later small tool industry. Horsehoof core-scrapers were present in the lower Mushroom Rock industry, and one was found on the surface of the Early Man Shelter deposit.

A bonus at the Early Man site was the preservation of some bone. In most sandstone shelters bone is only preserved in the upper levels and has disintegrated completely after a few hundred years in the ground. And in tropical Australia termites, which build their mounds against trees or rock walls, eat up any bone or other organic material very rapidly. Somehow bone in the lower levels of the Early Man Shelter escaped the attention of the termites. Some 2600 fragments of bone survived. Almost half the remains came from rock wallabies (*Petrogale godmani*), which still haunt the escarpments of Cape York. The other animals whose bones were found were kangaroos, possums, a bettong (*Bettongia tropica*), snakes, lizards, and the Tasmanian devil, which is now extinct in mainland Australia. These remains date to between 3000 and 6000 year ago. From the same levels came four bone tools. Three are slender bone points, ground at the tip, manufactured from animal fibulae (shin bones), probably of rock wallaby. The fourth is a fragment of a long bone with parallel longitudinal marks produced by a sharp-edged stone planing or scraping tool. There is no wear visible on these points suggestive of tool use.

The third site to be dug in Cape York was my own excavation of Green Ant Rockshelter in 1981.[9] This lies about 60 kilometres north-west of Laura, on the edge of the Koolburra Plateau. It is a small shelter but is covered with engravings, both fresh and patinated, and paintings. The shelter lies under a huge boulder at the foot of a slope, and its earth floor looked likely to have a substantial depth of deposit, whereas most sandstone shelters have rocky floors or only a thin veneer of sandy deposit above bedrock.

Green Ant proved to be an intensely interesting site. The shelter's back wall is adorned with engravings and paintings from different periods.[10] The most recent paintings appear to be those done in dry dark red pigment simply by rubbing a piece of ochre on the wall. Others are done in a lighter red, wet pigment and outlined in white. In this style is portrayed a Quinkan spirit figure in the centre of the wall, standing with arms outstretched as if to guard the site. These paintings overlie engravings, and there appear to be at least three different styles and periods of engravings. The most recent stand out fresh and white against the wall, others are so patinated that they are now the same colour as the parent rock.

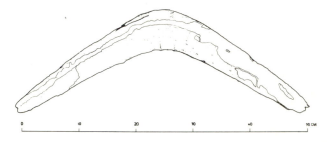

Figure 6.2 *Boomerang from Cape York. It has been attacked by termites, but it appears to be made from a wattle root and to be the returning type of boomerang.*

The engravings continued to a depth of about 85 cm below the modern ground surface and the occupation proved to span the last 8500 years. The sequence of tool types uncovered by the excavation was generally similar to that of the Laura sites but contained some surprises. One tool type was discovered that had never previously been found in Cape York. This was the geometric microlith.

One particularly exciting find was that of a wooden boomerang, found under a ledge in a rockshelter in the valley south of Green Ant[11] (figure 6.2). This is the first wooden boomerang found in a Cape York site. Its particular significance is that it disproved the earlier theory that Cape York Aborigines did not use boomerangs, since none was seen in use by early explorers or settlers. Stencils of boomerangs appear in the rock art in both Cape York and Arnhem Land, but until this find it was thought that boomerangs dropped out of use in both regions several centuries or more ago.

Further south in the Cape York region the limestone Walkunder Arch Cave at Chillagoe has recently produced a long cultural sequence in which bone is preserved. Occupation goes back more than 18 000 years, and the lowest level contained a horsehoof core, a waisted tool, shells and wallaby bones. Interestingly, burnt antbed or termite mound was found throughout the deposit, indicating that this was used as fuel in both Pleistocene and historic times.[12]

Walkunder Arch Cave is the oldest human occupation site yet found in north Queensland, but some argue that hunters had penetrated the Atherton Tablelands region just south of Chillagoe 45 000 years ago. This assertion is based on the long pollen sequence from Lynch's Crater, in which there is a huge increase in the amount of charcoal at the same time as the vegetation changes from rainforest to fire-adapted *Eucalyptus*. This change can only be explained, according to the pollen analyst, Peter Kershaw, by the arrival of man with his fire-stick.[13]

In north-west Queensland on the Barkly Tableland, traces of occupation more than 17 000 years old have recently been found.[14] This remote area north-west of Mount Isa contains spectacular gorges, permanent rivers and waterholes with abundant fish and shellfish and plant food such as the nuts of pandanus and cycad palms. Along 40 kilometres of river there is only one good rockshelter, the deep, well-protected shelter on Colless Creek.

A small excavation was carried out there, revealing an extraordinarily rich site with an average density of 50 000 artefacts per cubic metre of deposit. And in the uppermost cubic metre there were half a million pieces of bone. Occupation at Colless Creek certainly goes back beyond 17 550 BP – the oldest in a series of dates obtained on shell from the site.

The ancient environment was reconstructed through an analysis of sediments. Conditions in the vicinity of the shelter over the last 18 000 years were considerably drier than during the preceding phase of human occupation, which probably extended back beyond 30 000 years. The high degree of weathering of the deposit, the patination on the artefacts, and heavy staining on the bones suggest the base of occupation is at least 30 000 years old and perhaps considerably older.

During the last 18 000 years Colless Creek shelter and the surrounding well-watered region would have acted as an oasis in this arid area. The period around 17 000 years ago was a time of great aridity in other inland regions, such as the Willandra Lakes, and it may have been this climatic stress that drove people to such an 'oasis' at that time.

CHAPTER SEVEN

ARNHEM LAND AND THE WEST

ARNHEM LAND

In Arnhem Land in the Northern Territory the present East, South and West Alligator Rivers, together with the Wildman, Mary and Adelaide Rivers to the west, all apparently once joined together and formed one large, deeply incised 'Arnhem Land River'. This flowed down a gently sloping valley enclosed between Cobourg Peninsula and Melville Island out on to the Arafura Plain. There it joined the 'Arafura River', which flowed south from New Guinea and then west into the Indian Ocean.

By 24 000 years ago people had reached the Arnhem Land escarpment, which at that time lay about 350 kilometres inland. A drop in sea level of only 80 metres would have been sufficient to turn the whole of the Arafura Sea and the Gulf of Carpentaria into land, probably covered with savanna woodland and swamps.

The Arnhem Land Plateau stretches 260 kilometres from north to south and 200 kilometres from east to west. The edges of the plateau form a steep stone escarpment, rising as much as 250 metres above the alluvial plains. A series of large rivers flow through the escarpment in spectacular rocky gorges. The rivers are now estuarine and full of barramundi and huge salt-water crocodiles, but estuarine conditions only came into being with the post-glacial rise in sea level about 9000 to 7000 years ago.

The presence of fresh water, abundant food resources, and large rockshelters for protection against the elements made this an attractive area for prehistoric settlement. It is, therefore, not surprising that several rockshelters have been found with occupation extending back between 18 000 and 24 000 years. These sites are Nawamoyn and Malangangerr (plate 9) excavated in the 1960s,[1] and Malakunanja II and Nauwalabila (also known as the Lindner site) excavated in 1972–73.[2]

ARTEFACTS

Two successive stone tool traditions were identified at these sites. The more recent was distinguished by the introduction of stone spear points about 5000 years ago. This small tool tradition succeeded the earlier Australian core tool and scraper tradition. As elsewhere, this early industry was distinguished by chunky, steep-edged flakes and cores. Horsehoof cores were found in a 20 000-year-old level of Nauwalabila, and the 10 000-year-old basal levels of Ngarradj Warde Djobkeng.

The great surprise of these Arnhem Land sites was the presence in Pleistocene levels of stone axes with grooves around their sides and a ground cutting edge. Previously ground-edge axes had only been found in Australia in contexts belonging to the last few thousand years, but since then, further specimens have been found in the basal levels of other northern sites.

The axes (figure 7.1) are generally smaller than more recent examples. They were manufactured by the 'pecking' technique, which involves fashioning them with a hammer or 'hammer dressing'. A remarkable feature is the groove or nick that several axes bear, apparently to facilitate hafting the axe-head to a handle. Until the discovery of these axes with their hafting grooves, it was generally thought that the concept of attaching stone tools to handles for greater leverage was a much later development, but now evidence has shown that the technique of hafting was definitely in use during the Pleistocene. And a ground-edge tool has a much more effective cutting edge than a flaked tool.

Plate 9. *Malangangerr rockshelter, Kakadu National Park, Northern Territory, contained human occupation and ground-edge grooved axes dating back to 23 000 years ago*

These ground-edge axes have provided some of the world's oldest evidence for shaping stone by hammer-dressing or pecking. And so far only in Japan does the technology of grinding stone to make a sharp, chisel-like cutting edge have a similar antiquity, although ground-edge tools do occur in what may be equally early South-East Asian contexts. An age of about 15 000 years has been suggested for edge-grinding at Niah Cave in Sarawak, and edge-ground tools may date back to before 20 000 BP in Indochina.[3] These significant technological innovations of grinding and hammer-dressing thus appear to be older in the Australasian region than in Africa, Europe or the Middle East.

Two features of the Arnhem Land ground-edge artefacts support the idea that they originated locally rather than that they were imported. Firstly, unlike the ground-edge tools from Asia, the Australian artefacts are hatchets, rather than axes. Hatchets differ from true axes by being employed with one hand instead of two and by having a lower mass and shorter handle. The small size and light weight of the Arnhem Land examples make it clear that they should be termed hatchets rather than axes[4] (however, the traditional term 'axes' has been retained in this book). Secondly, the early use of hammer-dressing on ground-ege tools is confined to northern Australia.

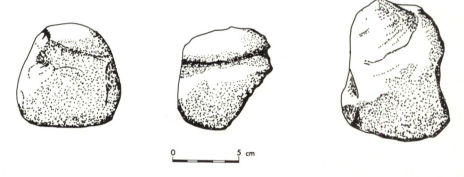

0 ____ 5 cm

Figure 7.1 *Pleistocene ground-edge axes from Arnhem Land, Northern Territory. All are bifacially flaked and the cutting edge is ground to a bevel; the grooves presumably assisted the attachment of handles. Left Axe from Malangangerr, made of hornfels, grooved on one surface (19 000–23 000 BP). Centre Axe from Nawamoyn, made of porphyritic dolerite, grooved on one surface and one broken margin (21 500 BP). Right Waisted axe from Nawamoyn, made of hornfels, indented on both margins (21 500 BP).* (After White 1967 and 1971)

Some of Australia's oldest grindstones have also been found in Arnhem Land. Three grindstones were found at Malakunanja II associated with charcoal dated to 18 000 ± 320 BP.[5] Two have flat to slightly concave grinding surfaces, and the face of one was impregnated with red and white ochre. The third has a circular grinding hollow about 10 centimetres in diameter on one of its faces. Similar grinding hollows were found in the lower levels of Nawamoyn and are common today in Arnhem Land rockshelters. It is likely that, as well as grinding up ochre to make pigment for painting artefacts, rockshelter walls or body decoration, grindstones and grinding hollows were used in the preparation of foods such as seeds and fruits.

Arnhem Land has great potential for archaeological research, since traces of prehistoric culture are preserved both in the floors and on the walls of rockshelters from early times to the present. Moreover, it seems likely that still older sites will be discovered, for only a handful of excavations have been carried out so far. This handful of excavated sites has nevertheless produced the world's oldest ground-edge hammer-dressed axes, and Australia's oldest grindstones, including the paint palette of an ice age artist.

KIMBERLEY SITES

The Kimberley region in the extreme north of Western Australia has long been thought to be one of the possible landfalls for early migrants or castaways swept southwards from the Timor or Indonesian part of island South-East Asia. Such migrants would have arrived on a broad plain, but it is uncertain whether it would have been grassland, savanna woodland, or mud and mangroves, with possibly an accompanying dearth of drinkable water. A few hundred kilometres inland the migrants would have encountered the high cliffs of the edge of the Kimberley escarpment, which forms the present rugged coastline.

The Kimberley escarpment is broken in places by plains and rivers flowing out to sea, through narrow gorges or broad river valleys like the Ord. It is in the Ord valley that two early occupation sites have been found, one of which certainly dates to the Pleistocene period. In Miriwun rockshelter on the Ord River, Charles Dortch of the Western Australian Museum excavated an occupation deposit in 1971 as part of a salvage programme before the area was flooded by the Ord River irrigation scheme.[6] The upper levels of the site contained small tools, but in the dark brown silty earth of the lower levels was a distinctive early assemblage. Tool types included relatively thick, denticulated or notched flakes, adze flakes, a few core-scrapers and small blades, and some pebble tools. Also found were some quartzite fragments, which may be parts of grindstones or anvils. The levels that produced these tools at Miriwun date to between about 3000 and 18 000 years ago.

One of the most remarkable discoveries was that two flakes recovered from below the horizon dated to 18 000 years were pieces struck from tektites. Tektites, or australites as they are called in Australia, are small glassy pebbles, up to about 2.5 centimetres in diameter, black or dark green in colour, and shaped like buttons, disks, teardrops, balls, or dumbbells. Their chemical composition is different from that of the rocks where they are found or from that of any terrestrial lava.

The origin of tektites is a puzzle. Some scientists believe that they are bits of terrestrial sedimentary rock excavated by the impact of meteorites crashing into the earth's surface, melted by the heat of impact, and congealed into glass as they are flung into the atmosphere to fall as a widely scattered shower. A more likely possibility is that they are the remains of gobs of lava fired at the earth by volcanic activity on the moon. A huge shower of tektites fell in the Australasian region 750 000 years ago. These australites are concentrated in a swathe across the southern half of Australia, particularly in Central Australia and in inland southern districts of Western Australia.

Analysis of one of the Miriwun tektites places it within the Indochinite group of tektites, the first tektite of this kind known from Australia. The seemingly remote possibility that this 18 000-year-old artefact (a very small flake) was brought from South-East Asia cannot be entirely dismissed until finds are made in Australia of whole Indochinites (i.e. pieces showing no artificial modification) in places where there is no association with human occupation. This Miriwun tektite may be the first ice age Asian artefact found in Australia, if Indochinites are shown never to occur outside Indochina.

In the Kimberley there may be a long continuity of technological tradition, both in grooved ground-edge axes and in serrated flakes. Kimberley serrated spear points are renowned for their fine workmanship and pleasing symmetry. They were made by pressure-flaking, a technique in which tiny flakes were pressed off by use of a bone, piece of wood or even one's teeth. Fine-grained stone was employed in their manufacture; more recently bottle glass or telephone insulators have been used. The use of these bifacially trimmed leaf-shaped points goes back at least 3000 years.

One particularly important feature of the Ord River sites is that organic material was well-preserved in most of them. It shows that, throughout the 18 000 years of Miriwun's habitation, the human occupants exploited a wide range of aquatic and terrestrial fauna. Food from the surrounding land included wallabies, possums, bandicoots, lizards and rodents; that from the river and lagoons, shellfish, reptiles, catfish, and goose eggs. The numerous eggshell fragments of the pied or semi-palmated goose (*Anseranas semipalmata*), which breeds only during the wet season, indicates that Miriwun was used as a wet-season camping place from late Pleistocene times until the European era.

MOUNT NEWMAN

Further west, in the Pilbara, new Pleistocene sites have been discovered. The first was the Mount Newman rockshelter, which overlooks the headwaters of the Fortescue River. Several rockshelters bearing traces of occupation were identified during a survey of the area before it was to be mined, and one, Newman orebody XXIX (PO187), was selected for a small test excavation.[7]

Ash, charcoal and ochre were found throughout the 1 metre deposit excavated, but no bone. Eleven hearths were found, one of which was typical of fire-pits used by modern Aborigines for baking animals. Most of the 400 artefacts found were simple flaked or retouched pieces, but two diagnostic implement types were found: steep-edged scrapers and notched scrapers. Radiocarbon dates revealed that the 1-metre deep deposit was 20 000 years old.

The Pleistocene age of habitation at Mount Newman raises the question of what conditions would have been like there 20 000 years ago. The site lies 7 kilometres from the bed of the Fortescue River, which now only flows after heavy rains. Normally it contains only a few pools of water on its upper section. The distance from the modern coast is about 360 kilometres, but in the Pleistocene the distance would have been more than 400 kilometres. Moreover, the rockshelter is located well within the present arid zone. But 20 000 years ago the Fortescue River, like Lake Mungo, may have been full of water, because of reduced evaporation in the colder glacial climate. The local environment would then have been far less arid than it is today. Pleistocene migrants may have gradually moved up the river, in the same way that they may have moved up the Murray and Darling until they reached Lake Mungo.

Eighteen kilometres to the north-east and close to the east side of the Fortescue River, another site, Newman rockshelter (P2055), yielded a date of 26 300 years on an early occupation layer.

Further south, bones of extinct marsupials and stone artefacts were found, although not in definite association with each other, in alluvial sediments on the banks of the Greenough and Murchison Rivers, east of Geraldton.[8] The excavators believe these sites to be more than 40 000 years old, but no datable material has yet been found in the lower layers, so their age can only be estimated on geological criteria, such as the degree of weathering. One significant aspect of these sites is that they are all located in the vicinity of springs, indicating that a reliable water supply was a major factor in locating Pleistocene campsites.

DEVIL'S LAIR

Devil's Lair is one of the earliest firmly dated sites in Australia, going back more than 30 000 years. This cave, in the extreme south-west, would have been not much more than 25 kilometres from the sea, even when sea level was at its lowest at the height of the last glaciation. Devil's Lair is now 5 kilometres from the coast, and 20 kilometres north of Cape Leeuwin. It is a single, dimly lit chamber with an earth floor of about 75 square metres largely covered with a layer of flowstone (a stone 'sheet' that sometimes forms on the floors of limestone caves) up to 20 centimetres thick. The name 'Devil's Lair' derives from the large quantity of remains of the Tasmanian devil found in the upper levels of the deposit.

In 1955 palaeontologist Ernest Lundelius excavated in the cave in search of a sequence of prehistoric fauna. As limestone caves provide excellent preservation conditions for bone, they are regular hunting grounds for palaeontologists, so other collectors followed him. One collector mentioned that there were possible artefacts in the cave, and a human incisor tooth was found. A salvage excavation was organized by Charles Dortch and Duncan Merrilees in 1970, to tidy up the disturbed material left by earlier excavators, line the pit with plastic, and then back-fill it to prevent further slumping of the deposit. The presence of artefacts in the deposit was confirmed, and six more seasons of investigation of the site and surrounding region followed.[9]

The Devil's Lair deposit is extremely rich in bone: the density of animals ranges from 70 to 2040 individuals per cubic metre. Some of the faunal remains in these bone beds were the prey not of owls or predators such as the Tasmanian devil, but of man. The case for humans as important predators rests on the unusually wide range of species present; artificial modification, including charring, of many bones; occurrence of some bones in undisturbed hearths; and the presence of items that must have been carried there by people, such as shells of fresh-water and even occasional marine shellfish. The people seem to have exploited most small to medium-sized animals, including wallabies, possums, bandicoots, native rats and mice, snakes, lizards, frogs, bats and birds, including emu eggs. Apart from absence of dingo bones and the presence of Tasmanian devil bones, the fauna represented is not very different from that of the present day.

Excavation revealed a deposit over 3 metres deep, accumulated over 37 000 years. The lowest levels that contain artefacts are dated to about 33 000 years ago and include a dozen pieces of limestone claimed to be artefacts, four small flakes of a stone foreign to the cave, one bone artefact, and several bones of extinct marsupial species such as the giant kangaroos, *Protemnodon* and *Sthenurus*. Some of the bones are fractured, and two are claimed by Dortch to be probable artefacts. If his claims are substantiated, this would be the best evidence yet found in Australia that man did prey on megafauna. Between about 28 000 and 6000 years ago occupation features, such as hearths, show that repeated, if intermittent, use was made of Devil's Lair. Most of the occupation was sealed below a layer of flowstone, formed 12 000 years ago.

The whole assemblage at Devil's Lair belongs to the early phase of Australian prehistory, although the artefacts are much smaller than those of most other Pleistocene sites. The early phase industries from both Miriwun and Devil's Lair contain small adze flakes and a variety of very small retouched tools made on flakes. It may be, therefore, that early phase tools tend to be smaller in western than eastern Australia, but much more evidence is needed before we can be sure whether this is the case or not. The comparatively small size of the Devil's Lair tools may also result from the fracturing properties of the raw materials used: quartz and a distinctive chert. The nearest known source of this rock is 120 kilometres east of Devil's Lair, but it is far more likely that it came from the now-drowned coastal plain, for similar chert was recently revealed by offshore drilling on the continental shelf.

Only about 170 stone and 100 bone tools were recovered from the area excavated at Devil's Lair. The stone tools are made from chert, quartz or limestone. Some undoubted limestone artefacts occur, but sometimes it is difficult to decide whether pieces of limestone that resemble choppers or rough cores are indeed artefacts, since most of them have been eroded by groundwater. Most of the stone artefacts are retouched flakes. Several are scrapers, perhaps intended to be hafted as adzes. Other tools have notched or toothed margins but most lack a distinctive form.

BONE ARTEFACTS

Even more important than the stone tools at Devil's Lair are those of bone, since bone and bone tools are preserved in so few Pleistocene sites. Those from Devil's Lair are at present Australia's oldest bone tools: the earliest is estimated to be 29 500 years old. A relatively large number and variety of types were preserved. The most common were split pointed bones, 1 to 15 centimetres long. Bone points are the next most common, some made from macropod shin bones and ground to a point, probably by a combination of abrasion and whittling.

A few tiny points have been found, which may have been used to pierce holes in animal skins to be sewn together. One is only 14 millimetres long and its point has been polished by use. Another 12 000-year-old bone artefact may be a pendant or bodkin. The broad end is perforated, and the edge of the hole has been smoothed by friction on the side next to the broad end. This shows that a piece of string or sinew has been passed through the hole, and suggests the object was used as a bodkin or suspended as an ornament.

ICE AGE ORNAMENTS

One of the most exciting finds from Devil's Lair was of three 12 000 to 15 000-year-old bone beads, the first indication in Australia that Pleistocene hunter-gatherers used such ornaments. The beads were made on short sections of naturally perforated long bones, and X-ray has shown that the perforation does extend right through. Experimental work has shown how such bone beads may have been manufactured.[10] A fresh kangaroo long bone is cut deeply around its shaft with a sharp flake, then snapped in half. The process is repeated about 2 centimetres from the broken edge and snapped again. The two ends of the bead are rounded by abrading with a piece of limestone, and the narrow cavity cleaned out with a sliver of wood or bone. The Devil's Lair beads are so far unique in Aboriginal culture and are the oldest known ornaments in Australia, indicating that life in the ice age was not merely a struggle for survival, but that there was time to devote to manufacturing non-utilitarian items (colour plate 5).

Other finds at Devil's Lair may also testify to the creativity and manual dexterity of its Pleistocene occupants. A perforated fragment of soft marl, which is definitely foreign to the locality, was found in a horizon about 14 000 years old. This might have been an ornamental pendant (figure 7.2).[11] The perforation, which may be artificial or natural, could also have served to polish

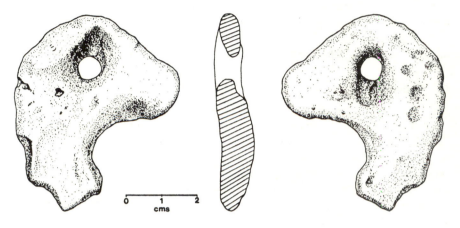

Figure 7.2 *A possible pendant of marl from Devil's Lair, Western Australia, about 14 000 years old.* (After Dortch 1980)

the tips or shafts of wooden spears or bone points. It resembles a bird's head, and the base of the 'neck' appears to have been fractured, so it may have originally been longer.

Finally, three pieces of limestone have been found, in 12 000 and 20 000-year-old horizons, which Dortch describes as 'engraved stone plaques'.[12] One of the flat surfaces of each 'plaque' is covered with faint straight lines, which could have been produced by a sharp, pointed tool of stone, bone or wood. Dortch argues that the lines must be man-made, and that they are either simple graffiti, or the plaques are art or ritual objects. Since similar linear engravings have been found in a few other West Australian sites (such as Orchestra Shell and Morfitt's Cave)[13] and elsewhere in Australia, the plaques are probably man-made. Further engravings, including definite motifs like animal tracks, may turn up in Devil's Lair, to dispel the shadow of doubt that hangs over them at present.

THE OLDEST CAMP YET

Until recently Devil's Lair was the oldest human occupation found in Western Australia, but a new discovery on the Upper Swan River has now shown that people were in the far south-west of the continent at least as early as in the south-east.

The new find is an extensive, open-air campsite on an ancient floodplain bordering the Swan River between Perth and Walyunga. It was found by an archaeological consultant, Bob Pearce, when he was driving past on the way to his holiday cottage. He had noticed men digging and could see that it was a clay deposit. In his own words, 'As I am interested in geology I just stopped to have a look. I spotted a couple of flakes by the roadside. It was the kind of rubble that most people would walk over and think nothing more about'.[14] What Pearce found were stone tools *in situ* in the clay at a depth of 70 to 90 centimetres. Some of the flakes were made of a distinctive chert containing fossils. This chert has only been found in Devil's Lair and other deposits older than 4600 years and came from an offshore source that was later submerged by the rising sea. Identical fossiliferous chert has now been turned up by drilling into the sea bed offshore, and is found on a number of other Western Australian archaeological sites in the Perth region.

Pearce alerted the manager of Midland Brick Company, who immediately halted work in that part of their clay pit. A small excavation was carried out by Pearce, and samples of charcoal associated with the tools were sent to Sydney University radiocarbon laboratory for dating, which was generously paid for by the company.

The great age of the occupation was not at first suspected, because the tools did not look particularly old and the deposit was not very deep. It was not until the first charcoal sample was processed a year later that its great antiquity was discovered. Meanwhile the government of Western Australia had given permission for the clay pit to go ahead and the site to be destroyed. Mike Barbetti, who runs the Sydney laboratory, acted with commendable speed. Phone calls alerted the authorities in Perth, and fortunately it emerged that the site, although released for destruction, was still intact. There was a collective sigh of relief that Australia had not inadvertently destroyed its oldest human occupation site yet discovered. It was a near miss, and a lesson for the future that permission must not be given to destroy sites, if it is suspected for any reason that they are of great antiquity, until they have been properly dated.

Further archaeological excavation of the Upper Swan site in January 1981 produced many more artefacts. Further dates confirmed the age as 38 000 years or older. Because this is close to the limit of radiocarbon dating, several samples were dated and gave very consistent and convincing results.[15]

About 900 artefacts have now been recovered from the site. Most are made of a deeply patinated dolerite. Stone chips (less than 15 millimetres long) account for 75 per cent of the finds and there are only thirty-seven tools showing retouch or use-wear. The small size of the tools is similar to other Western Australian Pleistocene sites such as Devil's Lair. The artefacts include small scrapers made of quartz and quartzite and pebble fragments showing wear on their edges. The presence of chips, cores and sets of flaked stone which can be re-fitted together suggests that this was a tool-manufacturing site and that it was relatively undisturbed.

The significance of the Upper Swan site lies in its very early date, which shows that the corners of Australia furthest from South-East Asia were populated by about 40 000 years ago. Indeed, this is the best evidence yet for the frequently cited estimate of more than 40 000 years of human occupation in Australia, which is suggested but not really proved at Mungo and Keilor. Human presence in the far south-west and south-east by 40 000 indicates the most likely time of first arrival in the continent as the period of low sea level around 52 000 years ago. Fortunately, new techniques are extending the range of radiocarbon dating back to about 60 000 years or even further, so it may well be that Australian sites older than 40 000 years will be discovered and dated during the next few years.

3. **Above** *Erosion at Lake Mungo, New South Wales, on the Walls of China lunette* (Australian Information Service)

4. **Below** *Koonalda Cave, Nullarbor Plain, South Australia* (D. J. Mulvaney)

CHAPTER EIGHT

THE EAST COAST IN THE PLEISTOCENE

It was not until the development of radiocarbon dating in 1950 that it became possible to determine the absolute age of prehistoric sites. During the 1950s several sites in Australia were excavated and dated, but none of these went back into the glacial period. Although it was widely argued that Aboriginal settlement of the continent must go back to times of low sea level in the ice age, there was still no firm evidence for the Pleistocene colonization of Australia.

It was, therefore, a great landmark in Australian prehistory when, in 1962, the National Physical Laboratory announced a 16 000-year-old date for the lower levels of Kenniff Cave in southern Queensland.[1] The circumstances of the announcement were characteristically Australian. John Mulvaney and his digging team were sitting round their campfire outside the cave, drinking billy tea and listening on their radio transceiver to the Royal Flying Doctor Service at Charleville. A telegram for the team from Melbourne was read out over the air, breaking the news of the Pleistocene age of the site. Mulvaney suspected a transmission error, with one zero too many, but his doubts were dispelled the next day when the age of 16 000 years was confirmed by a second telegram.

KENNIFF CAVE

Kenniff Cave lies 700 metres above sea level, near the crest of the Great Dividing Range, in a rugged region of sandstone cliffs and gorges, timbered hills and grassy plains. The cave, which would have provided an excellent shelter against wet or cold, lies in a sheltered valley called Lethbridge Pocket, above Meteor Creek. It is a roomy cave with low entrance but it averages about 3 metres of headroom inside (plate 10). Aboriginal paintings decorate the walls. The subjects are mainly stencils of hands and feet and items of equipment such as boomerangs, a shield and a hafted axe. Red, white, yellow and black pigments are used; the colour was blown from the mouth around the object held against the wall. The art had been recorded by a local amateur

◁ **5.** *Above* Bone bead from Devil's Lair, Western Australia, from a 15 000-year-old level (C. Dortch)

6. **Below** *Kartan tools from South Australia: horsehoof core and pebble tools*

Plate 10. *Excavation at Kenniff Cave, Queensland. The rockshelter bears stencilled hands on its roof and contained 19 000-year-old occupation. A latex soil profile is being taken off the rear wall of the excavation pit.* (Courtesy of D. J. Mulvaney)

fieldworker and senior radio operator of the Royal Flying Doctor Base, Reg Orr, through whom Mulvaney first heard of the site. In fact Kenniff Cave was already well-known locally because of the bush-ranging Kenniff brothers, by whose name it had become known.

Excavation of Kenniff Cave revealed occupation deposits going down 3.3 metres. Bone and other organic remains were not preserved, but stone artefacts were abundant. About 65 cubic metres of sand and ash were excavated and yielded more than 800 artefacts and almost 22 000 waste flakes or manufacturing debris. Kenniff Cave produced an early industry consisting entirely of scrapers and a later industry in which new specialized small tools were added to the scraper industry.

The older industry contained retouched tools made on flakes or large cores, which are generally termed scrapers (see figure 1.1). Their precise function cannot be established, but it is generally thought that they were used for planing or incising wooden objects, in other words they were tools for making tools. High-backed 'core-scrapers' and 'concave or nosed scrapers' are far more numerous in the earlier than later industry, and horsehoof cores are confined to the earlier horizons.

On the basis of further radiocarbon dates the earliest occupation of Kenniff Cave is now known to have occurred about 19 000 years ago. For 11 000 years there was no significant change in tool size, type, or manufacturing technique. Then, about 5000 years ago, the number of scrapers began to diminish and new small, finely worked tools were added to the existing toolkit. The most striking features of all these new tools were their small size and the probability that they were all composite tools that would be hafted into a handle. In the case of the long, juan knives, specimens exist in museums in which the stone knife is hafted in a handle of animal skin, fur, bark, and hair twine.

The importance of the Kenniff Cave cultural sequence is threefold. Firstly, it has an unusually wide range of artefacts and contains a small but representative sample of most of the major Australian prehistoric tool types, including all the small composite tools. Secondly, occupation extended over an extremely long time, from the present back into the Pleistocene. Thirdly, and most importantly, it was the site that provided the basis for the recognition of an earlier and a later technological phase in Australian prehistory. Mulvaney's broad concept of a two-part sequence has stood the test of time, although new discoveries have inevitably led to some modification of the original hypothesis.

Once the Pleistocene barrier had been broken, the search was on, and other early sites were found. Some were chance discoveries, but others were found because archaeologists now knew where to look.

BURRILL LAKE ROCKSHELTER

The earliest site found in south-eastern Australia was the Burrill Lake shelter, which was excavated in 1967–68.[2] The Burrill Lake site is a huge sandstone rockshelter, the largest known on the south coast of New South Wales. It is now signposted and open to the public, and there is also a replica of part of the site in the Australian Museum in Sydney. Facing east in a narrow, thickly wooded valley, it is sheltered both from onshore winds and the prevailing southerlies. The shelter floor is only 3 metres above modern sea level and lies about 180 metres from the edge of Burrill Lake. This is a coastal estuarine lagoon, usually open to the sea through a narrow channel. The site has fresh water nearby, together with all the food resources of woodland, estuary and ocean shore.

The excavation revealed that occupation of the shelter had begun 20 000 years ago. The discovery that humans had reached the south-east coast by that

time revolutionized archaeologists' thinking about the early settlement of
Australia. If people were so far south during the last glacial phase, a considerably earlier date had to be envisaged for the entry into the north of the
continent.

The cultural sequence at Burrill Lake had two major components: an older
and a younger industry, similar but not identical to those found at Kenniff
Cave. As at Kenniff, there was little technological change over 15 000 years,
until about 5000 to 5500 years ago, when new small tool types were added to
the toolkit.

BASS POINT

Not far north of Burrill Lake near Shellharbour is the open site of Bass Point.[3]
The hill on which the site is located drops sharply away on the seaward side, so
it would have been a campsite with a good vantage point. The offshore profile
is unusually steep in the region of Bass Point and Burrill Lake, so that even at
times of low sea level they would have been no more than 30 kilometres
inland. It was, nevertheless, a great surprise to discover that sporadic occupation on the site went back about 17 000 years.

The early stone tool industry at Bass Point lasted from about 17 000 to 3500
years ago. In the upper, younger, levels there is midden debris including
shellfish and the bones of fish, seals, birds and land mammals. By that time the
sea had risen, the hill had become a headland, and people were fishing and
collecting shellfish locally.

Bass Point is a significant site because it is the only open Pleistocene site to
have been found yet on the south-east coast, and it is one of only two
Pleistocene sites on this coast. Other ice age sites may still be found, but most
of them are probably now under the sea.

WALLEN WALLEN CREEK

Discoveries of ancient camps are generally made by chance, and one lucky find
of this sort was the discovery of an ancient 'transit camp'. This was used
sporadically by Aborigines for over 20 000 years, on the west coast of North
Stradbroke Island, about six kilometres south of Dunwich.[4]

Robert Neal, a post-graduate student at the University of Queensland,
found shells, animal bones, flaked stone artefacts and charcoal in a 2.5 metre
deep deposit at Wallen Wallen Creek, at the foot of a high sand dune about
400 metres inland from the present coastline. Geomorphic interpretation by
Errol Stock of Griffith University indicated that the site was formed at the base
of a large, well-vegetated sand hill near a water source. Twenty thousand years
ago sea level was some 150 metres lower and what is now Stradbroke Island
was part of the mainland, with the coast being between 12 and 20 kilometres

to the east. Wallen Wallen Creek was then a temporary sandy camping place on the main access route between the sea coast and the river valley and mountains to the west. As the polar ice caps began to melt about 17 000 years ago the sea gradually rose until it stabilized at its present level some 6500 years ago, transforming what was once a high coastal dunefield into an offshore island. The later phases of occupation formed next to an extensive freshwater swamp adjacent to the estuarine coastline. Other, even older prehistoric sites in the area may now lie deep beneath the waters of Moreton Bay.

This campsite has given scientists a rare chance to look back through the sands of time at profound changes in the coastal landscape and at the way Aboriginal lifestyles changed correspondingly, as the sea rose in the wake of the last global ice retreat. In recent times Aborigines were eating shellfish, fish and a few dugong there. The most recent artefacts are found in much greater quantities than those in the lower layers, indicating a major increase in human occupation of the offshore islands of Moreton Bay during the past few thousand years; this evidence accords with that from numerous shell middens on other sand islands such as Fraser and Moreton, revealed by archaeologists such as Peter Lauer, Jay Hall and Mike Rowland.

This is the first discovery of Pleistocene Aboriginal habitation on the east coast of Australia north of Sydney, and has pushed back the known date of Aboriginal occupation of south-east Queensland by at least 15 000 years. The site's evidence for continuous occupation of the near-coastal zone during the Pleistocene makes this site unique in the archaeological record of east coast Australia.

CRANEBROOK TERRACE

The oldest Aboriginal artefacts yet found in Australia came from gravels beside the Nepean River, at the foot of the Blue Mountains some 50 kilometres west of Sydney[5] (figure 8.1). Their discoverer was a Catholic priest, Father Eugene Stockton, who became interested in the archaeology of the Blue Mountains region when at the seminary at Springwood. He first noticed a few apparent stone artefacts in the Cranebrook gravel pits in the 1960s, and obtained radiocarbon dates in excess of 31 000 years on logs buried within the gravels. However, doubts were cast on whether the stones were really artefacts or naturifacts (made by natural agencies rather than by human hand), and whether the dated wood was really associated with the artefacts or not.[6]

It was not till 1987 that further evidence was gathered and published which indicates that at least some of the stones are artefacts, and that they must have been fashioned more than 40 000 years ago. (The wood cellulose of the first log dated proved to have been contaminated by much younger humic acid in the groundwater.) The artefacts were found in gravel pits on a terrace between the Nepean River and the village of Cranebrook just north of Penrith. Here a series of different sediments lie one on top of the other. The uppermost is six to nine metres of orange sandy-clay dating between about 40 000 and 45 000 years, which in places has been stripped off by river activity and replaced with younger (10 000 to 13 000 year old) but texturally similar overburden. This gravel-free overburden lies on top of a five to seven metre thick gravel layer with an undulating surface.

Stone artefacts have been found in the gravel layer, which was formed at a time when the river was much larger and more active than the present Nepean

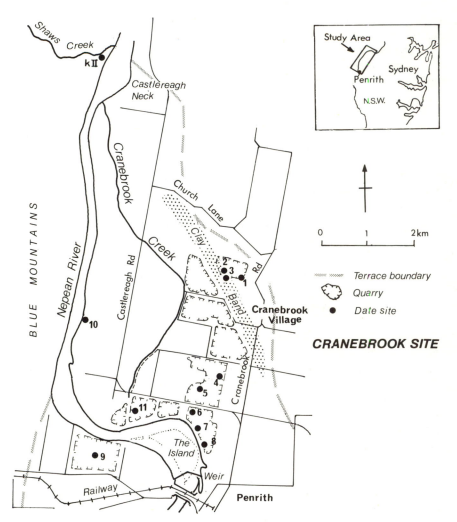

Figure 8.1 *Location of Cranebrook Terrace sites and Shaws Creek Shelter* (After Nanson, Young and Stockton 1987)

River. The period at which the gravel was deposited has been determined by
eleven radiocarbon dates of huge logs preserved within the gravel layer, and by
two thermoluminescence dates. On the basis of these dates the absolute time
of deposition of the gravels is believed to be between about 43 000 and 47 000
years ago.

Seven stones, which appear to be artefacts, have now been found well
within the gravel below as much as sixteen metres of alluvial overburden, one
right beside one of the dated logs. They resemble pebble choppers, steep-edged
scrapers and other core and scraper tools, typical in both form and size of the
old Australian core tool and scraper tradition. They are made of a wide variety
of stone: chert, rhyolite, dacite, quartzite, ignimbrite and siliceous mudstone.
One or two are weathered and may have been rolled along downstream in the
river bed before being deposited, but most are remarkably fresh and undam-
aged, as if they had been discarded where they were found, four hundred
centuries later.

Logs of several metres in length and up to a metre in diameter in the gravels
were identified as mainly Casuarina, Eucalyptus and Callistemon (bottlebrush),
which are all trees common on the forested floodplains of New South Wales
nowadays. Analysis of pollen, both from a core taken in the clay band and
from alluvium adhering to a large log within the gravel, confirmed that the
environment before the height of the last ice age was mixed grassland and
woodland similar to the present day, but the river had a very different flow
regime, much stronger and more variable. Later during the glacial period the
climate would have been much drier and colder.

The Cranebrook Terrace artefacts were not part of a campsite. Rather, they
occur in a coastal river valley at a relatively low elevation above sea level
which Aborigines occasionally visited for hunting and tool-making, between
40 000 and 47 000 years ago. The site's significance is that it seems to show
that Aborigines were down in the south-east of Australia more than 40 000
years ago, which means that they must have first entered the continent several
millennia earlier, perhaps more than 50 000 years ago.

The Nepean River terraces offer the prospect of a continuous archaeological
record from 45 000 years ago to the present. Stockton's excavation of a nearby
rockshelter, Shaws Creek KII, has revealed occupation from 15 000 years ago
to the present, and the two metre deep excavation has not yet reached
bedrock.[7]

The stone tools of Shaws Creek II shelter revealed the usual change from an
early core tool and large scraper tradition to small tools, particularly Bondi
points, in the upper levels. One particularly noteworthy find associated with a
radiocarbon date of about 14 700 years was a chert tool resembling an adze or
chisel, apparently bearing traces of resin. If correct, this is the first firm
evidence that tools such as adzes were fixed into a handle during the Pleistocene period.

LAKE GEORGE

At Lake George on the Southern Tablelands some hundred kilometres inland, a completely different type of evidence has been found that suggests that humans were there, not merely towards the end of the ice age, but more than 100 000 years ago. This evidence comes from a core drilled out of the sediments at the bottom of the lake by Gurdip Singh, a palynologist at the Australian National University.[8] Microscopic pollen grains and charcoal particles in the upper 8.6 metres of the core – covering the last 350 000 years – have been analysed and provide the longest continuous record of vegetation and fire history in Australia. The base of the 72 metre core is estimated to represent the years between 4.2 and 7 million years ago. The sediments extend down still further, to an estimated 134 metres, which means that the formation of the Lake George basin must be reckoned to date to 20 million years ago. The sediments indicate alternating lake-full to lake-dry conditions over the last 750 000 years, reflecting the effects of changes from eight glacial to eight interglacial periods.

Pollen analysis (palynology) was used to establish the kinds of plants that had grown in the area in the past. Because pollen grains of different plants have different forms, it is possible to identify the plants from which they came. It is not easy, however, to find out how many plants are represented, since different plants produce different quantities of pollen. Yet presence and absence of particular species can be determined, together with an approximate idea of relative frequencies.

The sequence (figure 8.2) shows that, about 120 000 years ago, there was a huge increase in the amount of charcoal in the sediment, indicating a much higher incidence of fires than before, although the last interglacial was no drier than the preceding two had been. At the same time there was a reduction in the number of fire-sensitive species and the first expansion of fire-tolerant, *Eucalyptus*-dominated vegetation in the 350 000 years of vegetation history represented by the upper part of this core. This change in vegetation has continued to the present day. The key question is, what sparked it off? Singh suggested that it was humans with their fire-sticks, and that nothing except human agency can explain the sudden change to a fire-tolerant vegetation dominated by *Eucalyptus*, indicating that humans reached the Lake George area during the mild, warm period of the last interglacial phase about 120 000 years ago. The Aborigines used fire not only for cooking but also as a hunting weapon, igniting the bush both to drive out game and to make fresh new grass spring up to attract browsing animals. This increase in the use of fire would account both for the change in vegetation and the great increase in charcoal remains washed or blown into the lake sediments at this period.

Since this theory was first propounded, archaeologists have been searching the shores of Lake George for early sites. There are no rockshelters in the area, so there is nothing to focus occupation in one place rather than another. It is thus no easy task, but some slight indications have now been found that Singh may be right.[9]

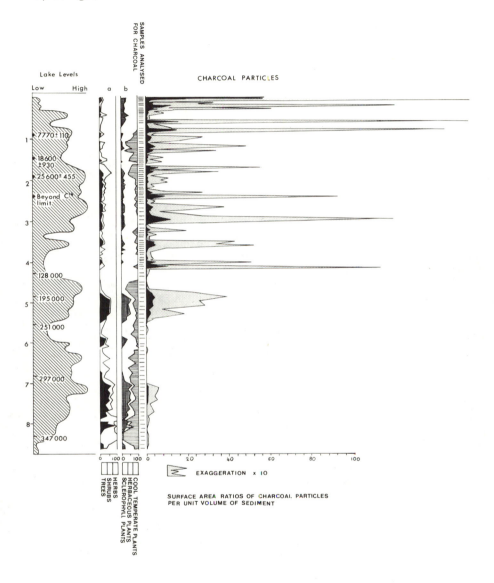

Figure 8.2 *The lake levels and vegetation and charcoal sequence from Lake George, New South Wales. The peaks and troughs on the lake level curve are approximate, and the dates beyond the limit of radiocarbon (C-14) dating are oxygen isotope dates inserted for comparative purposes only. (Based on Singh et al. 1980)*

In a gully (plate 11) on what would have been the lake shore during the ice age, some small amorphous flakes were found in aeolian sands dated to 17 000 to 23 000 years ago. But none was found indisputably *in situ*. A large excavation will be needed to try to uncover the remains of any prehistoric camp there, because if they exist, there is probably only a thin scatter of stone tools over a wide area.

Further discoveries were made in the Butmaroo sand quarry near the highest former eastern shore of the lake. Here in the tailings of sand-mining operations several large, heavy tools have been found. They include a horsehoof core and

Plate 11. *Fernhill Tree Gully, Lake George, New South Wales. A few stone artefacts have been found here in situ in Pleistocene sediments in field surveys as this one by the Canberra Archaeological Society.*

some coarse heavy scrapers, characteristic of the old Australian core tool and scraper tradition. None of these typologically old tools has yet been found still in position in the older aeolian sand, which is covered by younger sand that is

Plate 12. Diprotodon *skeleton found at Lake Callabonna, South Australia. The head is almost 1 metre long, and an adult would have weighed about 2 tonnes. Its teeth make it clear that it was a plant-eater.* (By courtesy of the South Australian Museum, Adelaide)

dated to the last 4000 years and contains small tools typical of the small tool tradition.

There are thus hints, but as yet no proof, that people were at Lake George in the Pleistocene. There are also no indications, as yet, of the sort of antiquity suggested by Singh, and this has been disputed by Richard Wright, who argues for a date of about 60 000 years ago.

Occupation of the Southern Tablelands during the Pleistocene does not now seem as unlikely as it once did. Indeed, analysis of pollen and sediments from the Lake George core has shown that there were considerable fluctuations in vegetation and lake levels. Moreover, Singh interprets the evidence as indicating that average annual temperature during the last glacial phase was about 6 degrees Celsius lower than today, rather than the 9 or 10 degrees suggested by earlier authorities. If this is so, Lake George would not have been so different a habitat from Lake Mungo, only considerably colder because of its higher elevation.

If further archaeological work shows that people were indeed at Lake George some 20 000 years ago, it will lend support to the concept of the rapid peopling of the continent, with almost every type of environment being inhabited during the Pleistocene. If it is further demonstrated that people reached Lake George during the last interglacial phase, 120 000 years ago, we will have to rethink radically our ideas about the antiquity of the human occupation of Australia.

At present the oldest sites yet found are of the order of 35 000 to 40 000 years at Swan River, Lake Mungo, Keilor and Cranebrook. Human occupation must be older than this, since these sites lie in the south of the continent, and it would have taken the first arrivals a considerable time to reach these areas. It is also improbable that archaeologists have chanced to find the very earliest sites that exist. Thus it is estimated that occupation must go back at least 45 000 to 50 000 years.

The problem about an antiquity of more than 100 000 years, as suggested by Singh, is that it is hard to imagine people being able at such an early date to make watercraft capable of crossing at least 50 kilometres of open sea. If the first Australians did step ashore at such an early date, we must envisage only a very few castaways, and salute their success in surviving and multiplying to fill a continent.

CHAPTER NINE

AN ICE AGE WALK TO TASMANIA

In the Pleistocene the most southerly part of the Australian continent was not Wilson's Promontory in Victoria but the South East Cape region of Tasmania. A drop in sea level of only about 60 metres exposed the floor of what is now Bass Strait, producing a land bridge of 15 million hectares (figure 9.1). The present islands of Bass Strait would at that time have been hills overlooking a broad plain.

Since beginning fieldwork in Tasmania early in the 1960s, Rhys Jones had always put forward the hypothesis that Tasmania was occupied by means of this land bridge at a time of lowered sea level. He had also argued that most of the Pleistocene sites would have been coastal, since during the height of the last glacial period extensive ice sheets covered the central highlands, and much of the present island of Tasmania was treeless and inhospitable. Archaeological work during the last decade has proved Jones's first prediction correct, but his second wrong. Due to his work and others such as Sandra Bowdler, Harry Lourandos, Jim Stockton, Don Ranson, Jim Allen, Richard Cosgrove, Steve Brown, Ron Vanderwal, Scott Cane, Kevin Kiernan, Greg Middleton, Albert Goede and Peter Sims, a great deal more is now known about Tasmanian prehistory, although many questions still remain to be answered.

CAVE BAY CAVE

On Hunter Island, 6 kilometres off what is now the north-west tip of Tasmania, an occupational sequence embracing the last 23 000[1] years has been found in a large sea cave at Cave Bay. Signs of both Aboriginal and European visits were found when the site was visited by Sandra Bowdler in 1973 at the suggestion of local residents. On the dusty floor there were shells and animal bones and on the walls numerous graffiti, the oldest of which read 'Walrus 1867'.

Excavation revealed that Pleistocene occupation of Cave Bay Cave began by 22 750 ± 720 BP (figure 9.2). Over the next 2000 years, half a metre of deposit built up, characterized by layers of thick ash, a few bone points and stone tools, and the smashed and burnt bones of various land animals.

Both the stone and bone tools resemble tools from mainland Pleistocene sites, yet are also forerunners of later Tasmanian forms. One bone point, 9 centimetres long, and made on a macropod shin bone, was associated with charcoal dated to 18 550 BP: the others were similar but belonged to levels of between 4000 and 6600 years ago. It has been suggested that these ice age bone points were used as awls or reamers for making fur cloaks. In historic times in the cold parts of south-east Australia similar bone points were observed in use by Aborigines for piercing holes to sew skins together with sinew thread. Sandra Bowdler argues that they were needles for making nets and baskets rather than for skin-clothing.

The ice age hunters, in the glacial cold of southern Australia, probably used the skins of wallabies and other animals they killed as clothing. Such fur cloaks may have gone out of use in some regions when the ice age was over, but in the Snowy Mountains and Victorian Alps, Aborigines were still snugly wrapped in possum-skin cloaks in winter in the nineteenth century.

No shells, fish bones, or mutton-bird bones were found in the lower layers of Cave Bay Cave, and the remains are best interpreted as the debris of occasional inland hunting parties. The sea at this time would have been 30 to 40

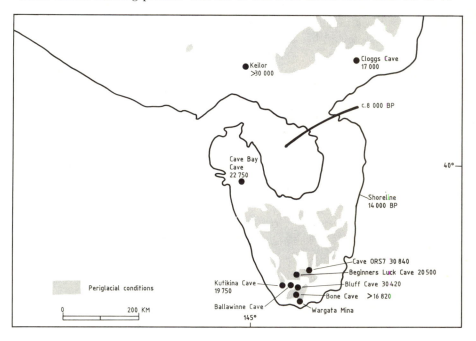

Figure 9.1 *Ice age sites in Tasmania, showing the coastline at 14 000 BP, and the drowning of the land bridge between about 12 000 and 8000 BP. (Based on Jones 1977)*

kilometres or more away from the cave, which would have looked out over the vast Bassian Plain. The marsupial animals in the ice age levels of the cave are, in order of frequency, the brush wallaby, the barred bandicoot, the tiger cat, the native cat, Tasmanian pademelon and the wombat. None of these are extinct animals, but the wombat, native cat and bandicoot are not found in more recent sites and were absent from Hunter Island in historic times.

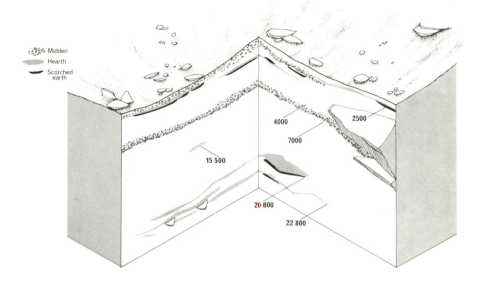

Figure 9.2 *The stratigraphy of the Cave Bay Cave site, Hunter Island. The 7000 BP date for the bottom of the lower midden has now been corrected to 6600 BP.* (After Bowdler 1977)

This early occupation was sporadic and fleeting, and it was followed by a phase of heavy rock fall, which may represent the peak of the last glacial episode about 18 000 years ago. The extreme cold would have caused water to freeze in the rock cracks and crevices, and the expansion of the ice would lead to widening of the cracks and the fall of rock slabs.

From about 18 000 until 7000 years ago, when the sea reached its present level, the cave was effectively deserted. One small isolated hearth, dated to about 15 000 years ago, indicates that humans were still present then, but otherwise the main occupants of the cave were owls and carnivorous predators. Large quantities of tiny intact rodent bones are indicative of the regurgitated pellets of owls, and masses of macropod and possum bones chewed into small fragments suggest the presence of the Tasmanian devil.

Then, about 6600 years ago, when the sea was close to its present position and marine shellfish were easily obtainable, the cave again came into use. The remains in the cave suggest the new occupants had a well-developed coastal economy. The contents of this midden are similar to those from the lowest levels of Rocky Cape South, excavated by Rhys Jones and dated to around 8000 years old. At Cave Bay Cave there was a dense shell midden, its base dated to about 6600 years ago, containing the bones of small macropods and mutton-birds, the shells of rocky coast species and a few fish bones. Bone points were present in layers older than 4000 years, and so were stone tools, such as quartz and quartzite flakes, and pebble tools.

Sandra Bowdler interprets this midden as representing the period when coastal people, with a well-developed fishing economy, had been pushed back by the rising seas to a 'Hunter Peninsula', just before the land link with Tasmania was finally severed. After this midden was deposited, the cave was not occupied for several thousand years, until Hunter Island was re-colonized 2500 years ago by Tasmanian seafarers.

THE SOUTH-WEST

Tasmania's south-west gave up a stone age secret on the afternoon of Sunday, 11 January 1981 to archaeologists Rhys Jones and Don Ranson, who were carrying out a two week survey for Aboriginal relics in the Gordon River Valley, threatened with flooding by a proposed hydro-electricity scheme.[2] The now uninhabited region is one of the world's last remaining temperate wildernesses and contains some of the densest rainforest in the world. This is some of the world's most inhospitable terrain.

When the first Europeans settled in Tasmania in the early 1880s, Aboriginal occupation was largely coastal, confined to a narrow coastal strip only a few hundred metres wide that was kept open by the use of fire. The people lived mainly off the resources of the sea and travelled up and down the coast. One or two tracks through rainforest were also kept open by fire, for example, from Port Davey across to the south coast, a short cut across the south-west corner of Tasmania, but there was little or no occupation through the rest of the south-west wilderness.

As well as the notorious horizontal scrub, which is very difficult to walk under or over, the rivers of the south-west are extremely swift-flowing and hard to cross. They would have been a formidable obstacle to Aborigines, but provided a means for twentieth century man to reach the heart of the wilderness. But only jet boats can make headway against the current, and they have to be carried around waterfalls and some rapids.

The first Aboriginal site to be discovered in the south-west rainforest was found on the bank of the Denison River 300 metres from its junction with the Gordon (figure 9.3). In the words of Rhys Jones: 'I noticed that on a bank a great tree, a *Nothofagus*, had fallen down, taking some of the earth with it. We stopped in the little boat we were in, walked up the bank, and found stone tools. Afterwards we found more, *in situ*, buried in a clay deposit on the high river bank. This was the first evidence we have had of any prehistoric occupation of this region by man – a very interesting discovery.'[3]

When the giant *Nothofagus* beech tree had fallen, its roots had exposed a patch of clay as they were wrenched from the ground. There was found a quartz pebble core with flakes chipped from it scattered around. The flakes, which would have been used as knives and scrapers, could be replaced exactly on the core, and were still as sharp as a surgeon's scalpel. Twelve tools were found, including a quartzite hammerstone. The campsite that these tools marked was originally thought to be very old, but a preliminary date on charcoal associated with the tools is 300 ± 150 BP. This means that the south-west must at least have been traversed by Aborigines in recent times.

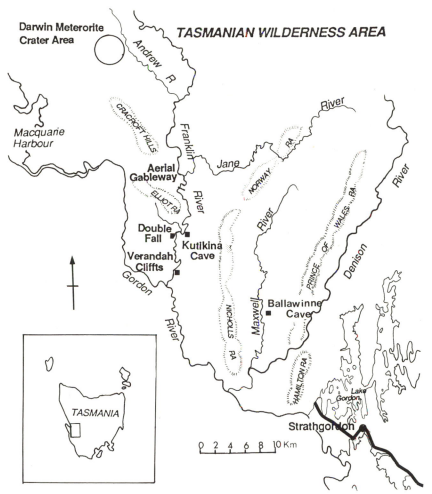

Figure 9.3 *South-west Tasmania*

The finding of these stone tools in dense rainforest was a million to one chance, but it was followed less than three weeks later by the discovery of rich Aboriginal cultural remains in a huge cave in the same primeval forest of south-west Tasmania.

KUTIKINA CAVE

The massive cave,[4] extending 170 metres into the cliff of limestone, is 35 metres back from the east bank of the Lower Franklin River and 10 kilometres from its confluence with the Gordon. It was found in 1977 by a geomorphology student, Kevin Kiernan, and named Fraser Cave after the Prime Minister, because 'we were trying to direct the attention of politicians to the area' (colour plate 8 and figure 9:4). Fraser Cave has now been given the Aboriginal name Kutikina meaning 'spirit' (pronounced to rhyme with miner).

Stone flakes and animal bones were noticed on the cave floor but the cave's discoverers did not realize their significance. Then, in February 1981, Kiernan revisited the cave on an expedition of the Tasmanian Wilderness Society and its archaeological potential was realized. Three weeks later he returned with Rhys Jones and officers of the National Parks and Wildlife Service of Tasmania.

The tools found include pebble choppers and thick, steep-edged scrapers of types typical of mainland Australia during the last ice age. The rocks used were mainly quartzite and quartz. Most remarkably, cutting tools were made from natural glass, or Darwin glass, as it is called after the Darwin meteorite crater. Darwin glass is a true glass which was formed when a meteorite crashed into the earth. The high energy collision melted the rocks around the collision point, forming glass. Small seams of these contorted glass 'impactites' occur around the meteorite crater, which is some 25 kilometres north-west of Kutikina Cave and was only discovered by geologists twenty years ago. The Aborigines, however, for thousands of years, selected the glass, collected it in bags, and carried it back to their cave for manufacture into sharp cutting tools.

Archaeological detective work by Tom Loy, involving residue analysis with high-powered microscopes, has revealed some of the ways in which ice age hunters used these glass artefacts. Examination of a tool's cutting edge, magnified 300 times, has revealed a residue of yellow fleshy tissue. This proved to be made up of two proteins, collagen which is found in some bones and tissue, and haemoglobin, which gives blood its red colour. The haemoglobin was crystallised, and it was found to be from the blood of a red-necked wallaby (also known as Bennett's wallaby). Haemoglobin crystals are like fingerprints; the shape and growth rate of the haemoglobin crystals of each animal species are unique. When the haemoglobin crystals from the tool were compared with those from a modern red-necked wallaby, they were found to be identical.

The bones in Kutikina Cave are also of great interest. Bone is preserved in few prehistoric occupation sites and, even where it is, it is usually almost impossible to distinguish the prey of human hunters from that of animals or from bones of animals who died there of natural causes. But here the bones must be the result of human meals for the long bones are smashed to extract the marrow, almost all the bones have been charred, and only certain body parts are present.

These bone deposits can give a unique picture of the hunting strategies of Pleistocene Tasmanians. The people were apparently eating mainly wallabies, especially Bennett's wallaby or the red-necked wallaby. It is interesting that among all the thousands of bones, no remains of any extinct species have yet been found.

The cave has a floor area of about 100 square metres, covered with a 1 to 2 metre deep carpet of bone debris, tools and fireplaces. Some 250 000 animal bones and 40 000 stone flakes have been found in less than one cubic metre of deposit. It was probably a base camp occupied by twenty to thirty people for a few weeks each year. They hunted the area for wallabies and other animals, bringing their game back to the cave to be butchered, cooked and eaten.

In places a faint glimmer of daylight penetrates through openings in the high roof, and under each of these 'skylights' is a mass of tool manufacturing debris where an ice age craftsman sat and flaked his stone choppers and knives. A few bone points have also been found. The type of tools and sediments revealed by Jones's small test excavation of one cubic metre caused him to suggest a Pleistocene antiquity for occupation long before the radiocarbon dates were received. These have proved his predictions correct.

The floor of the cave was capped by a thin, white, hard layer of calcium carbonate, often called moon milk. Found immediately below this was a 30 to 40 centimetre thick occupation layer of interleaving hearths, where people had been camping. Charcoal, ash and burnt earth in shallow depressions from old fires made this a dark coloured layer, fantastically rich in artefacts and charred animal bones. The top of this hearth layer has now been dated to 14 840 ± 930 BP.

Below the hearths was something quite different: small limestone blocks and angular fragments probably fallen from the roof. Such roof-fall would have occurred under very different climatic conditions from those of today. Stone tools and charcoal are present throughout this rubble layer and the clay below it, right down to bedrock. Dates from charcoal have shown that people first camped in this cave about 20 000 years ago.

The country around this Franklin River cave was completely different then. There were open plains instead of trees everywhere. Glaciers flowed down the high mountain valleys and the only trees were bands of forest along the rivers in sheltered valleys. This would have provided red-necked wallabies with a habitat of forest and grassland similar to their modern habitat, and they still roam the more open parts of the south-west today. The open heathlands would have been comparable to the cold, dry arctic tundra of Alaska, the Yukon, Russia or Patagonia, and icebergs would have sailed past the nearby coast.

Like their contemporaries in the northern hemisphere, the ice age hunters of Tasmania made use of deep caves to survive the freezing temperatures. The

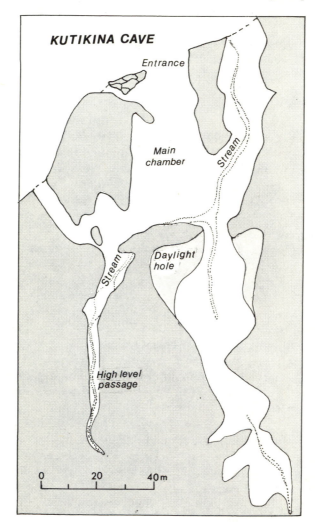

Figure 9.4 *Plan of Kutikina Cave, Franklin River* (After R. Jones 1987)

remains found in Kutikina Cave are similar to those from the caves of Dordogne in southern France. The stone tools are similar, the cooking methods are similar, even the hunting strategies are similar, although northern hunters concentrated on deer and the Tasmanians on wallabies.

Kutikina Cave is not unique; more than 20 other ice age camp sites in limestone caves have now been found in south-west Tasmania. The greatest number is on the lower Franklin River, but others lie in the valleys of the Maxwell, Andrew, Acheron and Florentine Rivers. One intriguing feature of all these sites is that, where the occupational deposits have been dated, they are almost all older than 13 000 years old. One factor in their abandonment around 13 000 years ago seems to be changing environmental conditions, including the spread of rainforest.

ROCK ART

The presence of ochre pigment in the Kutikina Cave deposit raised the exciting possibility that these ice age Tasmanians were practising art. In January 1986, the first rock art was found in south-west Tasmania, in the Maxwell River valley which runs parallel and about 12 kilometres to the east of the Franklin. Don Ranson of the Tasmanian National Parks and Wildlife Service was leading the first archaeological survey of this remote and rugged region.[5]

In all, six limestone caves were discovered which showed evidence of human occupation. One (M86/2) revealed on excavation an extensive cultural deposit. There were stone tools made of non-local materials, including quartz 'thumbnail scrapers', and bones of wallaby, wombat, devil, bandicoot, mouse and birds. Radiocarbon dates have now been obtained for charcoal in this deposit, and range from 18 000 to 23 000 years. The bottom of the cultural layer has not yet been reached, and continues on down below the excavated area for at least another 30 centimetres, so the site may well go back even further than 23 000 years.

The most exciting find of the expedition came near the end, on 21 January, when Steve Brown and Roy Nichols were examining hundreds of metres of passageways and caverns beyond the daylight section of a complex cave not far from the Maxwell River. Suddenly their torch beam lit up the outline of a human hand, stencilled in red ochre. Further examination of the walls of the chamber revealed a gallery of sixteen hand stencils in two groups. The stencils were made by grinding up iron oxide and mixing it with water and possibly animal fat into a red ochre paste, then placing the hand flat on the rock wall and spray painting it, probably by taking a mouthful of the paste and spitting it over the hand. At least five individuals were responsible for the art. Both left and right hands are equally represented. Some of the hand stencils are stunningly clear, standing out in a vivid red against the pale grey dolomite wall: others are quite indistinct. On one hand it is evident that the middle finger is missing at the first joint; this could be either an accidental or ritual mutilation.

In the same chamber there are small patches of red ochre on various parts of the ceiling. The chamber is in total darkness some 20 metres from the entrance, and would probably have been approached by the light of burning grass torches. Near the entrance to the passage which leads down to the hand stencil gallery five rock protuberances are emblazoned with dramatic large streaks of blood-red ochre. These may have acted as some kind of warning marker to a special area of ritual significance.

Beyond the main entrance to the cave there is a small occupation deposit in a narrow chamber, sealed by a thin, hard, white calcareous layer, dated elsewhere to about 14 000 years old. Below this layer are tiny fragments of ochre associated with charcoal.

The significance of this find is that it proves the ice age antiquity in Australia of hand stencils, and by implication of rock painting. Hand stencils are associated with paintings in very many younger Australian rock art sites, but until this find neither stencils nor paintings had been found in indisputable ice age contexts, whereas in the cave art of Europe hand stencils often accompany paintings dated from 24 000 to some 16 000 years ago.

The Maxwell River site also proves once and for all that Tasmanian Aborigines practised painting in prehistoric times. Ironically the island which has produced the first ice age stencils of Australia has a remarkable lack of more recent rock art sites, with less than 20 on record.

Significantly, the art of Ballawinne (pronounced Bal-a-win-ee and meaning 'ochre') Cave, as the Maxwell River site has now been named by Tasmanian Aborigines, is in complete darkness. This is extremely rare among Australian art sites, but more nearly parallels decorated caves of Europe such as Lascaux and Altamira. In prehistoric art, hand stencils are a world-wide motif, and this find shows that the first Tasmanians shared a common global cultural template in the marks they left behind on the walls of caves.

Once this first painted site had been found, the search was well and truly on, with archaeologists fantasizing about discovering 'the frieze of the leaping wallabies'! Eighteen months later another decorated cave was found in southern Tasmania, 85 kilometres to the south-east of Ballawinne Cave. This discovery was announced by Aboriginal archaeological consultant Darrell West, geomorphologist Kevin Kiernan, and archaeologists Richard Cosgrove and Rhys Jones in The Weekend Australian of 17–18 October 1987.[6] The cave, Wargata Mina (pronounced War-gata Mee-na, meaning 'my blood') and formerly Judds Cavern, lies deep within the southern Tasmanian rainforests in the Cracroft Valley, bordering on the World Heritage Area of the south-west. Wargata Mina is one of the largest river caves in Australia, with passages, alcoves and caverns extending over 1.7 kilometres. One has to negotiate a way through age-old stalagmites to reach the painted alcove, some 35 metres from the entrance and at the very last glimmer of daylight penetration. The chamber is the size of a suburban house, dark, dank and bedecked with curtains of stalactites. Yet, there on the wall are hand stencils, faint pale impressions of hands with red ochre sprayed around them (colour plate 10).

There are some eighteen stencils, very similar to those at Ballawinne Cave, and possibly dated to over 12 000 years ago. The stencils' age has been estimated through geomorphological evidence; the art is covered by a thick layer of calcium carbonate accretions, some of which extends continuously to a thick layer of flowstone on the floor and stalagmites more than a metre thick joining ceiling to floor. Likewise, some stalactites have grown in front of the stencils, demonstrating that they post-date the art. The age of this calcium carbonate deposition has been dated in other south-west Tasmanian caves, using *uranium thorium* and other radiometric methods, to the humid phase at the end of the glacial period about 12 000 years ago.

Both adult and children's hands were stencilled, and there are also extensive expanses of red ochre painted or smeared onto the walls. Some of these patches are several metres across, and some lie in total darkness at least 60 metres inside the cave. Analysis by Tom Loy[7] of tiny samples of the 'pigment' from two painted panels has revealed traces of blood proteins and red blood cells. This is mammalian, and almost certainly human blood. This seems to be the first time that blood has been biochemically identified as present in rock art anywhere in the world.

These cryptic signatures in blood and red ochre on the rock are a symbolic statement about identity, religion and land, reaching down across the centuries. Their similarity to early cave art in Europe and elsewhere bears witness to the evolution of humankind on a global scale and the cultural elements common in human behaviour.

SOUTHERN FORESTS CAVES

Archaeological discoveries in south-west Tasmania came thick and fast between 1985 and 1988. The impetus for further site survey and research came mainly from the battle for the Southern Forests between conservation interests and the forest industries, who were applying for renewal of licences for wood chip exports. The Australian National University's archaeological consultancy unit, ANUTECH, was commissioned by Australian Newsprint Mills and Huon Forest Products to carry out an archaeological survey. In addition, the Southern Forests Archaeological Project was set up independently by Jim Allen and Richard Cosgrove from the Archaeology Department at La Trobe University.

Both these initiatives have borne great fruit. The number of known Pleistocene occupation sites has risen to over twenty, and of ice age art sites to three, the known time of human occupation in Tasmania has been extended by almost 10 000 years, and the first human remains of apparent Pleistocene age have been found.

Nanwoon Cave in the Upper Florentine Valley yielded the human remains.[8] There had been previous research in the Florentine Valley by Albert Goede and Peter Murray, who had discovered Beginner's Luck Cave.[9] There it seemed that stone tools were associated with the bones of extinct fauna about 20 000 years ago, but it now appears that the megafauna dates from much earlier (about 40 000 years according to aspartic acid racemization dates) and the artefacts and fauna are not contemporary. At Nanwoon Cave on the other hand there appears to be no evidence of extinct animals, but instead, numerous stone tools associated with charcoal and burnt and unburnt remains of modern animal species. On the floor of the cave part of a human skull – an occipital bone – was found. This is now in the custodianship of the Tasmanian Aboriginal Centre but examination by physical anthropologist, Steve Webb, has been permitted. His conclusions are that the skull is that of a young adult, probably a woman in her late teens or twenties. The remains are gracile in form, but unfortunately too fragmentary to compare with human skeletal remains from mainland Australia. Their age is also unknown, although circumstantial evidence makes it likely that they are probably more than 12 000 years old.

Archaeological work by Richard Cosgrove and Jim Allen in the Southern Forests region has provided similarly dramatic evidence, pushing back the known time of occupation by at least 8000 years. Excavation of Bone Cave[10] in the middle Weld Valley yielded more than 17 000 year old occupation, and in Bluff Cave in the Florentine Valley and Cave ORS 7 on the Shannon River, the basal dates were 30 000 years.[11]

Bone Cave lies close to the Weld River at an altitude of 400 metres above sea level. Charcoal from a depth of 70 centimetres gave a date of about 17 000 years. Bone and stone artefacts and burnt bone are present in a small chamber, and systematic excavation was carried out in May 1988 by Jim Allen with a team from La Trobe University.

Bluff Cave is a small limestone shelter at an elevation of 400 metres above sea level, now surrounded by wet sclerophyll scrub and rainforest. The cultural deposit is sealed by a layer of calcium carbonate flowstone. Although only 60 centimetres deep, the deposit spans almost 20 000 years, with a date of 11 630 ± 200 BP on charcoal only five centimetres below the surface and a basal date of 30 420 ± 690 BP.

The site is extremely rich, with a small excavation of about one cubic metre yielding high concentrations of charcoal and some 30 000 stone flakes and many kilograms of bone fragments. Animal remains include red-necked wallaby, pademelon, platypus, wombat, grey kangaroo, native cat, bird bone and emu egg shell. The presence of emu egg shell would indicate occupation in late winter to early spring.

A wide variety of stone is used for tools, including chert, silcrete, crystal quartz, chalcedony, agate and hornfels. Many of the finished tools are 'thumbnail scrapers', first found in layers dated between 24 000 and 21 400 BP, whereas at Kutikina Cave, they first appeared around 17 000 years ago.

Darwin glass was also found, the lowest piece associated with a date of

27 770 BP. The Darwin meteorite crater is 75 kilometres to the west, and transport of this superb raw material would have necessitated a journey of over 100 kilometres along the main river valleys.

Further east is an unnamed sandstone rockshelter currently known as ORS 7, at 440 metres above sea level in the deeply-cut Shannon River valley. An *in situ* hearth, only 60 centimetres below the surface but at the base of the occupational material, gave a date of 30 840 ± 480 BP, associated with 179 artefacts. Three cubic metres of deposit were excavated by Richard Cosgrove, and contained about 2000 artefacts.

In the lowest layer artefacts are mainly unretouched flakes of quartzite and grey, fine-grained hornfels, together with some bones of red-necked wallaby, native cat and broad-toothed rat, and pieces of emu egg shell. Then, after 17 660 BP, there is a greater range in stone raw material used.

Some general patterns are beginning to emerge from these archaeological data, although much of the detailed analysis remains to be done. The ice age occupants of the Southern Forests are linked with those of the western valleys, such as the Franklin, in a single network. There are similarities in artefact types and usage, in art and in raw materials exploited. The presence of Darwin glass more than 75 kilometres journey from its source implies either long-distance resource exploitation, or exchange or trading networks. At the same time, differences between the western and eastern suites of Pleistocene sites in southern Tasmania indicate local adjustments to differing local environments and resources. Perhaps rather than a struggle for survival in a harsh southern land, what we are seeing is the efficient exploitation of a food-rich environment before and during the height of the last glaciation.

The findings at these sites have revolutionized views about Tasmanian prehistory. The age of human colonization of Tasmania has been pushed back at least 8000 years, and it is now clear that upland environments were exploited 20 000 years earlier than previously recorded in Tasmania and 10 000 years earlier than is known on the mainland.

Continual human presence in Tasmania over the last 30 000 years is remarkable in view of the glacial climate during much of this time, but it now seems that the land link with the mainland has been open intermittently over the last 55 000 years.[12] Prior to the onset of the last glacial age which lasted from about 25 000 to 10 000 BP, the land bridge seems to have been exposed three times, the longest spell being from 37 000 to 29 000 years ago. A drop in sea level of only 55 metres would expose a portion of the Bassian Rise, allowing entry to Tasmania.

Tasmania is further south than any other place in the southern hemisphere inhabited during the ice age. Not only were there glaciers on its mountains, but icebergs would also have come floating past the coast from the great Antarctic ice sheet only a thousand kilometres to the south. Into this freezing toe on the foot of the world moved the Aborigines, perhaps impelled into empty space by an.urge to explore. But these Aboriginal hunters stayed and weathered out the glacial cold in caves.

Fifteen thousand years later their descendants were able to leave the caves as the ice receded and the climate grew warmer, only to find that the melting ice caps had drowned their link to the mainland. They had survived 10 000 years of cold, and they were now to face a similar time of isolation. Tasmanian Aborigines of the nineteenth century were dubbed by anthropologists 'the world's most primitive people', but their most remarkable achievement was that they survived. And not only did they survive but they also preserved and developed the rich cultural traditions those first migrants had carried across the land bridge. The courage and skill of these Tasmanian Aborigines, braving the ice, snow and freezing cold to hunt wallabies within sight of glaciers, is eloquent testimony to the indomitable spirit of early humans. And to the several thousand people of Aboriginal descent in Tasmania, these sites are of tremendous significance as part of their heritage.

CHAPTER TEN

KARTA: ISLAND OF THE DEAD

A large offshore island without human inhabitants, called 'island of the dead' by mainland Aborigines, separated from the Australian continent for almost 10 000 years, yet with abundant evidence of a prehistoric population. These are all the ingredients of a classic mystery story, which scholars have been trying to solve since 1802.

Kangaroo Island, about 150 kilometres long and 50 kilometres wide, lies 14.5 kilometres from the coast of South Australia across Backstairs Passage. This strait is bedevilled by strong currents, heavy tidal swells, and steep breaking seas that make crossings in canoes or small boats a hazardous undertaking. The island was first visited by Captain Flinders in HMS *Investigator* in March 1802, and Nicolas Baudin, who followed in the same year. Both immediately noticed the lack of fires on Kangaroo Island in contrast to the adjacent mainland, where skies were constantly smoke-filled from Aborigines burning off the vegetation. When Flinders landed, he found no human inhabitants but only extraordinarily tame kangaroos and seals.

Kangaroo Island was settled later in 1802 by European sealers, who took with them Aboriginal women abducted from Tasmania and the adjacent mainland. Official settlement followed in 1836, and much of the land was cleared for agriculture. It was not, however, until a century after the first Europeans set foot on the island that evidence of prehistoric human inhabitants was discovered. In 1903, geologist Walter Howchin found some hammerstones at Hawk's Nest near Murray's Lagoon towards the centre of the island. In 1930 more stone tools were discovered, and Norman Tindale was invited to investigate.

It was Norman Tindale and his associate Harold Cooper who first seriously suggested that human occupation of Australia went back into the Pleistocene. They based this opinion largely on evidence from Kangaroo Island. Tindale's fieldwork in the early 1930s around the fresh-water, land-locked Murray's Lagoon produced hammerstones and some massive trimmed pebble implements.[1] Further work by Harold Cooper between 1934 and 1939 disclosed the existence of forty-seven campsites throughout the island. By 1958 the number had risen to 120 sites. Cooper collected some 1400 pebble choppers and horsehoof cores, and more than 150 hammerstones.

The large tool industry represented by these pieces was termed the 'Kartan' by Tindale, after 'Karta', the name given to the island by the mainland Ramindjeri tribe. It is characterized by the massiveness of its core tools (colour plate 6). The dominant implements are hammerstones and pebble choppers. The latter are made by hammer-flaking one side of a large quartzite pebble, usually oval in shape, and then trimming the margin to produce a sharp edge. Many are finely made and perfectly symmetrical, suggesting that their manufacturers were superb craftsmen with a strong aesthetic sense. Large heavy horsehoof-shaped cores are also characteristic of this Kangaroo Island industry, but they are less numerous than the pebble choppers.

The Kartan tools were generally found in fields where ploughing had brought them to the surface from about 30 centimetres below present ground level. Others lay in the higher ridges about Murray's Lagoon, on a shore-line 5 metres above the present one, suggesting that the Kartan campsites belong to a period when the lake was fuller than at present. Other tools were found in what is now almost impenetrable scrub country, but it seems likely that in earlier times the vegetation was sparser because of the effects of glacial climate combined with Aboriginal use of fire.

Most of the Kartan tools are made of quartzite, which must have been carried a considerable distance to these inland campsites. The nearest source of quartzite for the tools found at Hawk's Nest is at least 35 kilometres away on the north coast of the island. This factor could account for the lack of manufacturing debris and the few flakes in the Kartan industry.

How the former islanders, with their Kartan stone tools, first reached Kangaroo Island provided an intriguing problem for Tindale and Cooper. They both reached the conclusion that occupation must have taken place at a time of low sea level when Kangaroo Island was still joined to the mainland. This guess, for it was long before the advent of radiocarbon dating, was based on several different strands of circumstantial evidence. Firstly, there was the massive size and archaic appearance of the Kartan tools, unlike anything found on the mainland in more recent sites such as Devon Downs.[2] Moreover, their location suggested that the occupation had a considerable antiquity and derived from a time when the island's climate and environment were rather different from the present. And, if the people did not walk to Kangaroo Island, how did they get there? Backstairs Passage is notoriously rough, and at the time of European settlement none of the neighbouring mainland Aboriginal tribes had any watercraft capable of getting across it. Indeed, only frail bark canoes and rafts of reeds were used, both propelled solely by means of poles.

The absence of the dingo from Kangaroo Island and of the specialized small tools found in younger mainland sites supported the idea that the island was occupied during the Pleistocene, before the dingo was brought to Australia, and that subsequently it was cut off by the rising sea and isolated from later developments on the mainland. The development in the local fauna and flora of many subspecies also favours a considerable period of isolation.

Finally, there was an interesting myth about Kangaroo Island, widespread among Aborigines of South Australia, according to which the island is the home of the spirits of departed ancestors:

> Ngurunderi was a great Ancestral figure of the southern tribes in South Australia, who established Tribal Laws. After death, the spirits of men follow his ancient travel paths to the island of Nar-oong-owie (Kangaroo Island) and thence to Ngurunderi's home in the sky.
>
> Long ago, Ngurunderi's two wives ran away from him, and he was forced to follow them. He pursued them and as he did so he crossed Lake Albert and went along the beach to Cape Jervis. When he arrived there he saw his wives wading half-way across the shallow channel which divided Nar-oong-owie from the mainland.
>
> He was determined to punish his wives, and angrily ordered the water to rise up and drown them. With a terrific rush the waters roared and the women were carried back towards the mainland. Although they tried frantically to swim against the tidal wave they were powerless to do so and were drowned. Their bodies turned to stone and are seen as two rocks off the coast of Cape Jervis, called the The Pages or the Two Sisters.
>
> Ngurunderi dived into the water and swam out towards the island. As it was a hot day he wanted shade so he made a she-oak tree which is said to be the largest in Australia. He lay down in the shade and tried to sleep but could not for as every breeze blew he heard the wailing of his drowning wives. Finding he could get no rest, he walked to the end of the island and threw his spear out into the sea. Immediately a reef of rocks appeared. He then threw away all his other weapons and departed to his home in the skies, where those who have kept the Laws he gave the tribes will some day join him.
>
> To this day anyone who tries to sleep under a she-oak tree will hear the wailing that Ngurunderi heard beneath the giant tree on Kangaroo Island, the sacred island of the spirits of the dead.[3]

This story seems to be based on fact. Aboriginal oral history provides us with many accounts of the great climatic and geological changes that have taken place on the continent. There is a fascinating myth of the time when the earth blew up, which seems almost certainly to describe the volcanic eruption of Mount Wilson in the Blue Mountains near Sydney. Since erupting volcanoes have not been seen in the Sydney region for several thousand years this testifies to the incredibly long persistence of oral tradition. And on the Atherton Tablelands in Queensland, stories about volcanic eruptions seem to have lasted more than 10 000 years.[4] If memory of volcanoes can persist over thousands of years, there is no reason why traditions of rising seas drowning the land should not also persist. It has been estimated that Kangaroo Island was separated from the mainland about 10 000 years ago, but the drowning process continued until the sea stabilized at its present height between 5000 and 7000 years ago.

Archaeologist Ron Lampert, in an attempt to solve the riddle of stone tools on an island isolated for 10 000 years, surveyed the whole island in search of stratified occupation deposits that might establish the antiquity of the Kartan industry.[5] Only one cave was found that appeared promising: a small limestone cave beside a fresh-water lagoon, 8 kilometres from the south coast. This was named the Seton site after the local landowner.[6]

Excavation in 1971 and 1973 revealed an occupation deposit 1.5 metres deep, resting on bedrock. Dating of the deposit indicated that people first visited the cave about 16 000 years ago when the site would have been some 40 kilometres from the coast. They manufactured small scrapers from flint, and their diet possibly included the now extinct giant kangaroo, *Sthenurus*, bones of which were found in association with the earliest tools. Thereafter, the hunting site was visited infrequently, until about 11 000 years ago, when a period of intensive occupation began. Small flint scrapers were manufactured at the site, quartz was flaked and some quartz flakes were retouched for use as scrapers. Two small bone points were found in the 11 000-year-old level. These were made from kangaroo shinbones and the dull polish on their tips suggests they were used for skin-working. The Kangaroo Islanders' subsistence economy was broadly based; a wide variety of inland fauna were hunted, among which the modern grey kangaroo was of particular importance. Because of the rising sea-level Seton was by then within easy reach of the seashore and some marine shellfish formed part of the diet.

Then, abruptly, visits ceased. This abandonment of the Seton cave coincides with the time of final separation of the island from the mainland. The islanders' impending isolation would have become clear from daily and seasonal tidal fluctuations, which would gradually have produced breaks of longer and longer duration between the island and mainland.

Originally Lampert thought that Kangaroo Island was then consciously abandoned, but then he found several small sites belonging to the post-separation period. Some are coastal sites that contain small shell middens associated with flakes; shells from one of these middens gave an age of 6000 years. Other sites are inland, stratified open campsites with small flakes and scrapers, for example, Rowell's Site and The Sand Quarry site dated respectively to about 5200 and 4300 years ago.

This younger occupation is extremely sparse compared both with the earlier Kartan sites and with the very numerous shell middens of the adjacent coast of South Australia.

There are two possible explanations for the presence of sites on Kangaroo Island post-dating isolation from the mainland. Either a relict population survived on the island for several thousand years before becoming extinct, or the island was reoccupied occasionally from the mainland by Aborigines with watercraft. From considering varied evidences – palaeoenvironmental, archaeological and ethnographic – the case of a relict population is favoured. The demise of such a community before European contact might be explained largely by the steady deterioration of Kangaroo Island as a human habitat during the Holocene, though demographic imbalances and short term disasters could also have played a role.[7]

The case for a relict population, which eventually died out, is mainly based on the evidence that watercraft suitable for the crossing were not available in historic times, and that the island's stone tools show no sign of outside influence – despite significant changes and new tool types on the adjacent mainland. The extinction of the Kangaroo Island population was probably due to a variety of causes. The island could only have supported a few hundred people after separation, and such a small population is always at risk from naturally occurring imbalances in sex and age ratios and natural disasters. There is also evidence that there was a gradual deterioration in the island's environment, which became increasingly arid between about 5000 and 2000 years ago. Analysis of pollen from a core from Lashmar's Lagoon shows a change in vegetation towards drier shrubs, and there are strong signs that regular burning of the vegetation by Aborigines ceased after 2500 years ago. Burning of the bush was such a common practice in Aboriginal Australia that cessation of burning in all likelihood indicates that the last Kangaroo Islander had either left or died. Indeed, it was the absence of smoke from burning-off which made Flinders assume the island was uninhabited even before he landed.

The discovery of traces of a relict population stranded by the rising sea was not the only surprise produced by Lampert's research. In his search for the Kartan culture, he also found a non-Kartan industry on Kangaroo Island. This is exemplified at the Seton site. Others have suggested that the Seton industry of small flint scrapers might be the flake component of a Kartan industry, but Lampert has convincingly argued that Seton is not Kartan but post-Kartan, because among its 5000 pieces of flaked stone there was not one core tool and only a single piece of quartzite, the material out of which the heavy Kartan tools are made. Moreover there is an enormous difference in implement size between the two industries: the average weight of a Seton tool was 9 grams, whereas that of a tool from a typical Kartan assemblage was 900 grams. The assemblages are too different to represent merely different aspects of the same culture caused by seasonal or environmental differences. Indeed, not only are they not contemporary, but there is also little or no continuity between the two cultures.

Lampert suggests that the Kartan industry was brought to Kangaroo Island when it was joined to the mainland at least 50 000 years ago. It seems likely, but not certain, that there was a rise in the sea level between about 50 000 and 30 000 years ago. If there was, this would have caused the Kangaroo Island population to leave the island, to stay and become extinct, or to stay and survive in isolation for a long period. Any of these alternatives would account for the great difference between the Kartan and Seton industries. The latter would be a much younger industry, either a descendant of the Kartan or developed on the mainland and introduced to the island during the next phase of low sea level.

There was also a total change between the Kartan and Seton industries, from the use of quartzite to flint as raw material, perhaps because of the unavailability of the source of quartzite beach pebbles, covered by the rising seas. Tools also became much smaller. At other sites, such as Cloggs Cave and Burrill Lake, there was a very gradual reduction in the size of tools, quite unlike the dramatic change seen on Kangaroo Island. Another possibility is that the Kartan industry died out, and the Seton assemblage mirrors new technological developments that had taken place on the mainland whilst the Kartan was isolated. These questions are now being further investigated by young archaeologist Neale Draper.

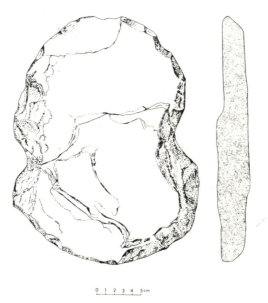

0 1 2 3 4 5cm

Figure 10.1 *Waisted axe from Kangaroo Island, South Australia. This axe is exceptionally large.* (After Lampert 1979)

A further discovery by Ron Lampert has complicated the picture even further. This is the discovery on the island of twenty-four huge, flaked stone tools with notches on each margin (figure 10.1).[8] Such waisted tools have also been found in mainland South Australia at Wepowie Creek in the southern Flinders Ranges and in the Mackay district of Queensland, 6 kilometres from the present coast in sugarcane fields at the base of Mount Jukes, which rises 500 metres above sea level.[9] The eighty waisted tools from Queensland have been examined by Lampert, who has shown that they closely resemble those from Kangaroo Island.

The use of these waisted tools is unknown. Lampert has remarked on their resemblance to the sago-pounders of New Guinea and thinks they may have been used to pound some hard foodstuff. Another possibility is forest clearance, as postulated for the New Guinea waisted axes (see chapter 1). Tindale suggests that they were used to kill large animals caught in fall-traps.[10] He draws attention to the Aboriginal practice in the Queensland rainforest in recent times of using large, heavy-bladed, sometimes grooved stone axes, with very long handles of the so-called 'lawyer cane' wrapped around the axe head and bound with cane lashings, to kill animals caught in pitfall traps.

MAINLAND KARTAN SITES

Kartan tools, although named after Kangaroo Island, were made by people occupying an area of more than 100 000 square kilometres, covering South Australia and the adjacent islands which then formed part of a single landmass. Kartan sites have been found on the mainland on the Fleurieu, Yorke and Eyre Peninsulas, but none has come from a stratified deposit.

One of the best-known mainland surface sites was at Hallett Cove. In 1934 Harold Cooper discovered at Hallett Cove, about 16 kilometres south of Adelaide, early, crude, heavily weathered stone implements lying on a ploughed hillside above a creek overlooking the beach. In the course of his 220 visits to the site over 36 years, Cooper found some 400 Kartan core tools, the largest of which weighed 5.5 kilograms.[11] The site has the essential requirements of campers: a permanent water supply, well-drained ground, and a commanding view. It also faces north-east, so it catches the warmth of the early morning sun.

One of the fascinating aspects of the Hallett Cove sites is that the Kartan pebble choppers, horsehoof cores, and hammerstones are all made of a poor quality siltstone found close to the camp, whereas at the foot of the cliff lie banks of fine-grained quartzite pebbles that are highly prized by more recent Aboriginal tool-makers. Why did Pleistocene tool-makers not use the better raw material? They probably could not do so, for when sea level was low the pebble bank would have been covered by a talus slope, now washed away by the sea pounding at the foot of the cliffs. In Kartan times the nearest pebble banks would have been a long distance away on the ice age shore.

More difficult to explain is early occupation on the Nullarbor Plain.[12] Two caves in the far south-west of South Australia were used before 20 000 years ago: Koonalda Cave and Allen's Cave. At Koonalda, occupation began by about 24 000 BP and at Allen's Cave near Eucla by at least 25 000.

At this time the region was not treeless, as it is today, but covered with mallee scrub. About 15 000 to 18 000 years ago, when the sea reached its lowest level of the last glaciation, the coast was about 160 kilometres further south than it is today and the Eucla–Koonalda region became treeless plains, with an estimated average annual rainfall of only 160 to 180 millimetres. Allen's Cave was virtually deserted at this time; no doubt the Aborigines had moved south on to the wide coastal plain that had emerged as a result of the fall in sea level. Sea level began to rise again about 12 000 years ago, bringing the coastline closer and thus again increasing the rainfall, water resources and mallee scrub.

Plate 13. *Yunta engraving from South Australia represents an emu walking away from its nest of eggs.* (R. Edwards)

Occupation of Koonalda Cave (colour plate 4) continued, however, until about 15 000 years ago, for this sink-hole had two big attractions for early man. It was a reliable source of water on an arid plain and its walls held nodules of flint, the best raw material for stone tool manufacture available in the continent.[13] The antiquity of use of these resources at Koonalda is significant, since it shows that man had learned to live in, or at least exploit the resources of, such arid areas as the Nullarbor Plain during the Pleistocene. Adaptation to arid environments clearly goes back into the Pleistocene, as was indicated also by the early occupation of Mount Newman rockshelter in Western Australia and of Puritjarra in central Australia. Koonalda's feature of outstanding importance is its early rock art (see chapter 11).

The long-suspected ice age occupation of the lower Murray River Valley has now been confirmed by the excavation of Roonka Flat near Blanchetown by Graeme Pretty (figure 10.2).[14] This has a complex history, going back 18 000 years. At that time the river flat seems to have been occasionally used as an open-air encampment by hunter–gatherers during the annual flood of the river. Charcoal (radiocarbon dated to 18 150 ± 350 BP) was found in four hearths, associated with stone cobble cooking structures and fresh-water mussel shells.

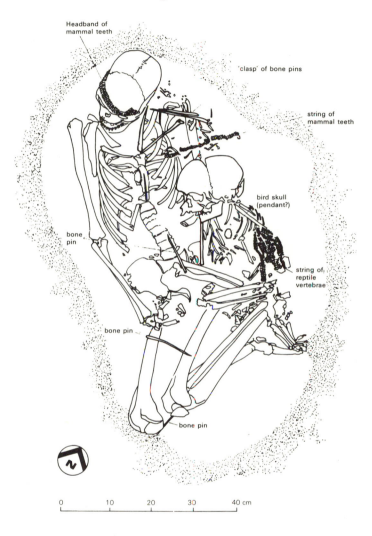

Figure 10.2 *Burial from Roonka, South Australia. The most elaborate status burial yet found in Australia. In a small chamber (tomb 108) a man and small child were buried together, splendidly attired, 4000 years ago. A skin cloak appears to have been wrapped tightly around the man's body and fastened with bone pins. Behind his left shoulder was a dense mass of small animals' foot bones, suggesting that the cloak was fixed at the shoulder with the paws of animal pelts hanging down. Bird bones found along the left side of the body probably mean that the cloak was fringed with bird feathers. The child wore a bird skull pendant, a necklace of reptile vertebrae, and had ochre staining on its feet.* (Courtesy of the South Australian Museum and G. Pretty)

EARLIEST OCCUPATION

There is good reason to believe that the Kartan choppers are the earliest tools in Australia. They are part of the Australian core tool and scraper tradition, but the oldest part of it. Various strands of evidence suggest the great antiquity of these massive stone tools. The only reasonable explanation for the absence of Kartan tools from the 16 000-year-old Seton site is that they pre-date it, and their similar absence from younger sites and post-glacial coastal dunes also indicates Pleistocene antiquity. In fact, their ice age antiquity is beyond dispute, the only question is 'which stage in the ice age'?

Comparisons of industries of the Australian core tool and scraper tradition show the Kartan to be the most archaic on two grounds: its massiveness and the high percentage of core tools to scrapers. Not only are there far more core tools in the Kartan industry, but they are also considerably larger and heavier than those of any other Australian industries. This is not due to their raw material, since Kartan tools were made of a great variety of different rock types. Finally, the waisted tools that are part of the Kartan industry suggest the possibility of great antiquity. Made of quartzite, like the Kartan core tools, the waisted tools are even more massive, weighing an average of 1837 grams, compared with 882 grams for Kartan tools. Their edges are also usually sharpened by crude bifacial flaking whereas all Kartan tools are unifacially flaked. They may have been hafted to a handle or they could have been used in a two-handed grip, one hand on each notched margin.

The massive, waisted tools of Kangaroo Island resemble, but exceed considerably in size, grooved axes found in 20 000-year-old contexts in Arnhem Land and the Kimberley. They more closely resemble those of New Guinea, both from the 26 000-year-old Kosipe site and the 50 000-year-old 80 metre Huon Terrace (see colour plate 2). And a similar waisted tool has been found associated with pebble tools in the Sai Yok site in Thailand.

It seems possible that the Kartan industry, including its waisted tools, formed part of the baggage of the earliest migrants into Australia. Examination of their distribution may, therefore, throw some light on the distribution of Australia's earliest population. In this analysis, a clear distinction must be made between true Kartan tools and other core tools found on ice age sites. True Kartan sites are concentrated in the region of South Australia around the mouth of the Murray and on the north-east coast of Queensland. Both these regions are high ground near fresh-water. They are among the few surviving remnants of Australia's continental shelf; if the earliest population were concentrated on the coast, most other sites would now be submerged.

The reasons Kangaroo Island has such prolific remains of the Kartan industry are probably twofold: sufficient altitude to place it above the present sea level and a particularly favourable location, close to both the sea and to the mouth of Australia's largest river, enjoying the resources of seashore, estuary, river and its own wooded hills and streams.

CHAPTER ELEVEN

ART AND TECHNOLOGY

THE DEVELOPMENT OF ROCK ART

By 20 000 years ago, not only had the first Australians successfully adapted to a new continent, but they were also developing complex art and ritual. What may be the oldest trace of rock art in Australia was excavated from a 20 000-year-old level in Devil's Lair.[1] The small piece of rock bears cut-marks that may be man-made engravings, and other engraved stone 'plaques' occur in a 12 000-year-old level. These incisions are similar to those found at Ingaladdi, in the Northern Territory, and to grooves produced in rain-making ceremonies at the nearby site of Delamere (plate 14). There has been some controversy about the validity of Charles Dortch's identification of the marks as man-made, and their human origin must be regarded as probable but not yet proven.

Engravings (also called petroglyphs or rock carvings) are made on rock surfaces using any implement in two basic methods. These are abrasion (linear friction by pushing an implement over the surface or rotating friction — drilling with an instrument under pressure) and percussion (applying vertical pressure by hammering). Friction produces an abraded or scratched groove or a rubbed or drilled area; percussion makes small pits, which may then be linked together into a line or motif.[2] Designs are made by percussion by pounding or hammer-dressing the surface with a lump of stone (direct percussion), or by pecking by indirect percussion, using a sharp pointed tool placed in position and then hit with a hammerstone. Indirect percussion by this hammer and chisel method gives clean edges, precise lines and some depth to an engraving in contrast to the shallow and more diffused outline of pounded engravings.

In places such as Red Gorge in South Australia some engravings occur on the cliffs in places now impossible to reach, showing that there has been rockfall and erosion since they were first chipped out. Tumbled rocks at the bottom of the gorge often bear parts of designs, the remains of which are still in position on the cliff above. Other designs are bisected by gaping cracks that have opened up in the rock. But the strongest evidence for great antiquity lies in the presence of a sheen on both the rock faces and the designs engraved

Plate 14. *Incised markings at the Lightning Brothers site, Delamere, Northern Territory, are believed to have been an important element in local rain-making ceremonies* (R. Edwards)

upon them. This surface sheen is usually called desert varnish, and it is found in hot desert regions in various parts of the world.

The dark desert varnish on Aboriginal engraving sites like Panaramitee[3] is thought to result from long periods of aridity such as occurred in late Pleistocene times. The engraved designs are usually covered with the same sheen as that of the rest of the rock surface, but, in contrast, modern graffiti on such rock faces leave ugly scars with high colour contrast.

The designs of the engravings are mostly not naturalistic. The circle motif predominates, together with what appear to be tracks of macropods and birds. Among them are many motifs, such as concentric circles and 'mazes', that we tend to term 'abstract', but they would certainly have had meaning for their makers. But we cannot penetrate the prehistoric mind. Inquiry by early ethnographers amongst Aboriginal people established that they did not know the meaning of the motifs, for this form of art was not practised by them, nor had it been within living memory; it was 'made in the Dreamtime'.

The interpretation of prehistoric art is very difficult. Researchers working in the first half of this century tended to be quite positive about the meaning of motifs, but the modern trend is towards extreme caution. Most researchers today do not give a name to a motif, except as a tentative label, unless identification is absolutely clear.

One possible indication of antiquity for these South Australian pecked engravings is that amongst the thousands of animal tracks there is not one representation of dingo tracks. This suggests that these engravings pre-date the arrival of the dingo in Australia.

Remarkable pecked engravings resembling human faces were found in the Cleland Hills, 320 kilometres west of Alice Springs in western central Australia.[4] The art has not been dated, but its heavily weathered condition suggests great age. Not far away is the Puritjarra occupation site, recently dated to more than 22 000 years. Parallels for these 'faces' have been found in equally weathered rock engravings in the Pilbara region of Western Australia.

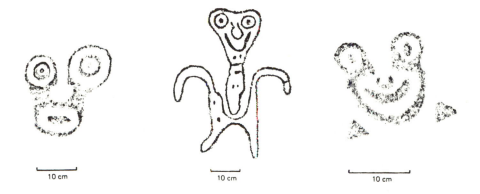

Figure 11.1 *Cleland Hills faces, Northern Territory. These weathered engravings were pecked out of sandstone on cliffs around the rockhole of Thomas Reservoir.* Left *Disembodied face with a distinct impression of sadness.* Centre *Happy face with a curious body.* Right *Face with a happy expression. There are two small triangles below the face and two long lines below, perhaps indicating a body.* (After Dix 1977; drawings based on photographs by R. Edwards 1968)

The sixteen Cleland Hills 'faces' are quite small – 10 to 20 centimetres wide and 30 centimetres long – and tend to be heart-shaped with eyes, nose and mouth (figure 11.1). One has a body with two legs and rather strange wing-like arms. Some believe that they are not faces at all, others that they are human or owl faces, and a recent suggestion is that they portray the full-face view of the giant extinct bird, *Genyornis*.[5] One reason for considering them to be human faces is that one or two also have bodies and some seem to show emotion. Two have their mouths up-turned at the corners in a classic 'happy face', while another has a completely different O-shaped mouth as if singing.

These 'faces' form only a small proportion of the designs at the Cleland Hills site. Of 387 motifs, 50 per cent are tracks and 33 per cent circles. Other sites from central and southern Australia have surprisingly similar frequencies of motifs, although some are as much as 1300 kilometres apart. The other constant features of these pecked engravings sites are their proximity to water, association with human occupation, advanced weathering, and surface patination.

TASMANIAN ENGRAVINGS

In Tasmania, similar pecked engravings occur and the dingo is likewise absent, both as a motif in the rock art and physically from the island, for the dingo did not arrive in Australia until after Tasmania was cut off from the mainland, about 8000 years ago.

The Tasmanian engravings are similar to those of central and south Australia. It has now been firmly established that Tasmania was first occupied during the Pleistocene, yet even before this early occupation was found, it had been postulated that the Tasmanian engravings were of Pleistocene antiquity. The basis of this claim was their high degree of weathering and similarity in style and motifs to mainland engravings. Because of this striking similarity, it seemed more likely that the engravings stemmed from an early period when Tasmania was joined to the mainland, rather than that they were an independent local development at a later stage when Tasmania had become an island.

There are several engraving sites in Tasmania, but the most extensive is Mount Cameron West on the north-west coast (plate 15). The site has been extensively recorded and excavations have been carried out there.[6]

The Mount Cameron West site was found by a local shepherd of the Van Diemen Land's Company in 1931. The site lies about 3 kilometres north of the high headland of that name and was uncovered by heavy wind erosion of the coastal sand dunes. Certainly the engravings were not visible when George Augustus Robinson must have walked within metres of the site on several occasions in the 1830s during his mission to gather the Tasmanian Aborigines still at large. A set of engravings was recorded in Robinson's journal at Cape Grim, but ironically whilst the Mount Cameron West ones have appeared, the Cape Grim ones have disappeared from view, presumably covered over again with sand in one of the frequent westerly gales that lash this coast.

The engravings at Mount Cameron West lie on two outcrops on a long beach exposed to the full force of the westerlies. An undercut cliff face provided an overhang under which prehistoric hunters camped, and the cliff face and large rock slabs that fell from it were decorated by early artists. The designs are non-figurative, geometric forms. The motifs include plain circles, concentric circles, overlapping and barred circles, crosses, rows of holes, trellis-like designs, and animal tracks. The engravings were made by pecking a

Plate 15. *Mount Cameron West engravings, Tasmania* (R. Edwards)

line of holes into the soft rock and then abrading the ridges between them to make deeply incised lines. Excavation of the site produced a few large pointed tools of hard rock, such as basalt and quartzite, which may well have been chisels of the ancient sculptors.

Excavation of the sheltered area behind the carved slabs did not reveal any Pleistocene occupation, and surprisingly, it now seems that the carvings date from only about 2000 or 1500 years ago.[7] Nevertheless, the artistic tradition goes back to the ice age, and other Tasmanian engravings, such as those at Sundown Point, may well be older. People camped in the Mount Cameron shelter a thousand years ago, leaving behind the remains of meals of mussel shells ·and birds. This camp debris formed a midden 1 metre thick, which gradually filled up the shelter and spilled over and covered some of the carved blocks in front of the campsite. The shelter was occupied from about 1350 to

850 years ago, but it was then abandoned and soon became buried by wind-blown sand.

The largest and most complex art site yet found in Tasmania, Mount Cameron West is also widely recognized as one of the most outstanding artistic achievements of any hunter–gatherer society. It is conceived on a grand scale, and the designs are so deeply incised that they have a sculptural quality.

Several other art sites have been found, such as Sundown Point and Green's Creek[8] on the west coast, which have as wide a range of designs as Mount Cameron West. The main motif everywhere is the circle, which varies from a few centimetres in diameter to more than 1 metre across at Mount Cameron West. Since 1986, three Pleistocene art sites have been found in caves in the south-west of Tasmania, as described in chapter 9. These comprise hand stencils and streaks of red ochre, in one case mixed human blood.

ANTIQUITY OF ROCK ENGRAVINGS

The first firm evidence of the great age of rock art came in 1929, when an engraved slab was found 3 to 4 metres below ground level in the Devon Downs rockshelter. This limestone shelter on the lower River Murray in South Australia was the subject of the first scientific archaeological excavation in Australia.[9] Methods of absolute dating were not developed for another two decades, but, when radiocarbon dating became available, samples of charcoal carefully bagged and stored twenty years before were dated. It emerged that the engraved rocks lay in a layer dated to some 3000 years ago, but this is a minimum age and the engravings are doubtless much older.

The first absolute age on Australian rock art came from Ingaladdi, west of Katherine in the Northern Territory, in 1966.[10] Around the large, permanent Ingaladdi waterhole lie a series of sandstone outcrops. Most bear rock paintings, and the back walls of some of the shelters are also engraved with animal tracks, human and animal feet, and simple linear grooves. These may have been produced in rain-making ceremonies; identical grooves were rubbed at the site of Delamere, 80 kilometres to the south, only fifty years ago. These ceremonies involved abrading grooves in the rock to bring rain (plate 14), and were associated with the myth of the Lightning Brothers, who are depicted in vivid multi-coloured paintings there.

In the excavation large fragments of engraved rock were found below a 5000-year-old layer, resting on a 7000-year-old occupation floor. The minimum age of the engravings is, therefore, between 5000 and 7000 years. They are probably much older, since these dates only indicate when the fragments fell into the occupation deposit, not when they were first carved onto the wall. The engraved rock fragments bear parallel linear grooves and a large 'bird track'; both these motifs are common in other art sites of suspected Pleistocene age.

Similar evidence of the antiquity of rock art was foundin the far north of Queensland by Dr Andrée Rosenfeld. The site she excavated had already been named 'Early Man Shelter' by its discoverer, Captain Percy Trezise.[11]

The Early Man rockshelter has produced the earliest firm date so far for the antiquity of Australian rock art. Heavily weathered and patinated engravings cover the back wall of the shelter in a diagonal frieze and clearly continue on below present ground surface (plate 16). Excavation revealed the presence of engravings on the rock wall below an occupation level dated to 13 000 years, which must be, therefore, older than this. They are pecked out on the shelter wall to form a long frieze, which rises obliquely, parallel to the ancient floor and to the natural bedding planes of the rock. The designs have been influenced by the natural contours of the rock surface; hollows have been emphasized by outlining or filled with engravings. Most common are gridded designs, simple three-pronged 'bird tracks', circular forms, and extensive maze-like patterns of lines.

Plate 16. *Engravings in the Early Man shelter, near Laura, Queensland, with its discoverer, Percy Trezise, seated in the foreground*

DATING OF DESERT VARNISH

Until recently, engravings could only be dated by circumstantial evidence, but an exciting breakthrough has just been made. This involves the dating of desert varnish, which can be a thick black shiny surface or a thin veneer, invisible to the naked eye.

Pioneering work on dating has been done by Deirdre Dragovich of Sydney University.[18] What has been developed recently is the cation-ratio (CR) method of dating rock varnish found on engravings. A first set of dates on varnish from inside engravings has been produced by Ron Dorn and Tom Cahill in conjunction with Margaret Nobbs on Karolta, one of the engraving sites she has recorded in the Olary region of South Australia.[19] The age determination of engravings by rock varnish is based on the premise that the varnish begins to form soon after the petroglyph is made. Dating the varnish provides a minimum age for the antiquity of the underlying engraving. The time lag between the age of the engraving and the onset of the first development of varnish has been demonstrated to be about 100 years at Karolta, on the basis of scanning electron microscope (SEM) observations of historic graffiti there.

The rock varnish can be dated by knowing the age of the underlying geomorphic surface, which in the case of Karolta involved obtaining Accelerator Mass Spectrometry (AMS) radiocarbon dates for surfaces near where the engravings are to be dated. Direct AMS radiocarbon dating of rock varnish on an engraving is not possible at present, because the varnish formed in an engraving has too little carbon for an AMS analysis, which requires a sample from an area of between 10 and 100 square centimetres.

A cation-ratio of (calcium + potassium)/titanium is then obtained for the same varnish on the same geomorphic surfaces where the AMS radiocarbon dates have been obtained. Only pinpricks of material are needed for the determination of varnish CRs, so sampling does not damage the engravings. The cation-ratio of $(K + Ca)/Ti$ in varnishes on surfaces whose age is known (by AMS radiocarbon dating in this case) are then compared with the cation-ratios of the engravings.

This method is new and somewhat controversial, but has been used effectively in North America, and the results at Karolta are internally consistent, even if startling. (They are consistent in that where one motif is engraved on top of another, the uppermost one's CR date is more recent, and when separate dates have been obtained on two parts of the same motif the dates are the same). If they are correct, engravings of circles, tracks of birds and macropods, and abraded grooves were being executed 31 500 years ago in the Olary region, and similar motifs were engraved right down the centuries until 1000 years ago. The surprises are the seeming lack of change in the subject matter of the engravings, and the great antiquity of this style of art, usually called the Panaramitee style. This has tremendous implications for the age of the meander tradition of the caves of the southern coast of Australia such as Koonalda, long considered to be earlier than the Panaramitee style of engravings. It seems that the antiquity of both art and occupation in prehistoric Australia are destined to be pushed further and further back.

ANTIQUITY OF ROCK PAINTINGS

There is every reason to believe that the art of painting has an antiquity similar to that of engraving in Australia, and in Tasmania Pleistocene ochred art has recently been found, as described in chapter 9. Some indications have also been found in Arnhem Land in the Northern Territory. The region contains the most complex and prolific rock art not only in Australia but also in the world. There are thousands of painted rockshelters. The paintings are generally naturalistic, documenting the local environment, life-style and material culture.[12]

It has been suggested that the art was produced over a long period. Although absolute dates for paintings cannot yet be determined, relative dating can be achieved by a careful study of styles and superimpositions, when one painting overlies another. A study of the art has been carried out over many years by George Chaloupka of the Northern Territory Museum in Darwin, who has recorded and analysed more than a thousand galleries. He believes the Arnhem Land rock art has considerable antiquity for the following reasons.[13] Pieces of ochre were found throughout the lower levels of most excavated sites; ochre 'crayons' with ground facets produced by use were found in a 19 000-year-old level at Nauwalabila and in an 18 000-year-old level at Malkunanja II, where an ochre-impregnated grindstone established that ochre was deliberately prepared. Another reason for suspecting that the paintings are very old is that some of those attributed to the earliest art phase, on stylistic grounds, have been found to be covered with a siliceous skin. When wet pigment is first applied to a rock wall, it sinks in, often to a depth of several millimetres. Later, dissolved silica may move through the rock, permeating the pigment, and then evaporating on the surface, forming a waterproof, transparent skin, which permanently preserves the paintings. These siliceous skins are not forming under present climatic conditions, and the last arid period when this process might have taken place occurred at about the height of the last glaciation, 18 000 years ago. Finally, all the paintings assigned to the early 'dynamic figure style' are in a faded red ochre, which has become bonded into the rock, so that in some places where part of a painting has fallen off the wall, the ochre has stained so deeply into the wall that the design can still be seen.

On the basis of superimposition, changes in style, and the motifs apparently portrayed in the paintings, Chaloupka has proposed a sequence of four styles. This chronological scheme is, however, speculative, since there is no way yet of dating rock paintings. The four styles are called pre-estuarine, estuarine, fresh-water and contact. According to George Chaloupka, the earliest art predates the post-glacial rise in sea level and development of estuarine conditions 7000 to 9000 years ago. His case is based on the apparent depiction of extinct animals, such as the thylacine, in the early art and the predominance of land animals among the motifs, whereas the later estuarine style is dominated by fish and crocodiles, often portrayed in the polychrome x-ray style, in which the spine or intestinal organs are shown as well as the exterior of a figure. The estuarine period was succeeded by a time when the salt plains became fresh-water swamps covered with lotus flowers and surrounded by graceful paperbark trees. This fresh-water phase is reflected in the appearance of goose wing fans in the rock paintings. The final period is that mirroring contact with Macassan fishermen from Indonesia and European settlers. Boats and ships, horses and guns were then painted, and there was much sorcery painting, until rock painting in Arnhem Land virtually came to an end with the death of the last main rock painter in 1972.

In the earliest style, the animals portrayed resemble kangaroos and wallabies, emus, echidnas, and the Tasmanian tiger or thylacine. The thylacine is locally extinct, but more than a dozen representations of striped animals have now been found (plate 17). The overall shape and physical features of these have been compared with other striped animals and the dingo.[14] It was concluded that thylacine designs can be clearly differentiated from those of dingoes, the striped numbats, kangaroos or wallabies. The characteristics of thylacines are well known from photographs, film and museum specimens (and a major search is under way in Tasmania to try to find living survivors).

Other extinct creatures that George Chaloupka has tentatively identified in the early paintings are the long-beaked echidna, *Zaglossus*, and the marsupial tapir, *Palorchestes*. Both appear to have been extinct in Australia for at least 18 000 years, but *Zaglossus* still exists in New Guinea.

Not only do animals resembling these locally extinct species appear in early style art, but the other creatures portrayed seem to be land-based animals of the inland plains. The animals apparently most frequently depicted are kangaroos, wallabies, emus, echidnas, bandicoots, rock possums and thylacines. The few fish that occur are all fresh-water species, in contrast to the many barramundi, salt-water crocodiles and other estuarine species of the succeeding period.

One fascinating aspect of the paintings of humans in the dynamic style is their evidence of personal adornment in the form of armlets, neck ornaments and head-dresses decorated with tassels and feathers (figures 11.2, 11.3). There even seems to be a stencil of a tooth necklace, reminiscent of that found on the Nitchie burial. Another remarkable feature of this style is the portrayal of zoomorphs – human figures with animal heads, some of which may represent flying foxes.

Plate 17. *Painting of thylacine (Tasmanian tiger) at Ubirr, Kakadu National Park, Northern Territory. Water has washed away the back of the figure*

In addition to large naturalistic representations of single animals and zoomorphs, there are many small, superbly drawn scenes of people and animals in narrative compositions from everyday life, such as dances and kangaroo hunts. As many as sixty figures appear in one painting. The scenes are full of expressive movements, which is why Chaloupka has named this the dynamic style. Previously it was known as *Mimi* art, because Aborigines had no direct knowledge of the paintings but described them as being the work of *Mimi* spirit people who live in the rocks. This is not surprising because the early *Mimi* or dynamic style is totally different in style and technique from the much younger and more familiar x-ray style.

In the Kimberley to the west, the so-called 'Bradshaw' figures are similar to the early *Mimi* (plate 18). They are depicted in red ochre, or at least only red pigment still survives, and average only 25 to 30 centimetres in height. Both *Mimi* and Bradshaw figures wear similar elongated head-dresses, pubic skirts, armlets and tassels and use the same type of barbed spear and boomerang. Barbed spears were not part of recent Aboriginal culture in the Kimberley – for the last 3000 years spears there seem to have been unbarbed but tipped with a pressure-flaked stone spear point. These paintings are not of importance to present-day Kimberley Aborigines, who say they cannot interpret the meaning of the scenes because they were the work of a bird, which painted spirits

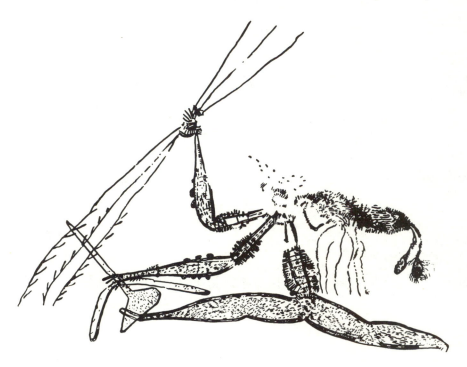

Figure 11.2 *Male figure in the dynamic style, Arnhem Land, Northern Territory. This hunter from Kolondjorluk site 2, Deaf Adder Creek, wears a long, tasselled ceremonial headdress and holds barbed spears, a boomerang and a hafted stone axe.* (After Brandl 1973, by courtesy of the Australian Institute of Aboriginal Studies)

that are invisible to humans.[15] The Bradshaw figures are very faint and weathered in comparison with the spectacular, later Wandjina spirit paintings (plate 21), and they are probably of a similar antiquity to the dynamic style in Arnhem Land.

Several changes took place in the development of this Arnhem Land rock art, which may have covered a considerable time span. One change is thought to reflect environmental change at the end of the Pleistocene. This was the

Figure 11.3 *Female figure in the dynamic style, Arnhem Land, Northern Territory. This female hunter from Kolondjorluk site 2, Deaf Adder Creek, holds spears and has a dilly bag suspended from her neck.* (After Brandl 1973, by courtesy of the Australian Institute of Aboriginal Studies)

development of the Yam figures, in which both human beings and animals were given the outward form of a yam (figure 11.4). This is the first known example of the portrayal of any edible plant in Australian rock art. The introduction of the yam style may indicate that yams (*Dioscorea* species) were becoming an important food source at the end of the Pleistocene period when rainfall increased. Chaloupka also points out that the encroaching sea may have led to the myth of the Rainbow Serpent, which makes its first appearance in the rock art of the Yam style. The Rainbow Serpent is generally associated in northern Australia with myths concerning rain and floods, which could reflect the rising post-glacial sea, which has been estimated to have swallowed up several hundred metres of land each decade. If Chaloupka is correct, the change from pre-estuarine conditions and the appearance of the Rainbow Serpent belong to the years between 9000 and 7000 years ago, which would make the Rainbow Serpent myth the longest continuing religious belief documented in the world.

The early phase of Arnhem Land prehistory came to an end when the sea reached its present level and the environment became estuarine. Elements in the more recent art are the x-ray style and polychrome paintings using a wide range of colourful pigments (see colour plate 11). The hunters for the first time

Plate 18. *Bradshaw dancing figures, Kimberley, Western Australia* (G. Walsh)

carried spear-throwers. This is an important clue to the time of development of the spear-thrower, which appears to have been independently invented within Australia. Spears are now multi-pronged or stone-tipped, and boomerangs gradually disappeared from their equipment. Boomerangs are now not used in Arnhem Land except as musical 'clap-sticks', imported from the desert people to the south.

In this naturalistic rock art the animals are portrayed with such realism and accuracy that it is possible to identify the particular species depicted. In this respect Australian rock art is similar to the cave art of Europe. And in both the European and Australian early cave art zoomorphic figures occur, such as humans with bird or animal heads.

Figure 11.4 *Anthropomorphic yam figures, Deaf Adder Creek, Arnhem Land, Northern Territory. The figures are painted in red; the tallest figure is 1 metre high.* (After Brandl 1973, by courtesy of the Australian Institute of Aboriginal Studies)

KOONALDA CAVE

One of the most remarkable discoveries yet made in Australia is the presence of ice age art in total darkness inside Koonalda Cave far below the Nullarbor Plain in South Australia. Koonalda is a crater-like doline (limestone sink-hole) in the karst scenery of this extensive, flat, arid plain[16] (colour plate 4).

Koonalda was a flint mine. Quarrying was done underground, at times with no natural light, and the quarried nodules were taken elsewhere to be made into tools. Hearths, charcoal and the residue of the quarrying process were found inside the cave, mainly in the first dimly lit chamber some 100 metres down from the entrance and 76 metres below the surface of the Nullarbor

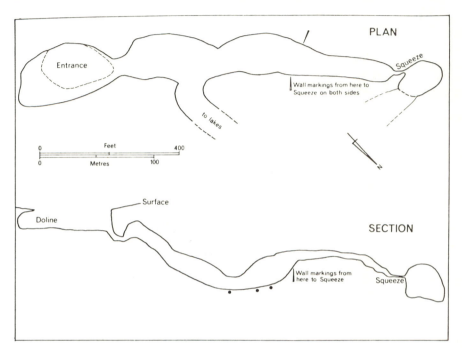

Figure 11.5 *Plan of Koonalda Cave, South Australia* (After Wright 1971)

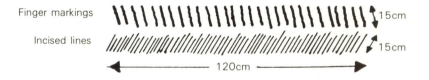

Finger markings

Incised lines

Figure 11.6 *Herringbone design from Koonalda Cave, South Australia, consisting of 74 diagonal incised lines in a row below 37 finger markings.* (After Edwards and Maynard in Wright, ed. 1971)

Plain. Excavation pits up to six metres deep produced evidence that flint miners had been visiting the cave between about 24 000 and 14 000 years ago.

The cave was thoroughly explored and found to contain a series of cathedral-size chambers, mirror-like lakes, narrow passages and steep boulder-

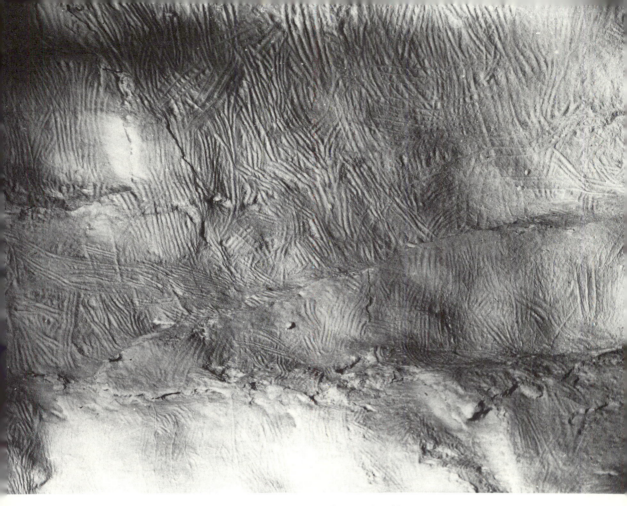

Plate 19. *Wall markings in Koonalda Cave, South Australia* (R. Edwards)

clad slopes. In total darkness, some 300 metres inside the cave, markings were found on the walls (figure 11.5). These markings are similar to the so-called 'macaroni' style of the earliest cave art in southern France and Spain.

The wall markings in Koonalda vary according to the texture of the wall. In one part of the cave, now known as the art passage, the walls are exceptionally soft and friable, with a surface the colour and texture of compacted talcum powder. There the slightest touch of a finger marked the wall. In other parts firm finger pressure was used to leave an impression, and elsewhere one or more strokes of a stone or stick were needed to scratch fine incised lines into the harder surface (plate 19).

Some large flat wall surfaces are completely covered with randomly criss-crossing sets of parallel finger-markings. Large groups of vertical and sometimes horizontal lines occur, together with a few definite patterns, such as regularly spaced grids or lattices. There are also two sets of four concentric circles, both about 20 centimetres in diameter. The most remarkable design of all is a 120 centimetre long herringbone design (figure 11.6). It consists of seventy-four diagonal incised lines in a row below thirty-seven short finger-markings. The fact that the number of the former is exactly twice the number of finger markings can hardly be accidental. This is, therefore, probably a deliberate design with symbolic significance.

Among these eroded markings, recent names, initials, dates and other markings made by recent visitors stand out fresh and clear. The fresh markings have small sharp ridges between the finger lines, which are smooth and compacted, whereas the old markings have less pronounced ridges and con-cavities. There is thus no difficulty in distinguishing between the old and the new.

There is strong presumptive evidence that this art is 20 000 or more years old. Charcoal from just below the surface of the passage before 'the Squeeze' gave a date of 20 000 years. The wall above was covered with incised markings, and the charcoal could have come from crude torches held by early man to light his way along the dark passages in these deepest recesses of the cave. Other markings are located in a cavity 15 metres below massive rock fall, indicating considerable antiquity. Others lie above a platform high in the dome of a large chamber containing a lake. This platform can only be reached through 'the Squeeze'. Beyond the platform, on a part of the wall that cannot now be reached, are further markings. Clearly part of the ledge has fallen into the lake far below since the markings were made. There is thus strong circumstantial evidence that the markings derive from the distant past and were contemporary with other prehistoric activity in the cave, some 15 000 to 24 000 years ago.

Some controversy arose after the discovery of the wall markings as to whether they should be regarded as 'art' or not. It was claimed that they were produced by accident, the sharpening of bone points, or by scraping off limestone powder for some particular purpose for instance, as symbolic signs, with the character of a message or script, which directed the prehistoric miners to the presence of flint veins. None of these pragmatic explanations, however, accounts for the definite designs that occur, nor do they accord with the evidence. If produced by accident, why are most of the lines vertical, and why do no haphazard smudged patches occur? If they derive from sharpening bone points, why was this done in total darkness? And if they were mining indica-tors, why are the markings restricted to one small part of the cave, whereas flint veins occur, and were mined, throughout the cave?

There are two other possible explanations. One is that the markings mirror the instinctive human impulse to make marks on blank surfaces. This is a well-documented reaction, common to *Homo sapiens* all over the globe, which may well be the first step in the development of art in all societies. The other possibility is that the markings were produced in the course of ritual activity. In hunter–gatherer societies most art forms part of religious ritual, and this is certainly true of traditional Aboriginal society in more recent times. The ritual may have been associated also with flint-mining in this remote, dark part of the cave.

Markings similar to those at Koonalda have been found in another cave on the Nullarbor in Western Australia. This is totally untouched by vandalism and is currently being studied and protected. Other sites with wall markings are Kintore and Cutta Cutta Caves in the Northern Territory and Orchestra Shell Cave[17] in Western Australia, but the possibility that animals' claws could have been used as engravers' tools complicates the problem of distinguishing between man-made and animal-made markings.

SNOWY RIVER CAVE, BUCHAN

In the wild gorge of the Snowy River north of Buchan a spectacular area of limestone cliffs and caves lies on the west bank. The region has become known as New Guinea, because of its rainforest vegetation and rugged terrain. Traces of Aboriginal occupation have been found in one cave, New Guinea II. The cave system leads far underground, but outside the entrance is a rockshelter, overlooking a slope covered with grass-trees, which leads down to the Snowy River a hundred metres away. The floor of the rockshelter is of earth interspersed with huge blocks of roof-fall. Excavations here in 1980 by Paul Ossa of La Trobe University revealed some traces of Aboriginal presence going back almost 20 000 years.

A narrow entrance and steep descent lead into a large chamber with high roof and several entrances. A permanent stream trickles across the chamber floor, but on a dry earth bank above the stream is an Aboriginal fireplace and midden heap, with shells clearly visible in the dim light filtering in from the entrance above. Aborigines evidently scrambled down into this deep cavern, but with what purpose in mind? A glance around provided an answer: the mud-covered, soft limestone walls formed a perfect canvas for prehistoric artists. Mud had been deposited on the walls by occasional flooding, leaving a smooth surface that could easily be marked with the fingers or a sharp object such as a bone or pointed stick (plate 20).

It has been suggested that the markings may have been made by the claws of animals scrambling to get out of the cave, but several features argue against this interpretation. The markings are not found indiscriminately all over the cave but tend to occur in 'panels' on the smoother sections of wall. They are not merely random markings but include some apparent patterns, such as a whole mass of diagonally crossing lines and circles. Finally, they are similar to the wall markings at Koonalda Cave, and to the 'macaroni' style of rock art found in ice age caves in Europe.

As at Koonalda, some of the Snowy River Cave markings are in inaccessible positions and in complete darkness. They may have been made in the course of secret ceremonies in this deep, dark cave and date from the very beginnings of Aboriginal art more than 20 000 years ago.

SUMMARY

There are inevitably many uncertainties in trying to identify tangible evidence of the awakening of early human intellect. What appears to be the oldest art yet found in Australia is barely distinguishable from random marks made by chance. The same process of development is found in the Upper Paleolithic caves of Europe, with which early Aboriginal art seems to be contemporary. In the caves of southern France and Spain early macaroni style wall markings evolved over thousands of years into the glorious naturalistic art of Lascaux and Altamira. In Australia, the tentative finger designs of Koonalda Cave are later than those of Europe, but they are several thousand years older than the paintings of the Lascaux bison hunters.

Certainly hands were being stencilled and ochre mixed with blood and applied to rock walls in Tasmanian caves during the last glaciation. Ochre pigments were being ground up for use 18 000 years ago in Arnhem Land, and 19 000-year-old ochre 'crayons' were found in Kenniff Cave in southern Queensland. Even further back in time, ochre was being used at Lake Mungo in a 30 000-year-old burial and a 32 000-year-old campsite. Moreover, the ochre was not local to the area but had to be transported from several kilometres away.

One problem in trying to trace the development of Aboriginal art in the ice age is that engravings and paintings do not normally occur in the same region, so the relationship between the two is hard to determine. Pleistocene art in Australia is largely represented by engravings – a difficult medium with limited possibilities – but in Arnhem Land it has been argued that the dynamic style paintings belong to the Pleistocene period. If this is correct the dynamic hunting and dancing scenes are the earliest known narrative paintings in the world.

There is ample evidence that art has been part of Australian Aboriginal life for over 10 000 years. Only a few traces are left of ice age art, but the marvellous quality, variety, vigour, and complexity of more recent Aboriginal art testify to strong artistic traditions of great antiquity.

TECHNOLOGY

The emerging picture of ice age technology is of a varied and efficient toolkit, including stone, bone and wooden tools, and no doubt many other items made of organic materials that have not survived in the archaeological record. The stone tools are remarkably similar all over the continent, even when made from very different raw materials, and they appear to belong to a single technological tradition. This Australian core tool and scraper tradition is characterized by pebble choppers, horsehoof cores, steep-edge scrapers, notched and other types. These are primarily tools to make tools; they are used for manufacturing, maintenance and processing tasks, and they were also used for preparation of some vegetable food.

Proof is still lacking that the ice age inhabitants of Australia wore skin clothing, but there is strong circumstantial evidence. The whole toolkit used for skin-working in historic times has been found in Pleistocene sites. The bone points found have use-wear on their tips consistent with piercing skins. Bone points were found in ice age levels in Cloggs Cave at the foot of the Snowy Mountains and in Cave Bay Cave on Hunter Island, at that time a hill within sight of the Tasmanian glaciers. Bone points may have served a number of different purposes as they did in historic times, but it would be most surprising if fur cloaks in Australia only came into use after the end of the ice age, given the long continuity of other traditions.

Stone tools played a very small part in traditional Aboriginal equipment: most artefacts were of wood, bone, shell or plant material. Unfortunately, after even a thousand years in the ground, almost everything has disappeared except items made of stone. Very special conditions are needed to preserve wooden tools, in particular a constantly wet or dry environment. These conditions are found in peat bogs, but there are regrettably few such bogs in Australia, the world's driest inhabited continent. It was thus a great day for Australian archaeology when the first early wooden tools were discovered in Wyrie Swamp in South Australia.[20]

Although archaeologists are well aware of the potential of such environments, the artefacts in Wyrie Swamp came to light by accident. Roger Luebbers was doing fieldwork in the Millicent district of South Australia, when he fell, slipped a disc, and ended up in hospital. Whilst convalescing, he got talking to the man in the next bed, Mr Hans Van Schaik, who casually mentioned that there were boomerangs in a peat bog on his land. As soon as he could, Luebbers investigated and discovered that most of the peat had been removed, but in the remaining part was a 10 000-year-old lakeside camp, containing both stone and wooden tools, which had later been flooded and preserved by the swamp (colour plate 7).

From 10 200 to 9000 years ago Aborigines visited the shores of the shallow swamp, hunting game, gathering plants, and manufacturing stone tools. Their

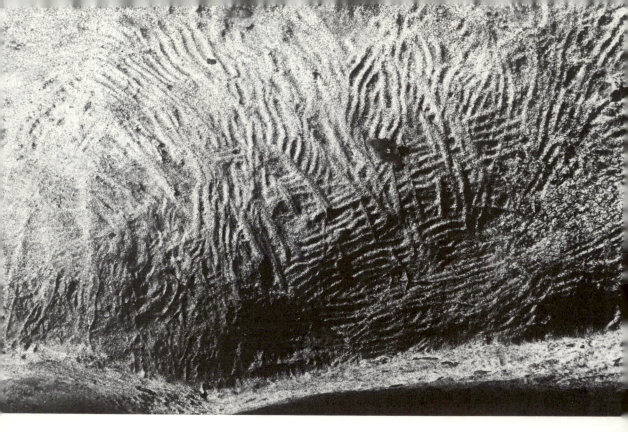

Plate 20. *Wall markings in Snowy River Cave, eastern Victoria*

stone toolkit included the core tools and scrapers characteristic of other ice age sites. However, conditions of preservation were so good that the residue of organic materials remained on some of the working edges. Microscopic examination revealed that they had been used to process not only wood, but also plant foods. Associated with this typical Australian core tool and scraper industry was the missing element from all ice age sites hitherto excavated in Australia: the wooden artefacts.

Twenty-five wooden tools were recovered, complete or in fragments. The types represented were a digging stick, pointed stakes (about 40 centimetres long, possibly also for digging), a short simple spear, two barbed spears, and nine boomerangs, three of them complete. The barbed spears were a real surprise – no one had thought they went so far back in time in Australia, and they are the oldest examples of this implement type found anywhere in the world.

Boomerangs too were a weapon of ice age Australia, and the Wyrie Swamp examples are the oldest in the world. So-called boomerangs have been found in other parts of the world, such as those in a Florida swamp in the United States, but the latter are throwing sticks, not true boomerangs. The South Australian boomerangs are clearly the returning type, shown by the fact that the two ends are oriented in different aerodynamic planes. The curvature and lateral twist they exhibit are the classic properties of a well-designed aerodynamic missile. The wing span is 29 to 50 centimetres and the arms join in a sharp elbow.

Analysis of the pollen in Wyrie Swamp[21] has revealed the type of environment these boomerang throwers lived in. This was woodland dominated by *Casuarina* trees (she-oaks) around a shallow fresh-water swamp, rich in bulrushes and other plant foods. Earlier, between about 26 000 and 11 000 years ago, the woodland was more open, reflecting the dry cold period of the last phase of the last glaciation, which witnessed the drying-up of the Willandra Lakes. It seems likely that the boomerangs of Wyrie Swamp were used to bag some of the numerous waterfowl that haunted the wetlands 10 000 years ago.

Australian prehistoric technology was not static. There was a gradual development towards less massive, more efficient and more varied tools: later ice age industries have fewer core tools, smaller scrapers, and a greater range of types. This decrease in size reflects progress towards greater efficiency in the use of raw material. It has been calculated by Rhys Jones that over a period of a thousand human generations, stone tools became eight times more efficient. (These figures are based on an increase in the average length of working edge per unit weight of tool from 0.5 mm per gram 25 000 years ago to 4 mm per gram 5000 years ago.)

The earliest industry in Australia is generally believed to have been the Kartan, with its huge horsehoof cores and pebble choppers. This may well have been a forerunner to the core tool and scraper tradition found so widely by about 20 000 years ago. The presence of large waisted tools at Pleistocene sites in Australia and New Guinea suggests a common origin for the early industries of Greater Australia and South-East Asia. The concept of grinding the blade of a tool to a chisel-like cutting edge is also found in early sites in northern Australia, New Guinea and South-East Asia.

The world's earliest known ground axe blades come from Arnhem Land, from a 23 000-year-old level in Malangangerr Shelter. Some of these ground-edge axes also possess encircling grooves, which have been hammered or pecked to provide a grip for an attached handle. This is the earliest evidence in the world for such stone dressing techniques. These practices of grinding and hafting may be an Australian invention, the idea perhaps springing from the ancient pecked rock art of central and western Australia. On the other hand, parallels have been drawn[22] with the similar early ground and hafted tools of sites in Japan and South-East Asia, such as Sai Yok in Thailand. In New Guinea there seems to be a progression from large flaked waisted tools to smaller ones with ground edges. The same progression may have occurred in Australia from the large Kartan flaked waisted tools to the small edge-ground axe heads with waists or encircling grooves of Arnhem Land.

Since both hafting notches and edge-grinding are specialized techniques, there may have been a fairly rapid dispersal of certain technological ideas around the Australian continent. The presence of waisted tools on Kartan sites would thus reflect the toolkit of the earliest migrants. Their absence from later sites in southern Australia may be because they dropped out of use since they were unnecessary in a non-tropical environment.

Other stone artefacts that appear early in Australia are grindstones, for grinding up ochre or hard fruits, seeds and vegetable foods. Grindstones appear in Arnhem Land by 19 000 years ago, and in the Willandra Lakes region they were used for seed-grinding by about 5 000.

Of ice age wooden technology we have but a single glimpse: the twenty-five wooden artefacts of Wyrie Swamp. Yet even in so small a sample is represented the characteristic equipment of traditional Aboriginal Australia. Then, as now, women were equipped with digging sticks, men with spears and boomerangs. A strong, fire-hardened wooden spear was a highly effective weapon which has been used throughout Aboriginal occupation of the continent. The barbed, javelin-type spear was a refinement that was unexpected in the ice age, but it would have been an effective weapon with which to spear large kangaroos. When such barbed spears enter man or beast they are difficult to dislodge, and tend to cause death through loss of blood. The boomerangs from Wyrie Swamp are even more sophisticated weapons than the barbed spears. It is fitting that the world's oldest boomerangs have been found in Australia. It is also a salutary thought that 10 000 years ago Aborigines understood the principles of torque and aerodynamic flight sufficiently to design and make returning boomerangs, something most of us cannot do today.

In summary, prehistoric technology in Australia was neither simple nor primitive. The toolkit was limited in range and highly portable, but it was adapted to cope successfully with a wide variety of environments and harsh conditions which, 20 000 years later, were to prove too much for many European 'explorers' and settlers.

SUMMARY

The time of arrival of the first Australians is also still in doubt, although the likely limits can now be stated with some certainty. No archaeological evidence has yet been found to support suggestions made by Gurdip Singh and Charles Dortch for human arrival 120 000 years ago in the last great interglacial.[23] Several deposits belonging to the last interglacial, such as the Golgol lunette series at Mungo, the inner coastal barrier system of northern New South Wales, and deposits on Kangaroo Island, have been carefully scrutinized but found sterile of human occupation.

There is thus no positive evidence but some negative evidence that people were not in Australia 120 000 years ago. But as we have seen, they were in far south-west Australia by 38 000 years ago and in south-east Australia at Lake

Mungo and elsewhere certainly by 35 000 and more probably by 40 000 years ago. And by 20 000 years ago, people had already penetrated far inland in the Pilbara, Central Australia and on the Nullarbor Plain, and deep within the mountain ranges of southern Queensland, the Australian Capital Territory and Tasmania.

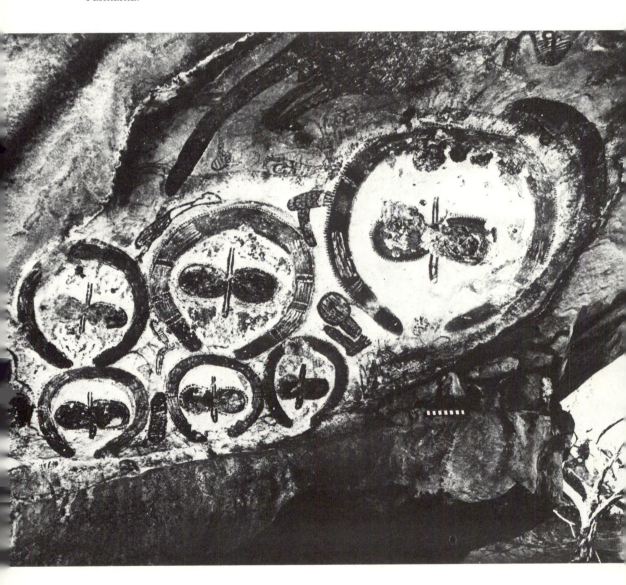

Plate 21. *Wandjina art site, Kimberley, Western Australia* (G. Walsh)

The most likely time for entry into Australia was at a time when sea level was low, and such a time was the period around 52 000 years ago. In fact, sea level was lower then than at any time during the previous 100 000 years and was not to sink so low again for another 30 000 years. Even so, more than 50 kilometres of open sea had to be crossed before landfall on the great southern continent.

Plate 22. *Aborigines flaking stone at Point Plomer, near Port Macquarie, New South Wales.* (Dick Collection, by courtesy of the Australian Museum)

CHAPTER TWELVE

EXTINCTION OF THE GIANT MARSUPIALS

There are many Aboriginal legends about giant mythical beings of the Dream-time, and some of these stories handed down from generation to generation may well enshrine memories of the giant creatures that roamed Australia more than 15 000 years ago. One such story tells of the hunting of giant kangaroos with fire and weapons in western New South Wales.

Long ago, many people were camped at the confluence of the Lachlan and Murrumbidgee Rivers. The day was very hot and a haze rose from the windless plan so that the horizon danced, and mirages distorted the landscape. Everyone lay motionless, resting in the heat. Suddenly, a tribe of giant Kangaroos were seen away in the distance and the headman leapt to his feet with a galvanizing cry. The camp became a scene of wild excitement and fear. Children were quickly seized and everyone dispersed into the bush. In those times, however, the men had no weapons and were defenceless against the enemy. The Kangaroos relentlessly advanced on them through the bush and without mercy crushed their victims with their powerful arms. When the animals were finished, few of the tribe remained. The headman, however, lived, and in desperation he called the remaining band together to discuss methods of defence. At that meeting the men devised the weapons of spears, shields, clubs and boomerangs, some of which are still used today in many parts of Australia. Many young women had lost their children as they fled, and needing a device in which to carry their babies they made the ingenious bark cradle.

But Wirroowaa, the cleverest of the men, thought of enlisting the help of the Great Spirit. To do this, however, he needed to paint his chest with sacred designs in white clay which had to be collected from the banks of the river bed where the giant Kangaroos were camped.

Fearlessly he set out across the plain for the river bed. He turned over a hollow log with his foot and found a big, brown-banded goanna, his beady eyes blinking and his wide yellow jaws apart. Quickly killing the goanna, Wirroowaa slit the belly open with a stone tool and extracted the body fat. This he smeared all over his skin until it glistened in the hot sun; then he rolled in the dust until he was as brown as the earth, and then picked up a branch of leaves to hold before him. This was the first time a man had used the technique of camouflage. Completely disguised, he quietly crept on towards the Kangaroo camp and without being observed stole the sacred clay.

Behind him a small breeze had come up, and the nearer he got to the river bed the stronger the breeze became. Two sticks which first were gently rubbing together soon became warm, then red hot, and suddenly a spark flew from the smoking twigs into a patch of dry grass. A fire was made. Wirroowaa quickly smeared his body with the clay, making sacred designs which would bring the presence of the Great Spirit to him.

The wind gradually grew in volume and spread over the grassy plain. The little breeze became a gale. The Great Spirit came and told Wirroowaa to keep to the dry patches of ground. Some of the people had already been caught in the fire, but others picking up their babies in the bark cradles, rushed to the treeless area. The giant Kangaroos appeared on the horizon but were driven back immediately by the fire. The danger from them was over for a while.

But the leader, the headman, was dying and Wirroowaa painted him with the sacred clay so that the power of the Great Spirit would be with him. Then the old man spoke. He said that one day the giant Kangaroos would be overcome. Each man must carry spears and clubs, and bark must be stripped from trees to make shelters for each family, so that the sun would not weaken the people as it had in the past. Shields were also to be used in defence.[1]

Humans probably arrived in Australia before 50 000 years ago, gradually spreading around the continent and using fire in hunting. The giant marsupials would have been relatively slow-moving prey and vulnerable to hunters until they learned defensive behaviour against these new predators. It may be significant that in the areas where the earliest occupation has been found, such as the Willandra Lakes and Perth region, the megafauna apparently disappeared earliest. Indeed, although it is dangerous to argue from absence of evidence, it is noteworthy that megafauna are absent from both Koonalda and Allen's Caves on the Nullarbor Plain. Since occupation of these caves had begun by at least 20 000 years ago, megafauna may already have been extinct in this arid region by that time.

Those huge browsers that survived the initial impact of man the hunter finally seem to have met their end during the Great Dry at the end of the Pleistocene. The one thing they all had in common was large size and a gigantic thirst, so as the lakes and waterholes dried up, one by one, they became doomed to extinction. Some, like the red kangaroo, managed to adapt, others evolved smaller forms, the rest died out. The period from about 25 000 to 15 000 years ago was a time of stress: stress from diminishing water supplies, changes in vegetation and climate, and from the ever-present hunters with their spears and fire-sticks. Wooded areas near the coast probably acted as refuge areas, which would account for the megafauna's apparent survival there longer than in the arid inland. It seems that, directly or indirectly, Aboriginal occupation of the continent had as great an impact on Australian fauna in the Pleistocene as European settlement was to have in recent times.

Since 1830 it has been known that giant animals (megafauna) once existed in Australia. In that year Sir Thomas Mitchell, Surveyor-General of New South Wales, found in the Wellington Caves west of Sydney a tooth of *Diprotodon optatum*, the largest marsupial known to have lived. Indeed, one of Mitchell's party tied a rope to a projection in order to lower himself into the cave, only to find that the projection was the bone of a giant marsupial. At that time much of the continent was unknown to Europeans, and early explorers such as Ludwig Leichhardt quite expected to come across live *Diprotodon* in their travels. However, it emerged that the megafauna were all extinct, and people turned their attention to the questions of when and why these extinctions took place, and what part hunters played in their disappearance. The question of Aboriginal impact on the environment is important, for there are those who argue that Aborigines were merely parasites, whereas others regard the Australian vegetation as an Aboriginal artefact. Aboriginal impact on fauna will be examined here, and that on the flora in chapter 16.

The extinction of Pleistocene megafauna must not be confused with the much earlier extinction of the dinosaurs, who met their end about 65 million years ago. Down the ages many creatures have become extinct, but such extinctions were usually gradual and extinct animal families were replaced by new ones. Then at the end of the ice age the extinction rate accelerated. An extraordinary number of large vertebrate animals disappeared over much of the globe. There was extinction without replacement. In Australia about one-third of the large mammals that existed 50 000 years ago were extinct by 15 000 years ago. Most of these were giant marsupials.

The world's largest marsupials were the *Diprotodons*, browsers of wombat-like build but the size of a rhinoceros (plate 12). But the highest number of extinct species is found in the family of kangaroos and wallabies, the Macropodidae (literally meaning 'big feet'). There were giant wallabies, *Protemnodon*, which were larger in size than the largest living kangaroo (the big red, *Megaleia rufa*), which stands up to 2 metres tall and weighs as much as 90 kilograms. Some giant kangaroos did not die out but simply became smaller. For example *Macropus titan* was twice the mass, 30 centimetres or more taller and had more complex teeth than its descendant, the large living grey kangaroo, *Macropus giganteus*. Other extinct kangaroos such as *Sthenurus* were not much bigger than modern kangaroos but were different in form (figure 12.1).

The largest and most peculiar macropod of all was *Procoptodon goliah*, a massive 3 metre tall kangaroo with short, broad face. The name *Procoptodon* means 'front crushing teeth'. In all living kangaroos the two lower incisors grow forward, but *Procoptodon* had its upturned like the koala's. The molars were huge, with high transverse furrows and ridges. Such powerful jaws were highly adapted for chewing tough plant food, and the shortening of the face increased biting power. It seems that *Procoptodon* browsed on shrubs and trees, using its very long fore-limbs to pull down high branches (figure 12.2).

In most marsupial families there was at least one giant form that became extinct. Among the wombats, *Phascolonus gigas* was twice as large as modern wombats and weighed half a tonne or more. There was a giant echidna, *Zaglossus*, which still exists in New Guinea. And the massive extinct goanna, *Megalania*, was far larger than the largest living lizard in the world, the Komodo dragon of Indonesia. *Megalania* grew to 6 and possibly 9 metres long and appears to have had the same sharp teeth and claws found on the largest living Australian lizard, the perentie of central Australia, which reaches 2.5

Figure 12.1 *The extinct* Sthenurus, *a short-faced kangaroo adapted for browsing.* (After P. Murray)

Figure 12.2 *The extinct giant kangaroo,* Procoptodon, *which stood 3 metres tall and had only a single huge toe on the hind foot.* (After P. Murray)

metres in length. *Megalania* may well have given rise to some of the Aboriginal legends concerning monsters such as the bunyip and yowie.

Among the birds was an extinct flightless bird, *Genyornis*, larger and much heavier than the modern emu, with a beak about 30 centimetres long. *Genyornis* was possibly similar to the *Moa* of New Zealand, which was hunted to extinction by the first humans to reach those islands.

Finally, there was one predator, *Thylacoleo*, known as the marsupial 'lion' (figure 12.3). The size of a leopard, *Thylacoleo* was equipped with very large powerful teeth. An additional weapon was an enormous claw on each front foot. With all this armament, it seems likely that *Thylacoleo* was both a carnivore (meat-eater) and an active predator. Marsupial 'lion' is an appropriate name because it seems likely that *Thylacoleo* killed like the big cats, using its large front claws as weapons for stabbing or for grabbing the prey while strangling it. It also seems to have fed like a cheetah, biting through the rib

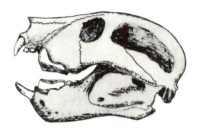

Figure 12.3 *Skull of the marsupial 'lion'*, Thylacoleo. *Thylacoleo was a leopard-sized meat-eater, equipped with large, powerful teeth. Its two lower incisors and the central pair of the six upper incisors were enlarged as 'tusks', resembling the stabbing canine teeth found in flesh-eaters. On each side of its upper and lower jaw were two huge teeth, up to 6 centimetres long, which could slice flesh like sharp shears.* (After Mincham and Richardson 1971)

cage to gain access to its victim's internal organs, but leaving the rest of the skeleton virtually intact.[2]

Other animals became extinct, or at least appear to be extinct, on the Australian mainland, but survived in Tasmania. The Tasmanian devil, *Sarcophilus*, appears to have survived until a few hundred years ago on the mainland and is still alive and well in Tasmania. The Tasmanian tiger, *Thylacinus*, is more of a problem (figure 12.4). The youngest thylacine bones to have been found on the mainland are about 3300 years old. These remains came from Murra-el-elevyn Cave on the Nullarbor Plain. Another cave on the Nullarbor, Thylacine Hole, contained an incredibly well preserved thylacine skeleton 4600 years old.[3] The extreme aridity had preserved the carcase so well that the tongue and left eyeball were still recognizable. (The remains are now being carefully conserved in the Western Australian Museum.) It might be assumed, therefore, that thylacines are now extinct in mainland Australia, except that sightings of a striped thylacine-like creature have occasionally been reported from areas as far apart as Victoria and northern Queensland. The thylacine was alive in Tasmania in historic times, but one has not been captured or photographed for the last fifty years. Sightings, however, have been reported, and the World Wildlife Fund has mounted a project to try to find thylacines and save them from extinction. Whatever the outcome, the Tasmanian devil and tiger are in a different category from the giant animals that became extinct all over Australia, and should be considered separately from the megafauna.

Figure 12.4 *The Tasmanian 'tiger'*, Thylacinus cynocephalus. *The largest marsupial flesh-eater.* (After P. Murray)

CHRONOLOGY OF EXTINCTION

The debate about the Aborigines' part in megafaunal extinction in Australia has been severely clouded by uncertainties concerning its chronology.[4] Early researchers were misled by apparently very low dates for some megafauna, such as the claim that *Diprotodon* was present as recently as 6000 years ago. These claims have now been disproved.

One of the main problems in obtaining reliable dates on megafauna has been the difficulty of dating bone, so palaeontologists have had to rely on stratigraphic association with more reliable datable materials, such as charcoal and shell. Bone is particularly susceptible to contamination, especially by younger calcium carbonate carried downwards by groundwater, which makes radiocarbon dates less accurate. Bone dates, therefore, tend to be too low; this has been demonstrated by comparing dates derived from charcoal, shell and bone in the same archaeological layer. Analysis of the fluorine content of bones can be used to tell whether bones found together are broadly contemporary or not, but fluorine analysis does not give absolute ages.

In spite of all these problems, within the last decade the general chronological framework of Pleistocene extinctions has been established. The main

Table 12.1. *Some occurrences of extinct fauna in Australia since 40 000 BP*

	Date BP	Fauna	Site
Period of extinction of megafauna	> 37 000	Thylacoleo Zaglossus Zygomaturus Sthenurus	* Mammoth Cave, WA
	31 600 ± 1300	Diprotodon Thylacoleo Macropus titan	* Arundel Terrace, Keilor, Vic.
	26 600 ± 650 25 200 ± 800	Macropus titan Diprotodon Protemnodon Genyornis Sthenurus	Lancefield, Vic.
	>26 300 ± 1500 <18 800 ± 800	Diprotodon Procoptodon Protemnodon Phascolonus Thylacoleo Macropus titan Sthenurus	Lake Menindee Lunette, N.S.W.
	> 31 000	Sthenurus Protemnodon	* Devil's Lair, W.A.
	22 980 ± 2000 c. 19 000	Sthenurus Zygomaturus Diprotodon Protemnodon Sthenurus	Cloggs Cave, E. Vic. Rocky River, Kangaroo Island, S.A.
	c. 19 000	Diprotodon Sthenurus	Spring Creek, S.W. Vic.
	20 650 ± 1790 <20 000	Macropus titan Sthenurus Macropus titan	* Beginners' Luck, Tas. Titan's Shelter, Tas.
	< 19 300 ± 500	Diprotodon Macropus titan Protemnodon Procoptodon Sthenurus	* Lime Springs, N.S.W.
	16 100 ± 100	Sthenurus	* Seton, Kangaroo Island, S.A.
Period of later extinctions on mainland (caused by dingo?)	4650 ± 153 4550 ± 112	Thylacinus	Nullarbor Plain, W.A.
	3280 ± 90	Thylacinus	Murra-el-Elevyn, Nullarbor, W.A.
	c. 500	Sarcophilus	s-w Western Australia

* Indicates sites where the fauna seem to be associated with human occupation.

concern here is the part hunters may have played in Pleistocene extinctions. The most reliable dates associated with extinct fauna during the time-span of known human occupation in Australia are set out in table 12.1.

Three phases of extinction appear to have occurred during the last 40 000 years. In the earliest phase, the largest animals became extinct, and this process seems to have been largely completed by 20 000 years ago. The megafauna that still remained after then tended to be only a little larger than modern species. In the second phase, some of these diminished in size, others, like *Sthenurus*, died out altogether. By the end of the ice age, all seem to have gone.

Later there was another phase of extinction on mainland Australia, but this time only two medium-sized flesh-eating predators were the victims: the Tasmanian devil and the thylacine. The reason for at least the demise of the thylacine on the mainland seems to have been the arrival of a more efficient predator, the dingo. No dingo bones have been found in ice age faunal deposits, and the oldest firmly dated ones go back only some 3000 years at Fromm's Landing rockshelter in South Australia and Wombah midden, New South Wales.[5]

It is now generally thought that the dingo was brought by hunter–gatherers to Australia about 4000 years ago and in any case certainly after 8000 years ago, when Tasmania was finally severed from the mainland by the post-glacial sea rise. This would account for the dingo's absence from Tasmania and older mainland sites, but presence in younger sites and historic times on the mainland. It would also account for the extinction of predators such as the Tasmanian devil and tiger on the mainland, but their survival in Tasmania, where they were free from the dingo's competition.

CAUSES OF EXTINCTION

Three possible reasons for the extinction of the megafauna in the late Pleistocene period have been proposed: climatic change, overkill, and habitat alteration by man-made fires. Early writers sought to correlate extinctions with climatic change, particularly with the so-called 'Great Arid Period' around 4000 years ago. When it became clear that the latter did not exist and that the extinctions occurred much earlier, Rhys Jones and Duncan Merrilees, a palaeontologist from Western Australia, published in 1968 the conclusion they had reached independently, namely that man was primarily responsible, both through direct hunting of the giant animals and by habitat alteration through use of fire.[6] Jones produced a neat model of humans entering the continent and rapidly hunting the megafauna to extinction. There is a virtual absence in Australia of 'kill sites', that is, places where large animals have been killed and butchered by big-game hunters. Some Pleistocene sites contain only megafauna, others only human occupational debris. A very few, such as Seton,

Devil's Lair and Menindee, contain both, but they have produced no clear evidence of the killing or butchering of megafauna. But along with a number of other sites, they provide good evidence that humans and megafauna were contemporary. Evidence of what seems to be deliberate breaking, cutting and burning of megafaunal bones comes from Mammoth Cave in Western Australia.[7] The age of the bones is greater than 37 000 years, and this is the best evidence yet that Aborigines preyed upon the large extinct animals.

WESTERN NEW SOUTH WALES

Several possibilities have been put forward over the years as kill sites. In 1955 the first reports were published of an archaeological site on the shore of Lake Menindee in the Darling River basin in western New South Wales.[8] This site, like Mungo, was in a sand dune bordering a lake that was once full of fresh water. Bones of both extinct and modern species, fireplaces apparently dating to 18 000 and 26 000 years, and about 300 tools were found. These included bone points, a few large stone tools of Kartan type, horsehoof cores, adzes, and specialized small tools, such as stone points, belonging to the last few thousand years. The fact that both young and old tool types were found in the same level along with the bones of extinct fauna shows that there had been some mixing by deflation of the sand dune so things of different ages lay together on an eroded surface. This throws suspicion on the apparent association of man and megafauna at the site.

At most other sites in the Darling River region, there is almost no overlap between megafauna and human occupation. For example, in the lunette at Lake Victoria, another now-dry lake near the River Murray in the far south-west of New South Wales, more than 177 occurrences of extinct species, 67 human skeletons and numerous middens have been found, but not one of the extinct animals was in association with cultural material.[9]

At Lake Mungo and the other Willandra Lakes, megafauna is conspicuous by its rarity. Only a few remains of one species, *Procoptodon*, have been found as yet. These came from the southern shore of Lake Garnpung in sediments that also contain middens dated to about 31 000 BP, and from the northern shore of Lake Mungo from within the Mungo sediments, dated between 25 000 and 19 000 years ago. At one of the Garnpung sites the *Procoptodon* remains were associated with artefacts and some of the bone was burnt. At Mungo, however, the fauna found in the human occupation sites are all modern species.

The scarcity of megafauna at Mungo has been cited as evidence that the huge Pleistocene species had become extinct before 30 000 years ago as a result of overkill by human hunters. Another explanation to account for the lack of extinct giant fauna in the Mungo occupation sites is that people were camping at Mungo when giant animals were around, but they concentrated on hunting small animals and fishing. In almost all of the hundreds of archaeological sites known in Australia the bones of small animals predominate markedly. There are only a few sites where large animals such as kangaroos make up a major part of the faunal assemblage. It could, therefore, be argued that the earliest migrants were adapted to a maritime economy concentrating on fish, shellfish and small game, and that big game hunting did not develop until much later. This hypothesis would account for the co-existence of man and megafauna but the general lack of kill sites.

To sum up the situation in western New South Wales, the disappearance of most megafauna seems to have occurred primarily before 25 000, and probably before 30 000 years ago. This was the period of high water-levels in the Willandra Lakes, and hence does not support the theory that the giant marsupials became extinct because of the increasing aridity from about 25 000 to 15 000 years ago. The only major change that took place in the region before or at the time of the extinctions was the arrival of man with his fire-stick, so this evidence supports human agency as a cause of the death of the megafauna.

LANCEFIELD SWAMP

In 1974 a bone bed containing extinct species was discovered in Lancefield Swamp in Victoria, and, embedded amongst the bones, a large quartzite blade of indisputable human manufacture was found (figure 12.5). Large scale excavations were carried out in 1975–76, for Lancefield was the first site to combine the presence of extinct fauna, artefacts, reliable radiocarbon dates on charcoal, and clear stratification.[10] And in the constantly wet environment of Lancefield Swamp pollen was preserved, which provided valuable information about the past vegetation of the area.

In the first season of excavation 3000 bones were recovered from only 5 square metres of the swamp, representing a minimum of 72 individual animals: an average of 14 individuals per square metre. The whole swamp, with an area of 2000 square metres, has been estimated to contain the skeletons of more than 10 000 extinct animals. The bones lie about 1.5 metres below the surface in a 20 centimetre thick bone bed. Two samples of charcoal associated with the bones have both given radiocarbon dates of about 26 000 years ago.

Only one additional artefact was found associated with the bone bed: a piece of flake, only 3 centimetres long, of the same quartzite as the original blade. Other artefacts typical of the small tool tradition were found in the much younger layers above, but none was made of the same material as the Pleistocene flakes. These flakes belong to the same time as the formation of the bone bed, so they indicate that humans visited the swamp at the same time that the giant fauna were dying there.

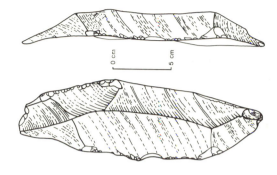

Figure 12.5 *Quartzite blade from Lancefield Swamp, Victoria, about 26 000 years old* (By courtesy of American Association Advancement of Science from *Science* 1978, vol. 200, p. 104)

FAUNAL ANALYSIS

This is strong circumstantial evidence for big game hunting, but causes of death other than by human hand have been proposed by David Horton,[11] who has carefully analysed the faunal evidence. He found that 'some special selective event was causing death', because the animals in the swamp were restricted to a very few, large species and were nearly all adult rather than juvenile animals. The only species represented were the giant kangaroo, *Macropus titan* (90 per cent), the huge extinct wallaby, *Protemnodon* species (8 per cent), and less than 1 per cent each of *Sthenurus*, *Diprotodon*, *Genyornis*, and *Dromaius*. Except for *Dromaius*, the modern emu, they are all extinct. They are also all large animals and flightless birds; no small animals suffered the same fate of death at the swamp.

In addition to the remarkably low variety of species, there was also a curiously restricted age range. Eighty per cent of the giant kangaroos were more than seven years old, and only eight per cent were less than two years old. This is not a random sample of a normal population that became bogged or died of other natural causes at the swamp; nor is it the normal result of predation by man or carnivores, neither of whom are likely to be so selective in the age of their prey. However, it could be a random sample of a kangaroo population that had stopped breeding for a number of years because of environmental stress, such as drought, because during drought female kangaroos stop reproducing. This explanation would account both for the extinction of some large species and the diminution in size of others.

The pollen and geomorphological evidence support the theory of a dry period at Lancefield around 26 000 years ago, with the waterhole gradually drying up amid treeless plains. During a long drought, large animals are compelled to gather around the few remaining waterholes as other sources of water disappear. Animals that need to drink every day are restricted for their food supply to food within a narrow radius determined by the distance they can forage each day without drinking. For large, slow-moving animals in hot weather this foraging distance would not be great. If there are no other sources of water within this radius, they are inexorably tied to the one waterhole, until the drought breaks or they die of hunger or thirst or become the prey of carnivores or human hunters.

Such predators may certainly have played a part, but the Lancefield slaughter cannot be the result of predation alone. No butchering marks are visible on any of the bones, no bones are burnt, and the articulation and fragmentation of the bones generally argue against them being the remains of human or carnivore meals. Some scavenging by carnivores did occur, for the toothmarks of the marsupial 'lion', *Thylacoleo*, appear on some bones. However, the strongest evidence in support of Horton's 'last waterhole' theory is the low diversity in species and age of the animals that died, which is otherwise impossible to explain. The one characteristic that megafauna had in common was large size, which made them especially vulnerable to drought.

HABITAT ALTERATION

It has been claimed by Duncan Merrilees and Rhys Jones that man altered the environment by use of fire and this contributed to the extinction of the megafauna. If fire were used in the Pleistocene in a similar fashion to that observed by early settlers and more recently by ethnoarchaeologists, it probably contributed to increases in the number and diversity of local animal communities. Traditionally, small areas are burnt at intervals to clear the way for easier travel, as a hunting aid, and to promote the growth of new grass on which kangaroos and wallabies can feed. This regular, light, mosaic pattern of burning creates a varied array of habitats and conserves the modern macropod species, providing both good grazing and the shelter of unburnt areas, and lessening the occurrence of the disastrous blanket burns that often devastate parts of Australia nowadays.

Nevertheless, there is one type of habitat alteration by use of fire that might have had a profound effect on megafauna: the destruction of particular fire-sensitive species that formed their food supply, since many of the large animals that became extinct in Australia were browsers.

OVERSEAS PARALLELS

A theory of overkill by hunters as the worldwide agent of destruction of megafauna has been proposed.[12] This theory suggests that megafaunal extinction never precedes but always follows closely man's arrival or his development of big-game hunting techniques. There is no doubt that on certain islands the extinction of fauna followed closely on the arrival of man the hunter. When the first Maoris reached New Zealand in about AD 700, they quickly became moa-hunters and hunted these giant flightless birds to extinction. Early archaeological sites, particularly on the South Island, dating between AD 700 and 1600 show that the moa was important in both Maori diet and technology, but that it rapidly decreased in number and range of species under the onslaught of the islands' first human hunters and their fire-sticks. The fire-lighting activities of early Maoris certainly wrought significant destruction and change on the vegetation and increased the rate of erosion.

On the other islands the same story has been repeated. The island of Madagascar witnessed the disappearance of the local fauna, the lemuroids, within a thousand years of human settlement about AD 1200. On the volcanic islands of Mauritius and Reunion the swan-like, flightless bird, the dodo, was eradicated soon after the arrival of European settlers with their guns, and pigs that ran wild and ate the eggs. The year 1681 saw the death of the last bird and the birth of the phrase 'dead as a dodo'.

On the continents of Africa and Eurasia the picture is not as clear-cut, for there men were present long before the Pleistocene extinctions, which were also not total as they were on islands. In Africa, fifty animal species comprising 30 per cent of Pleistocene big game disappeared some 50 000 years ago. This is seen as a result of the development of big-game hunting techniques.

In America the first big-game hunters apparently swept through the continent from Alaska to Tierra del Fuego in only a thousand years, decimating the giant beasts and triggering changes that led to the extinction of mammoths, mastodons, ground sloths, horses, camels and twenty-six other families of megafauna. These late Pleistocene extinctions were unique in their intensity, rapidity, and selection of larger herd animals. Extinction struck only large terrestrial herbivores, their ecologically dependent carnivores, and scavengers. Small animals were not affected, nor were the giants of the sea, such as the world's largest mammals, the whales. The Pleistocene megafauna of America had survived all environmental changes until the arrival of man – they disappeared 'not because they lost their food supply but because they became one'.

KILL SITES

The best evidence yet that hunters exploited megafauna comes from Lime Springs, a spring-fed swamp south of Gunnedah in north-eastern New South Wales. This site has been investigated by David Horton and Richard Wright, aided by teams of diggers from Sydney University.[13] The swamp is two metres deep. It contains more than 2500 stone artefacts and the fragmented teeth and bone of *Diprotodon*, *Procoptodon* and *Macropus titan*, together with the remains of smaller animals. About one quarter of the bone is burnt, and the amount of burnt bone increases when the number of stone artefacts increases. The lowest artefacts are small, amorphous flakes of chert and quartzite, succeeded by large flakes, horsehoof cores and other implements of Kartan type. A distinctive tuff is the dominant raw material for these large tools.

At Lime Springs for the first time megafauna and artefacts have been found together in a sequence that appears to span a long time. Here a broad spectrum of megafauna survived to a date more recent than 19 300 years ago. Kartan-type tools were in use during this same time period, and there is a clear association between the cultural material and the megafaunal bone, which endures through a stratigraphic succession. This adds to the evidence from other sites that humans and megafauna had a long period of co-existence in Australia. Lime Springs has also provided proof that Aborigines not only shared the land with the giant creatures, but also hunted and ate them.

The main arguments against climatic change as the prime agent of extinction of the megafauna are that the extinctions occurred all over Greater Australia, from the mountains of western Papua through the arid heart of the continent to the temperate forests of Tasmania. The megafauna were as diverse in form as the environments they occupied, so it seems unlikely that their extinction can be attributed to climatic change. Droughts do not affect the whole continent, refuge areas were available, and the giant animals had survived dry periods and climatic changes before. Moreover, the main period of extinction precedes the main late Pleistocene climatic change. The only new element in the equation was man, who may have caused the extinctions by a combination of hunting and his use of fire, which drastically altered the animals' habitats. The weight of circumstantial evidence favours human hunters as the decisive factor. Aborigines were not parasites on the land, but to a significant extent the Australian vegetation and fauna are artefacts, artefacts created by Aborigines with their fire-sticks.

PART IV

THE RISING OF THE SEAS

CHAPTER THIRTEEN

TASMANIA: EIGHT THOUSAND YEARS OF ISOLATION

No other surviving human society has ever been isolated so long or so completely as were Tasmanian Aborigines over the last 8000 years (figure 13.1). (The land bridge was gradually inundated between 12 000 and 8000 BP – see chapter 9.) The storm-wracked waters surging through Bass Strait ensured that there was no contact with the mainland 250 kilometres away, and none of the new developments there penetrated Tasmania. Nor did the dingo reach Tasmania. Dingoes were found all over mainland Australia, so they must have arrived in south-east Australia after the disappearance of the land bridge.

To archaeologists the most interesting question is not why Tasmanians had curly hair, but what effect 8000 years of isolation had on the culture of these three or four thousand Aborigines, stranded on an island of 67 870 square kilometres – about the same size as Sri Lanka or Ireland.

The evidence from a few ice age sites suggests that, at the time the island was cut off, the Tasmanians' toolkit was similar to that found on the mainland (see chapter 9). A more comprehensive picture of early Tasmanian technology and diet is provided by the earliest occupation of Rocky Cape caves, excavated by Phys Jones.[1]

ROCKY CAPE

On the rugged headland of Rocky Cape on the north-west coast are two old sea caves cut into the face of great quartzite cliffs. The presence of Aboriginal shell middens in the caves had been known since the end of the last century, but the first scientific excavation of the sites was not carried out until 1965. The work revealed the importance of Rocky Cape, and the area was declared a National Park in 1967.

Holes dug into the sites earlier by amateur collectors made the excavators' task difficult, but some undisturbed parts of the deposits were found, from which the cultural sequence could be established. The huge shell midden in the South Cave was 3.5 metres deep, representing about 4000 years of occupa-

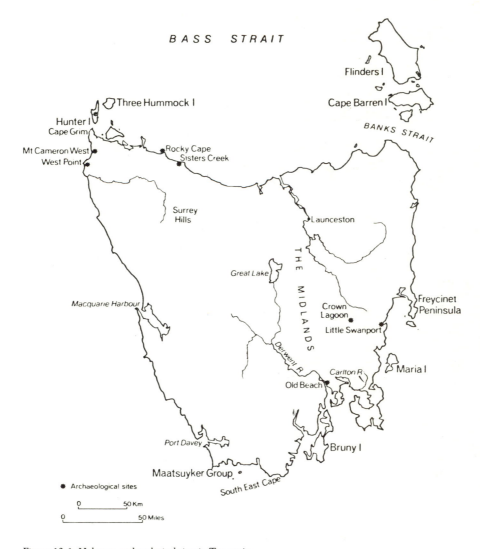

Figure 13.1 *Holocene archaeological sites in Tasmania*

tion, from 8000 to about 3800 years ago. By then the cave had become so full
of food refuse that the midden heap almost reached the roof.

Inside the cave, a small inner chamber had already been sealed off 6800
years ago by midden accumulation outside its mouth (plate 23). The archaeologists found these cramped living quarters just as they had been left.[2] Piles of
big abalone shells were dumped around the walls, but in the centre the floor
had been swept clear for comfortable sitting round the fireplace. Here five

Plate 23. *Inner chamber of Rocky Cape South Cave, Tasmania. The small piles of abalone shells against the walls have lain undisturbed since the cave's inhabitants vacated the inner chamber 6500 years ago.* (W. Ambrose, by courtesy R. Jones)

small ashy hearths, placed close to the rock wall for maximum heat reflection, were found. Food refuse included bones of seals, fish, a few birds and small mammals, shells of rocky coast species, bracken fern stems, a lily tuber and split sections of the pith of the grass-tree. Faeces found in the rubbish dump were at first thought to be human, but analysis showed them to belong to Tasmanian devils, which no doubt scavenged there when the cave was unoccupied. Stone scrapers and a stone mortar, with pestle neatly placed on top, had been left behind by the last occupants for their next visit, a visit that never took place.

When the main chamber as well as the inner chamber became choked with refuse, the occupants seem to have decided that, rather than clearing it out, they would move to another cave about 300 metres to the north. This North Cave had been used intermittently since 5500 years ago, and its use continued until AD 1500.

Rocky Cape south and north caves together contain over 6 metres of midden, spanning 8000 years. This is the longest and most complete record in existence of the technology and diet of coastal hunter-gatherers anywhere in Australia.

STONE AND BONE TOOLS

Flaked stone tools, found in all levels, included scrapers, unretouched flakes and large choppers (figure 13.2).[3] The tasks for which these tools were used have been established with a reasonable degree of certainty from analysis of their shape, microscopic traces of use-wear along their working edges, and observations recorded in historic times of Tasmanian Aborigines using stone tools. Tasmanians used stone tools overwhelmingly for cutting purposes and for manufacturing wooden tools, especially spears. Sometimes shells were used for the same tasks. Large scrapers and choppers were used for general chopping and hammering, and to chop toe-holds in trees when climbing the trunk to catch possums. Holes were also chopped in the bark of the cider gum tree, *Eucalyptus gunnii*, in order to tap its sweet, semi-intoxicating sap, which was the nearest thing to an alcoholic drink available in prehistoric Australia.

These Tasmanian stone tools were all hand-held; the concept of hafting was apparently unknown in Tasmania, although hafting was employed in mainland Australia in the Pleistocene. There was continuity in technological tradition in Tasmania from ice age to historic times, the same tool types and manufacturing techniques continued throughout. But within this general continuity there was also change.

The two major changes revealed were a steady decrease in the size of the stone tools, and the increasing use over time of better raw materials, such as chert, spongolite and siliceous breccia, brought from quarries as far as 100 kilometres away on the west coast. These changes are linked: the better flaking qualities of the new raw materials made it worthwhile to carry them over long distances, but this also meant that more efficient and economical use was made of the exotic stone than had been of the local veins of hard quartzite and beach pebbles of shale and argillite used in the oldest levels. At first stone tool manufacturing was carried out in the caves, but when the exotic raw materials began to be used, stone tools were fashioned, or at least roughed out, at the quarries and transported to Rocky Cape ready-made.

Bone tools were also present at Rocky Cape. Seven thousand years ago people here were using a considerable number and variety of bone artefacts: large, rounded tipped points or awls made from macropod shin bones, small, sharp needle-like points (without an eye), broad spatulae, and an assortment of split slivers of bone fashioned to a point at one end. The people were using one bone tool to every two or three stone ones.

A remarkable change took place over the next four thousand years: bone

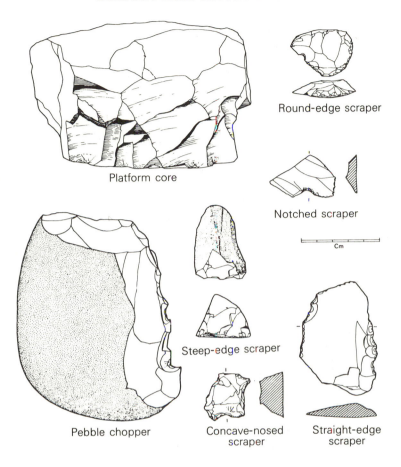

Figure 13.2 *Stone tools from Rocky Cape, Tasmania* (After Jones 1971)

tools dropped out of use. By 4000 years ago only one bone tool was being used for every fifteen stone ones, and by 3500 years ago they had disappeared from the Tasmanian toolkit altogether. This disappearance of bone tools in Tasmania about 3000 years ago has been confirmed by the evidence of several other sites in both the north-west and east of the island. Moreover, no bone tools were observed in use by any of the Europeans who recorded Tasmanian culture, including George Augustus Robinson, who recorded virtually every detail of the years between 1830 and 1836 he spent camping in the bush with Tasmanian Aborigines.[4]

It has been suggested that bone tools dropped out of the equipment of Tasmanian Aborigines because they stopped making skin cloaks. In the colder regions of the mainland in historic times, bone awls or skewers were used to pierce holes in skins for 'sewing' together possum or kangaroo skins into cloaks or rugs, which were often also fastened with a bone pin on the shoulder. The use-wear and form of the Rocky Cape points suggest they had a similar use, although other uses, such as netting needles, are possible. Yet, when Europeans arrived in Tasmania, they found no bone tools and no warm possum-skin rugs, but only skimpy cloaks of wallaby skin fastened with tied pieces of skin. It might be argued that possum skin cloaks were necessary in the Pleistocene but not once the glacial cold dimished, but, if so, why were Aborigines in New South Wales and Victoria still snugly wrapped in voluminous possum skin in the nineteenth century? Tasmania lies further south in the Roaring Forties, and can be cold even in summertime.

Other artefacts and technical skills may also have been lost or abandoned over the long period of isolation. Mainland Australian Pleistocene culture, as we have seen, included boomerangs, barbed spears, and the techniques of hafting handles to tools and grinding the edge of axes, but none of these items existed in the Tasmania of AD 1800.

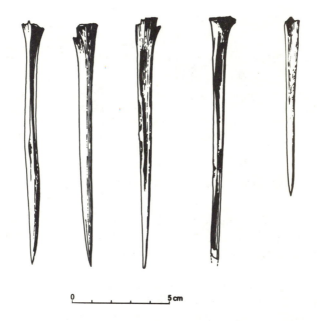

0 _____ 5 cm

Figure 13.3 *Bone tools from Cave Bay Cave, Tasmania, similar to those from Rocky Cape. The large tools are points and spatulas from the Holocene period; the small, sharp point is from an 18 000-year-old level. (After Bowdler 1974)*

DIET

Even more surprising is the incontrovertible evidence that after eating fish for many thousands of years the Tasmanians dropped fish from the diet about 3500 years ago. Early explorers were amazed that the Tasmanians did not eat scale fish and did not even seem to regard it as human food. Those who could bring themselves to believe this astonishing fact ascribed it to the extreme primitiveness of Tasmanian culture.[5] Certainly the Tasmanians had no nets or fish-hooks, so it seemed logical to some scholars, steeped in Darwinian evolutionary theory, that these most primitive representatives of the human race should be unable even to catch fish, one of the basic foods of mankind.

This concept of a people too far down on the evolutionary ladder to have learnt how to catch fish was not seriously challenged until fish bones were found in the middens of Rocky Cape. Yet fish bones were not at the top, but at the base, of the middens. The Tasmanians had once eaten fish but later gave up this excellent source of food.

In Rocky Cape South Cave there were 3196 fish bones in the lower half of the midden, dated to between 3800 and 8000 years ago, and only one fish bone in the younger, upper half. (The latter was a small vertebra which could easily have been brought inside a seal or cormorant.) The fish remains from the Rocky Cape sites, including the inner cave, have recently been analysed in great detail by palaeo-ichthyologist (prehistoric fish remains specialist) Sarah Colley.[6] She identified 31 different types of fish from rocky reefs, bays and estuaries. The data suggest that all the rocky reef species were caught by a simple baited box trap and the others by tidal traps made of boulders, such as the one on Sisters Beach six kilometres east of Rocky Cape.

The average weight of the prehistoric fish was calculated by Jones from bone size as half a kilogram, and he estimated that they provided about 10 per cent of the total caloric intake in the diet in the fish-eating period. Shellfish contributed about half the total flesh weight throughout the whole occupation; the main species collected were warreners, and some abalone. The other major foods were fur seals, some southern elephant seals, and small quantities of wallabies, birds (especially cormorants), bandicoots and other land mammals. During the fish-eating phase ninety fish were caught for every one bird, two wallabies, three seals, and four other land mammals. The pattern would seem to be a steady diet of shellfish, fish and perhaps vegetable food, enlivened by the occasional bagging of a young seal or wallaby. Plants probably did not contribute a great deal to the food supply, for in the high latitude and marked seasonality of temperate Tasmania they were less abundant than on the Australian mainland, and there was scarcity during the cold, non-growing period of winter. And Tasmania had none of the major staple vegetable foods found on the mainland, such as native millet or yams.

The amount of food energy represented in the middens consumed over 8000 years would be sufficient to maintain a group of a few families camping there for five to ten days each year. This may well have been in winter, for winter was the time of stress in Tasmania, at least in historic times, when people fanned out in small groups along the coastline and lived on the only food which was readily available, shellfish.

The cessation of fish-eating was confirmed by other sites, such as Blackman's Cave on Sisters Creek, another sea cave in a cliff 8 kilometres east of Rocky Cape. The midden here, accumulated between about 6000 and 4000 years ago, contained fish and similar material to the lower part of the Rocky Cape sequence, with the interesting addition of crab claws, and many more small mammals, such as possums, rat kangaroos, bandicoots and rats.

Two sites, one on the west coast and one on the east, are examples of the later, non-fish phase: West Point midden and Little Swanport midden.

WEST POINT MIDDEN

Sixty kilometres west of Rocky Cape is the massive midden of West Point, one of the largest and richest occupation sites ever excavated in Australia. It looks like a grass-covered hill and commands an extensive view out over the reefs, bays and islets to seaward and the swamps and tea-tree scrub behind the site. Formed on an old sand dune resting on a pebble bank, the midden rises 6 metres above the surrounding country and measures about 90 metres long by 40 wide. On its surface were seven or eight circular depressions, about 4 metres across and 0.5 metre deep. It seems certain that these were the foundations of dome-shaped huts, which were in use in historic times in Tasmania (figure 13.4). These huts were constructed from a framework of pliable branches, such as tea-tree stems, thatched with bark, grass or turf, and lined inside with skins, bark or feathers.

When George Augustus Robinson was travelling along the western coast in the 1830s, he saw many such huts, often grouped into villages, close to a

Figure 13.4 *Tasmanian huts.* Left *A simple bark windbreak.* Right *Framework of a round dome-shaped thatched hut of the type used on the west coast.* (By courtesy of the Tasmanian Museum and Art Gallery)

source of fresh water and a good foraging area. West Point is such a site; it was situated next to what would seem to have been an elephant seal breeding ground. Elephant seals do not now breed closer to Australia than Macquarie Island, 2000 kilometres to the south, but between 1300 and 1800 years ago young seal calves were being killed at West Point, indicating that there was probably a seal colony next to the village, which was occupied in summer when the young seals were being weaned.

Seals were the major component of the diet at West Point, providing about 65 per cent of the calories consumed; another 25 per cent came from abalone and other shellfish, and the rest from sea and land birds, wallabies, small marsupials, and lizards. Among 20 000 bones from 75 cubic metres of deposit, there were only 3 fish vertebrae, which could easily have been transported there accidentally. Fish swim now in the waters off West Point and are readily speared or trapped, but the prehistoric inhabitants clearly did not eat fish. However, they did eat seal, which would have provided a much richer source of energy than fish. And seals could be killed without entering the water, which around Tasmania is cool in summer and icy cold in winter.

Rhys Jones has estimated that a band of forty people could have camped there for three or four months every year for the five hundred years or more that the site was occupied. If a family occupied each of the hut sites, this would give a population for the village of about forty.

The way of life of these people was semi-sedentary; they probably spent about a quarter of each year in their village. Men would have clubbed young seals to death, while women dived for shellfish. The women were excellent swimmers and could stay under water for a long time, as observed by Robinson, the French explorer Labillardière and others. They dived down, pried the shells off the rocks with small wooden wedges, and put them into rush baskets suspended from their necks. Crayfish were also obtained by diving, sometimes in 4 metres of rough water; the fish were grabbed from under rocks and thrown up onto shore. Long thin fronds of giant kelp were sometimes used as an underwater 'rope' to get down to such depths, for this type of 'seaweed' grows on the seabed and sends up fronds of up to 60 metres in length. Women also used to swim up to 1 or 2 kilometres across open sea straits to reach offshore islands, such as the Doughboys (rocky stacks about a kilometre offshore) and Trefoil, where muttonbirds nested. The muttonbird nests in burrows, making its nestlings easy prey for human predators. It is also an energy-rich food because of the high fat and oil content of the flesh.

No male activities needed much swimming skill, and some men could not swim at all. The reason for this may be that women with their higher percentage of subcutaneous fat were better adapted to withstanding the cold water in these latitudes than were men. To protect themselves from the cold, both men and women used to rub their bodies with seal or muttonbird fat mixed with red ochre. In eastern Tasmania shellfish were not so important in the diet, and a woman told Robinson that whereas the women in the west prided themselves on their ability to dive for shellfish, those from the east and inland regions could climb trees for possums. In mainland Australia it was men who cut toe-holds up trees hunting possums, and it seems that in Tasmania women made an unusually large contribution to diet. In many ways they were the force that kept Tasmanian Aboriginal society going. Women not only produced most of the food, but, when travelling, they carried spears and game, all equipment, babies and toddlers. They also mined ochre. And on one occasion in an unexpected storm they were seen by Robinson to build huts over the men where they sat down!

In addition to the food quest, the West Point people spent time manufacturing thousands of stone tools. More than 30 000 stone artefacts were found in the midden, most of them steep-edged scrapers that were probably used for making digging sticks, spears and clubs. They closely resemble the industry of the upper part of the Rocky Cape sequence, and bone tools are similarly absent.

HUMAN REMAINS

The first prehistoric human remains to be found in Tasmania were excavated from the midden at West Point.[7] Several human teeth were found, including one molar with severe erosion of the roots due to periodontal disease. Then three small cremation pits were found, two in the middle and one at the base of the midden dating to 1800 years ago. The pits were filled with burnt and broken human bones. It seems the bodies were cremated, then the bones systematically broken, collected together with the charcoal, and deposited in little pits, about 45 centimetres wide and dug some 30 centimetres down into the sand or sandy midden.

In one pit were the foot bones of several wallabies and the talons of a large hawk. In another was a necklace of thirty-two shells, each pierced with a small circular hole. These were no doubt personal belongings of the dead. This is fascinating evidence that the shell necklaces worn by Tasmanians in the eighteenth century and their practice of cremation go back at least 1800 years. Since cremation was practised at Lake Mungo 26 000 years ago, it is likely that it also formed part of the beliefs and customs the first Tasmanians transported across the land bridge into what was to become their island home.

The human remains at West Point were fragmentary, but they showed great similarities to modern mainland Australian Aborigines.[8] In 1973, a reasonably intact burial in a sand dune near the Mount Cameron West engraving site was exposed by a gale.[9] A skull was set in an upright position facing north-east with two long bones crossed in front of it. In an arc around it on the western side were a series of carbonized remnants that appeared to be the remains of poles, set in the sand in the form of a wooden 'wigwam', like the structures

Plate 24. *Little Swanport midden, Tasmania*

observed as erected over burial pits on Maria Island, off the east coast of Tasmania, by the explorer François Péron. Carbon from the 'poles' and flecks associated with the skull were dated to 4260 ± 360 BP. The skull proved to be that of a woman, which shows that status burials were not reserved for males. She seemed to have been partially cremated and the bones smashed after death. Her teeth showed no decay, but there was chronic periodontal disease and molar wear. Her skull, whilst displaying typically Tasmanian features, falls within the range of mainland Aborigines, supporting the concept of the kinship of Tasmanian and mainland Australians.

LITTLE SWANPORT MIDDEN

In historic times most of the Tasmanian Aborigines lived in the eastern half of the island, isolated by mountains and rainforests from the west coast. The terrain is still rugged but mostly composed of savanna grasslands, open sclerophyll forests, lakes and moorlands, and the coastline is indented by many sheltered bays and estuaries. Such a different environment from that of the north-west led to expectations that the east might have had a completely different cultural sequence and economy, but these were dispelled by excavations on the central east coast.[10]

Several middens were excavated by Harry Lourandos, and no fish bones were found in any of them, except at the very base of the Little Swanport site. This is a huge midden, the existence of which was reported as long ago as 1891. It is the largest of a series of middens lying on the shores and islands of a sheltered tidal estuary on the central east coast (plate 24). Two metres thick, the midden consists of oysters and mussels collected from the nearby muddy banks of the estuary. Crayfish remains were also found throughout the deposit, but there were very few bones or artefacts. The Little Swanport site was, therefore, a specialized fishing camp rather than a home base camp, but fishing activities were confined to shellfish. There were no fish bones at all in the upper part of the midden, but in the lowest zone, dated to between 4750 and 3550 years ago, remains of at least thirteen fish of the leatherjacket or Aluteridae family were found. These small, fast-moving fish still dart around the estuary today, but, as in western Tasmania, it seems that for some reason they were dropped from the diet about 3500 years ago.

SOUTH-WEST TASMANIA

In the far south-west of Tasmania, the Louisa Bay area has been investigated by Ron Vanderwal.[11] There, in a series of cave and open midden sites going back about 3000 years, fish bones are totally absent. Bone tools are also absent, except for one bone point made from a wallaby shin bone, which was found in the lowest level of an undated layer of shells in a sand dune.

South of Louisa Bay lie the Maatsuyker Islands, across a strait that takes the full force of the frequent southerly gales and is dangerous even for modern craft. Yet Aborigines in their frail, paperbark vessels braved these dangers to hunt seal on Maatsuyker. Maatsuyker is 15 kilometres from the mainland, although it is likely that the neighbouring De Witt island, which lies between the mainland and Maatsuyker, was used· as a staging place. This would then involve two voyages of 10 and 7 kilometres. Middens and seals have been found on Maatsuyker but none on De Witt, so a direct voyage may have been made. Given the wind and current directions, embarkation was probably from west of Louisa Bay, making a voyage of 20 kilometres. And there are sufficient remains of prehistoric camps on Maatsuyker to show that such visits were reasonably commonplace in summer to hunt seals and nesting muttonbirds.

These voyages to the Maatsuyker Island group mark the most southerly penetration by hunter-gatherers in Australia and must rank among the greatest maritime exploits of stone age people anywhere.

REASONS FOR ECONOMIC CHANGE

Tasmanian traditional material culture apparently included only about two dozen items: wooden spears with fire-hardened tips, throwing clubs, the women's club–chisel–digging stick, wooden wedges or spatulae, baskets woven from grass or rushes, possum-skin pouch bags, water buckets made from kelp (figure 13.5), fire-sticks, kangaroo skin cloaks, shell necklaces, canoe-rafts, huts and a few stone tools.

That the simplest material culture should be found among the people who experienced the longest isolation in the world is significant. Rhys Jones sees analogies with the reduction in the number of faunal species on islands that become separated from their parent continents. He considers the 4000 people

Figure 13.5 *Tasmanian water container made from bull-kelp. The kelp is folded onto two wooden skewers, making a flexible water bag.* (After Péron and Freycinet 1807–16)

isolated on Tasmania and divided into several different language groups were too few to maintain indefinitely their Pleistocene culture, and that they were, therefore, doomed – 'doomed to a slow strangulation of the mind'.

Certainly the evidence for the religious life of the Tasmanians is very limited, which may indicate a limited religious life. Compared with the richness of religious life on the mainland, it was apparently largely confined to burial cermonies and dances depicting mythical and historical themes. But by the time George Augustus Robinson made his record of Aboriginal life, the population had been decimated and large ceremonial gatherings would hardly have been possible. Tasmanian material equipment was reduced to the minimum necessary for survival, yet the Tasmanians may not have been a doomed society. And their discontinuation of fishing need not have been a maladaptation, a deliberate but mistaken cultural decision to put a taboo on fishing. There may be much simpler and more plausible economic reasons why the Tasmanians stopped eating fish.

One possibility is that this change in diet was a positive response to a changing environment. An increase in the seal population may have been the cause in the west, and the fashion may then have spread over the island. At

Louisa Bay in more recent times people ate seal all the year round: in summer they hunted them on offshore islands, in winter elephant and fur seals came ashore on the mainland. Or the climate may have become colder about 4000 years ago, causing the Tasmanians to switch to high energy foods, such as seals and sea birds, and to abandon fish, an item of less nutritional value that required considerably more energy and immersion in cold water to catch.

Hunters in high, cold latitudes need foods rich in fat yielding high energy. Thus, for the Tasmanians, seals and sea birds were better than fish or shellfish. Indeed, 'Had the Tasmanians the service of a consultant nutritionist, they would probably have been advised to give up fishing and concentrate their energies on more profitable foods. There is evidence in the post-3000 BP archaeological record that this is just what they did.'[12]

Finally, in contrast to the 'doomed people theory', there is a strong case that the Tasmanian population was on the increase and that the society, rather than deteriorating, was branching out in new directions over the last two thousand years.

The interesting idea has been put forward that Tasmanian watercraft were only invented about 2000 years ago, in the west of the island where they were needed most. It has long been taken for granted that Pleistocene Tasmanians had watercraft, but there is no reason why they should have. Tasmanian watercraft are unlike any craft on the mainland (figure 13.6). They were made from three bundles of paperbark (*Melaleuca*) or stringybark (*Eucalyptus obliqua*). Each bundle was bound with a network of bark or grass string, forming a sausage-shaped craft, tied at both ends, with a slightly hollow centre and upcurving bow and stern. The central bundle provided most of the buoyancy, and the side ones acted as stabilizers. The boat was propelled by a long pole or by swimmers pushing it along; paddles were unknown. These canoe-rafts can hold six or seven people but they were generally not taken more than 5 to 8 kilometres off the coast.[13] The problem was that, when saturated, the bark had a density similar to water, so after a few hours the craft lost its rigidity, became waterlogged, and sank.

There is no evidence at present that watercraft were used anywhere in Tasmania before about 2500 years ago when Hunter Island was revisited, after being vacated when it was first severed from the mainland. Similarly, Bruny Island was vacated about 5000 years ago and re-occupied about 3000 years later. One strong point in favour of the above theory is that it accounts for the absence of watercraft in north-east Tasmania. With far fewer rivers, bays, and offshore islands, there was no real need for boats there, so it is not surprising that the invention of a group on the opposite side of the island was not adopted. Further fieldwork will have to be done to test this hypothesis, but it is supported by some cultural developments in the same period.

It now appears that the Mount Cameron West engravings, which used to be thought a relic of ice age art, were probably carved only about 2000 years ago.

The style is certainly ancient, but the execution apparently fairly recent. On the other side of the island is a stone arrangement on the Bay of Fires, which was constructed less than 700 years ago.[14] Robinson during his 'Friendly Mission' in 1830 came across similar arrangements on the west coast.

The Bay of Fires stone arrangement is located on a ridge overlooking a pebble beach. About 56 metres long, it consists of a single line of 93 flat stones, in places resembling a garden path. The stones are set into an underlying midden so that their top surfaces are flush with the ground surface. A small test excavation in the midden revealed that another stone alignment lay stratified below. The sequence of events seems to have been that a linear stone

Figure 13.6 *Tasmanian watercraft* (By courtesy of Tasmanian Museum and Art Gallery)

arrangement was built on the surface of a sand dune. Then, about 750 years ago people camped by the line of stones. Shell material and discarded quartz tools accumulated around and over the original arrangement, and a new ceremonial structure was built. A further stone arrangement was subsequently found by archaeologist Scott Cane 115 metres to the north. It has 43 stones and extends for six metres in a north–south direction. The stones resemble those of the more southerly lower stratified alignment.

On the pebble beaches nearby are many curious birdnest-shaped pits, some with low walls around, and stone cairns, made from many rocks piled high together. Construction of these features must have required a lot of time and effort, but no one knows whether they are historic or prehistoric, or what purpose they served.

Whatever the function of the Bay of Fires stone arrangements, they show that new initiatives to do with intellectual life were being taken during the last thousand years, by minds not yet numbed by long isolation. After surviving more than 30 000 years on their remote island, the Tasmanian Aborigines continued to cope as their land was gradually taken from them by European settlers. They fought a strong guerilla war against the invaders, and, although most fell to European bullets or disease, a few survived on the islands of Bass Strait and continued the existence of their people. While dispossessed and decimated, they did not die out.

Truganini was not 'the last Tasmanian'. Today there are some 2000 descendants of those seal-hunting and muttonbirding Aborigines of Bass Strait. They call themselves Aboriginal, they look Aboriginal, they are regarded as Aboriginal by Aboriginal communities in other parts of Australia. It is to the white man's eternal shame that he tried to wipe out the Aborigines of Tasmania; it is to their credit that he failed.

Not only have present day Tasmanian Aborigines been denied their identity, but prehistoric Tasmanian culture has also been consistently misjudged and undervalued. This is because it has been judged from the journals of George Augustus Robinson, journals not written until the 1830s, which record only the remnants of culture of a people decimated after three decades of fighting for survival. It has been said that Tasmanian Aborigines lacked the rich ritual life of the mainlanders and did not hold large ceremonies involving several hundred people, but by the time of Robinson's travels there were only about 300 tribal Aborigines at large in all Tasmania, and they were fully occupied with a guerilla war.[15]

Another myth that should be laid to rest is that the Tasmanian Aborigines did not know how to make fire. The only evidence for this is that Robinson never observed anyone making fire because fire-sticks were always carried. An argument based on flimsy negative evidence is always suspect, and it seems unlikely that the Tasmanians could have made some of the water crossings that they did, such as those to Hunter and Maatsuyker Islands, and keep fires alight on hearths in the boats during the whole voyage. And there is no lack of charcoal in middens on the islands.

Prehistoric Tasmanian Aborigines may have had a simple toolkit and limited ceremonial life, but they survived more than 30 000 years on their rugged island, they successfully weathered the glacial cold further south than any other people, they produced some of the finest rock engravings in the world, and they achieved a successful balance between hunters and land and a population density apparently equivalent to that on the Australian mainland.

CHAPTER FOURTEEN

RISING SEAS AND CHANGE

The end of the ice age was a period of dramatic change. Rising temperatures dried up the lakes of inland Australia while rising seas drowned vast areas around the coasts. Not surprisingly, many Aboriginal myths reflect these events. The evaporation of inland lakes and formation of huge salt pans are commemorated in a number of stories that tell of the time when all the waters of the earth were fresh but then became salty. The story of 'The Salt Lakes of Kiti' tells how greed turned rich fertile plains into a desert of salt lakes.

> Gumuduk was a tall, thin, medicine man, who belonged to the hills country. He owned a magical bone of such power that he could use it to make the rain fall in season, the trees bear much fruit, the animals increase, and the fish multiply. Because of such good fortune the hills people always had plenty of food.
>
> However, the tribe that lived on the fertile plain below the Kiti range captured the medicine man and his bone, convinced that they, too, would in future have more food.
>
> But instead of bringing them prosperity, the theft resulted in a calamity which totally destroyed their country. For the medicine man escaped and was so angry over the indignity he had suffered that, plunging his magical bone into the ground, Gumuduk decreed that wherever he walked in the country of his enemies salt water would rise in his footsteps.
>
> Those waters not only contaminated the rivers and lagoons, but completely inundated the tribal lands. And when these waters dried up, the whole area was changed to an inhospitable desert of salt lakes, useless to both the creatures and the Aborigines.[1]

The drowning of the coastal plains must have had a profound impact on those who lived there, particularly as they had no means of knowing that the seas would ever stop rising. As the world's ice melted and the oceans rose, not only were hills on the continental shelf transformed into islands, but immense areas were also submerged. About one seventh of the land mass of Greater Australia – two and a half million square kilometres – was inundated by the rising glacial melt-water. And around the shore of South-East Asia an area the size of the Indian sub-continent went under. Over 10 000 to 15 000 years, the average rise was between 1 and 3 centimetres a year, but the sea's advance was erratic. Sometimes it rose quickly, sometimes it stood still, and occasionally it even retreated. When the sea was rising most quickly, it could, within one generation, have drowned a strip of land over a hundred kilometres wide, which would greatly reduce a coastal tribe's territory.

All over the world the event seems to be commemorated in legends about a great flood, and in Australia the stories are so detailed and specific that there can be no doubt that they recall events thousands of years ago. Various explanations are given for the separation of offshore islands from the mainland. From Mornington Island come legends of the seagull woman, Garnguur, who pulled her raft backwards and forwards across what was then a peninsula to form the channels that now separate the island from the mainland. Elcho Island was similarly severed from the mainland when the Djankawu brother tripped and accidentally pushed his stick into the sand there, causing the sea to rush in. The narrow seas between Milingimbi in the Crocodile Islands and the mainland were made by the Creation Shark. And the separation of Kangaroo Island from South Australia, which occurred about 10 000 years ago, is remembered in the legend of Ngurunderi drowning his wives as they fled across on foot.[2]

The drowning of great expanses of the mainland is related in a number of stories from both northern and southern Australia. A time when Port Phillip Bay (near Melbourne) was dry land and excellent hunting ground is recalled in a legend of the Kulin people,[3] and in South Australia a story about a great flood inundating Spencer Gulf is told.[4] The rising of the seas was indeed one of the major events in the prehistory of Australia. Coastal people became islanders, or were forced back from the coast as their tribal territory was inundated.

THE GREAT BARRIER REEF ISLANDS

Archaeological work on Queensland islands has been concentrated largely on those close to the mainland and under threat from sand-mining, tourism or other development. Little of this research has been completed, and it is but a drop in the ocean of the prehistory of offshore islands, for in the Barrier Reef there are 1200 islands, and it seems that all the major ones were inhabited by Aborigines at the time of European settlement. All the archaeological sites excavated so far on islands of the Great Barrier Reef and the adjacent coast are less than 3000 years old, with the exception of the open site of Mazie Bay on North Keppel Island excavated by Mike Rowland, which appears to have been occupied for about 5000 years, probably since shortly after the island was cut off from the mainland by the rising sea.[5]

The Keppel Islands now lie 13 kilometres from the mainland, but the journey to the island could be made in two legs: 4.5 kilometres to Pelican Island and then 8.5 kilometres to South Keppel. The islanders were rather isolated because of this distance from the mainland, and the effects of isolation can be seen in their language, physical appearance and material culture. Their

7. **Above** *Barbed spear from Wyrie Swamp, South Australia, approximately 10 000 years old*   ▷
(R. Luebbers)

8. **Below** *Kutikina Cave (previously Fraser Cave), Tasmania. Wallaby hunters inhabited this limestone cave between 15 000 and 20 000 years ago.* (By courtesy of R. Jones)

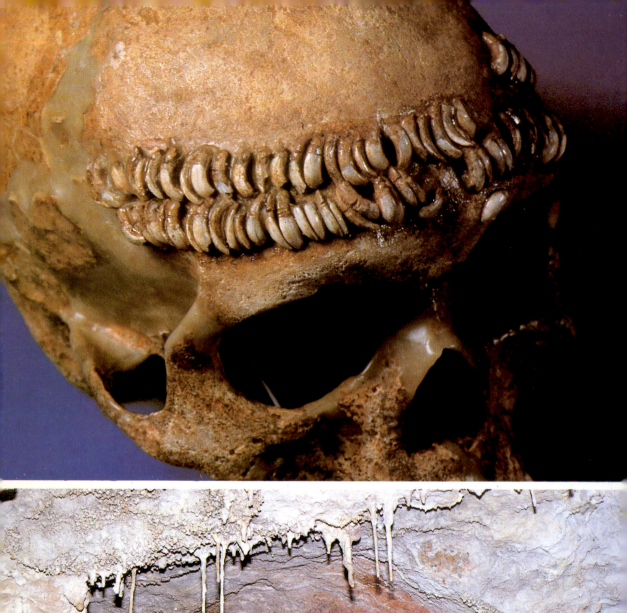

language was unintelligible to the mainlanders, and they spoke so quickly that mainland Aborigines said they 'yabbered like crows'. Physically, the Keppel islanders were also distinctive. The skulls studied show a high percentage of 'auditory exostoses', that is, bony, protruding growths in the region of the ear, which may be the result of inbreeding through isolation.

Keppel islanders' material culture was also different from that of the mainland. They had no boomerangs, shields or ground-edge axes, and only one type of club, but they possessed other items apparently absent from the adjacent coast such as necklaces made of shell and of 'bits of red toadstool', fish-hooks (made of coconut or turtle shell) and stone drills for manufacturing the hooks. For transport, they had one-piece bark canoes, not the three-piece ones of the mainland, but their usual means of transport was what have been termed 'swimming logs' (figure 14.1). At the time of the visit of W. E. Roth, then Protector of Aborigines in Queensland, to the Keppel Islands in 1897, these logs were the only form of water transport. They were hand-propelled and were paddled from island to island and even on occasion to the mainland.[6] This co-operative use of logs as craft seems to be unique to the Keppel Islands; elsewhere logs were used by only one person at a time, and they were straddled as floats, particularly in waters infested by crocodiles or sharks.

It seems that the Keppel islanders were more or less isolated for some 5000 years. A small population of about eighty-five people exploited their limited territory of 20 square kilometres, including about 38 kilometres of coastline: there would have been about two people to each kilometre of coast, a similar population density to that found among other coastal groups, such as the Bentinck islanders or the Anbara of Arnhem Land. Over the centuries the language and physical characteristics of the Keppel Island people changed as a result of evolution in a small, isolated community, and their material culture became almost as simple and limited in range as that of the Tasmanian Aborigines.

The survival of prehistoric people stranded on islands has been studied by Rhys Jones, who has come to the conclusion that 'totally isolated populations of between 1000 and 4000 people are perfectly viable over extremely lengthy periods, but . . . ones of under about 350 or 400 are vulnerable in the long run. In hunter–gatherer conditions, the limiting viable population may be somewhere in the range of 400 to 600 depending on local circumstances and the vagaries of chance.'[7]

It may be significant that this estimated minimum viable population of about 500 is also the average size of a 'tribe' in Australia.[8] A 'tribe' is the traditional name used by some anthropologists for the major social and kinship group of Aboriginal society, characterized by possession of a common language, territory, identity and culture. (Although the term 'tribe' has been much criticized, there are as yet no satisfactory alternatives to use.) It now appears that it may also be the minimum number of people in a group necessary to

◁   **9. Above** *Burial from tomb 108 Roonka, South Australia. A double-stranded band of notched wallaby teeth encircled the forehead of this man buried at Roonka on the Murray River over 4000 years ago* (By courtesy of the South Australian Museum and G. Pretty)

10. Below *Stalactites have almost covered these traces of ice age hand stencils in the Wargata Mina Cave, Southern Forests, Tasmania.* (Photo S. Brown)

ensure long-term survival. Tribal territory varied greatly in size depending on the food resources available, so the desert groups had huge territories and coastal groups very small ones.[9]

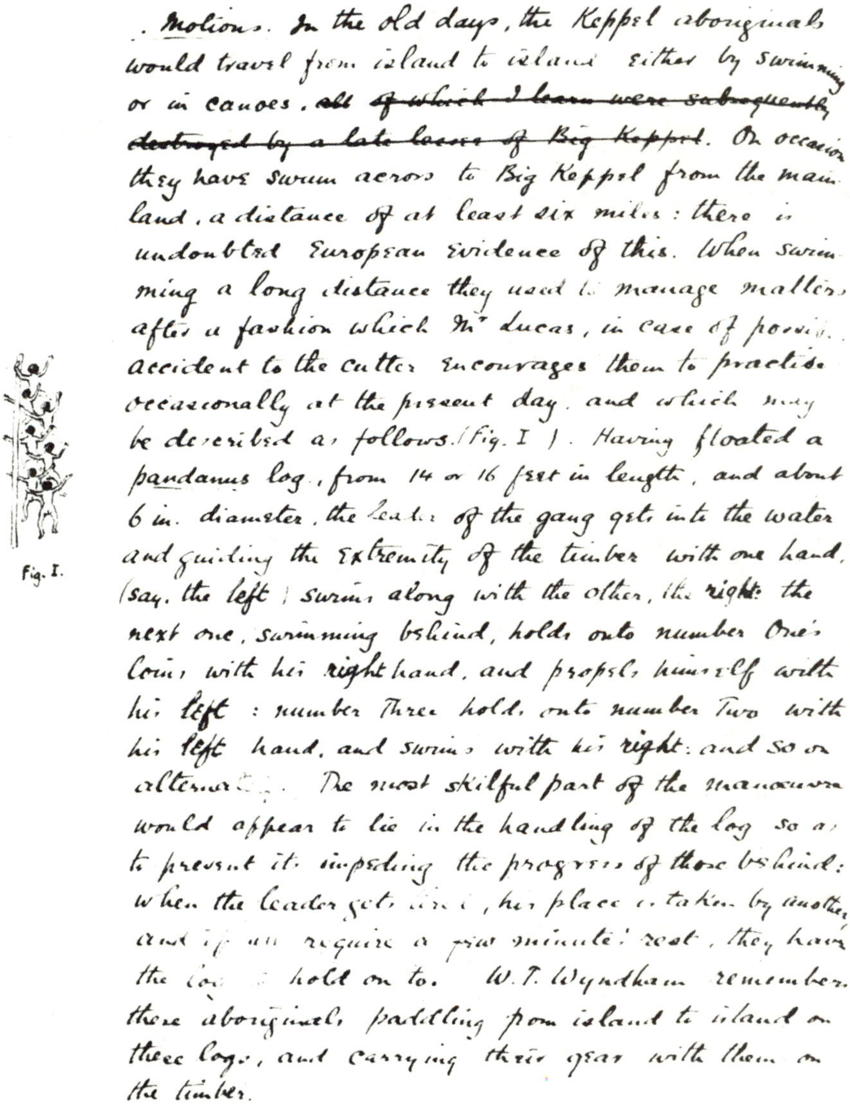

motions. In the old days, the Keppel aboriginals would travel from island to island either by swimming or in canoes. ~~all of which I learn were subsequently destroyed by a late lessee of Big Keppel.~~ On occasion they have swum across to Big Keppel from the mainland, a distance of at least six miles: there is undoubted European evidence of this. When swimming a long distance they used to manage matters after a fashion which Mr Lucas, in case of possible accident to the cutter encourages them to practise occasionally at the present day, and which may be described as follows (Fig. I). Having floated a pandanus log, from 14 or 16 feet in length, and about 6 in. diameter, the leader of the gang gets into the water and guiding the extremity of the timber with one hand, (say, the left) swims along with the other, the right: the next one, swimming behind, holds onto number One's loins with his right hand, and propels himself with his left: number Three holds onto number Two with his left hand, and swims with his right: and so on alternately. The most skilful part of the manoeuvre would appear to lie in the handling of the log so as to prevent it impeding the progress of those behind: when the leader gets tired, his place is taken by another, and if all require a few minutes' rest, they have the log to hold on to. W. T. Wyndham remembers these aboriginals paddling from island to island on these logs, and carrying their gear with them on the timber.

Figure 14.1 *A page from W. E. Roth's manuscript report on* The Aborigines of the Rockhampton and surrounding coast districts, *1898 (By courtesy of the Queensland State Archives and the Premier's Department)*

THE MAINLAND

Less catastrophic than being trapped on offshore islands, but still traumatic, was the effect of rising seas on the mainlanders. The land submerged by the encroaching ocean was equivalent to loss of the whole of the present state of Western Australia. On the gently sloping coastal plains of northern Australia the sea at times ate up 5 kilometres of land in one year. Even in southern Australia, in the Great Australian Bight, the coastal strip was consumed at a rate of about 1 kilometre every fifteen years.

The loss of territory would have been much less severe on the east coast of Australia, where the continental shelf slopes down fairly steeply. Over 15 000 years a strip of only about 20 kilometres wide was submerged along the south coast of New South Wales. In recent times the territories of Aboriginal tribes on this coast extended inland a considerable distance. Most encompass the drainage basin of one river and stretch from the shoreline up to the top of the coastal escarpment, at least 30 kilometres inland. There is no way of knowing how far back in time this territorial organization goes, but it may well be quite ancient. If so, it would mean that the coastal tribes were pushed back by the rising sea into their own hinterland, rather than into the territory of other tribes. This would have been a much less traumatic event than that experienced in the Gulf of Carpentaria.

It is thought that the sea rose fairly rapidly until about 7000 years ago, and then more slowly until the present level was reached about 5000 years ago. This means that the coast of New South Wales has been much as it is today for the last 5000 to 7000 years, but before that a fairly steep coastal slope stretched down to the shore. Under these early conditions there would have been only a narrow tidal zone, with the sea deepening rapidly offshore. The amount of food people could have obtained from the deep water of such a shoreline would have been substantially less than in later times, when the sea level had stabilized.

The rising of the seas drowned large tracts of land, but at the same time stabilization of the sea level extended estuaries and tidal reefs, the zones of the shore most productive of fish and shellfish accessible to Aborigines. Lagoons formed at the mouths of rivers held back by sandy barriers, which previously had been swept away by the constantly rising sea. And the drowning of river valleys led to the development of many food-rich small bays and inlets, such as those in the higher reaches of Sydney Harbour.

Thousands of Aboriginal middens have been found on the south-east coast of Australia. These refuse dumps consist mainly of shell, but they also contain other remains of food, such as bird, animal and fish bones, together with broken, lost or discarded tools. Unfortunately plant remains are rarely preserved, so it is difficult to interpret the total diet from the midden remains.

The most favoured campsite was a foredune close to a rock platform on the north side of a headland. Such a site offered easy access to shellfish, a landing place for canoes, proximity to drinking water, shelter from the prevailing winds, and soft sand for a bed. In addition, fish in the lagoons could be caught with multi-pronged spears or with shell fish-hooks and line made from twisted strands of inner bark from trees or other vegetable fibre.

A comparison of the occupation sites along the coast with those further inland indicates that the shoreline was much more densely occupied than the hinterland. Whether this was always the case is more difficult to determine. Almost all the sites known along the south coast of New South Wales were first occupied within the last 5000 years, but an equal number of older sites on earlier shorelines may now lie submerged under the ocean. The archaeological evidence, along with that for environmental change, suggests an increase in population resulting from increased food resources. This theory[10] is supported by evidence from two sites on the east coast which span the period of rising seas. At Bass Point midden there was a dramatic increase in intensity of occupation about 4000 years ago. Similarly at Burrill Lake rockshelter human activity increased over the last few thousand years. This increase in human use is revealed not only by more stone-working at the sites, but also by increased man-induced sedimentation. When people were living at a site, the deposition of sediment occurred more quickly than when there were no humans present.

THE EARLY POST-GLACIAL SCENE

The end of the Pleistocene was a time of change. Some areas became less attractive human habitats, others acquired better food resources and a more tolerable climate. And in some regions the effect of the drastic loss of land to the rising sea was to push occupation into less favourable zones, which had been previously uninhabited or visited only occasionally. There is now evidence that virtually the whole of Australia was occupied by Pleistocene hunters, at least by 20 000 years ago. In a few regions, such as the northern tablelands of New South Wales, the Snowy Mountains and the centre of the arid mallee region of north-western Victoria, not a single Pleistocene site has been found among the dozens of younger ones known, but this may well be due to a lack of much archaeological work in the area or poor site visibility rather than a genuine absence of sites.

These regions are all poor in food resources compared with the coast and the large inland rivers. Thus if they were inhabited during early times, short seasonal hunting visits are more likely than year-round occupation. The suggestion that the abundance of young sites but lack of older ones in these areas is simply due to a higher loss rate of early sites may be valid for the coast, where earlier sites are now under the sea, but it does not hold for inland regions. Stone tools have the same lasting qualities, whether 5000 or 25 000 years old; erosion applies to young and old sites alike; and there is generally little depth of soil above bedrock in which older tools could lie hidden.

The evidence suggests a comparatively small early population spread thinly around the continent and concentrating on the places where food was most abundant: the coast and large inland lakes and rivers. The most inhospitable parts of mainland Australia in the ice age were the Snowy Mountains and the desert core of the continent. We now know that people were camping at least occasionally on the fringes of the Snowy Mountains in treeless country at 730 metres above sea level at Birrigai Shelter in the A.C.T. at 21 000 BP, and in the region north of Uluru (Ayers Rock) at Puritjarra more than 22 000 years ago.[12] And in western New South Wales it seems that people adapted to the drying up of the Pleistocene lakes by changing their staple food to flour made from grass seeds.

Some mountain regions, like the Blue Mountains near Sydney, had a comparatively mild climate, and they were inhabited at least seasonally in glacial or early post-glacial times. The large, well-protected rockshelters of Walls Cave near Blackheath and Lyre Bird Dell at Leura (respectively 910 and 915 metres above sea level) were inhabited about 12 000 years ago, when the local environment was probably rather drier than it is today.[13] Even today both sites provide excellent shelter from the elements. The King's Table shelter, 800 metres above sea level, was definitely occupied about 14 000 years ago (the earlier occupation claimed by Eugene Stockton is uncertain). Another 12 000-year-old site in a valley on the northern side of the Blue Mountains is Noola rockshelter.[14] Occupation in the same area at the Capertee shelters goes back 7500 years.[15]

The distribution of tools shows us the human response to the changing environment. Areas such as the Willandra Lakes were largely abandoned in favour of large rivers like the Darling and Murray, and in these regions eroded dunes bordering the old lakes are littered with ancient core tools and chunky scrapers, but there is hardly a trace of the succeeding small tool tradition. Elsewhere, as on the coast, the opposite is true. As well as adapting to change by altering their settlement patterns and staple foods, these prehistoric people either invented or adopted new tools and technology, leading to still more change and development.

CHAPTER FIFTEEN

ARRIVAL OF THE DINGO

Some time after 6000 years ago, the dingo appears in Australia and new small tools are added to the existing toolkit. Dingoes were certainly introduced from Asia, probably deliberately but possibly as castaways. The origin of the new small tools is more debatable. It has been asserted that they were independently invented in Australia,[1] but many archaeologists think that some new tools and technology were brought into Australia by diffusion of ideas and possibly migration of people from outside. What has to be explained in this prehistoric mystery is why the dingo and a number of distinctive new tools are suddenly added to the core tool and scraper tradition over 5000 years ago all over Australia except on distant offshore islands, and why different new tools are found in different parts of the continent (figure 15.1). Was Australia completely isolated from Asia after the rising of the seas, or did new people migrate to or visit the island continent, adding fresh elements to Aboriginal culture?

The stone tools, the historical documents from which prehistory is written, will be discussed first. To the archaeologist each tool tells a story, adding one more piece to the jigsaw puzzle of the past. The outstanding characteristics of the small tool tradition are the symmetry and delicate trimming of tiny, slender blades made from fine-grained, often colourful stone. Three major types of small tool are discernible: points, backed blades and adzes.

POINTS

Stone points are generally presumed to have been hafted onto the tip of a spear as projectile points. They occur with trimming on one or both faces (unifacial or bifacial) but one variety does not pre-date the other, since at some sites, such as Yarar in the Northern Territory, they are in use simultaneously.

The evidence from the Yarar rockshelter showed that unifacial and bifacial points were of similar dimensions, averaging 3.5 centimetres in length.[2] The function of both would seem to have been as spear points. Among the broken

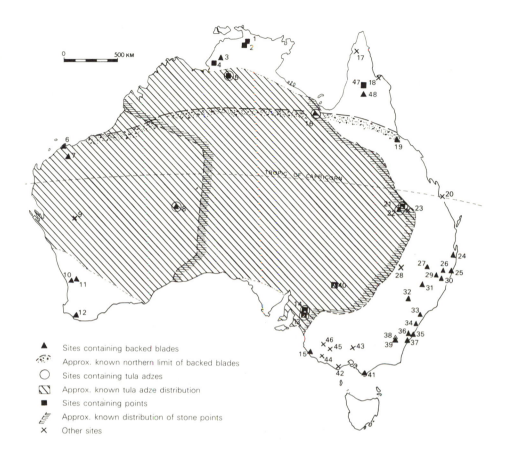

Figure 15.1 *Archaeological sites from the Holocene Period*

1. Tyimede, N.T.	17. Weipa Middens, Qld
2. Ngarradj-Warde-Djobkeng, N.T.	18. Bathurst Head, Qld
3. Daly River, N.T.	19. Jourama, Qld
4. Yarar, N.T.	20. Keppel Islands, Qld
5. Ingaladdi, N.T.	21. Kenniff Cave, Qld
6. Skew Valley, W.A.	22. The Tombs, Qld
7. Millstream, W.A.	23. Cathedral Cave, Qld
8. Puntutjarpa, W.A.	24. Broadbeach, Qld
9. Wilgie Mia ochre mine, W.A.	25. Wombah Midden N.S.W.
10. Orchestra Shell Cave, W.A.	26. Seelands N.S.W.
11. Frieze Cave, W.A.	27. Graman, N.S.W.
12. Northcliffe, W.A.	28. Brewarrina fish traps, N.S.W.
13. Fromm's Landing, S.A.	29. Bendemeer, N.S.W.
14. Devon Downs, S.A.	30. Moore Creek Quarry, N.S.W.
15. Mount Burr, S.A.	31. Bobadeen, N.S.W.
16. Colless Creek, Qld	32. Capertee, N.S.W.

33. Lapstone Creek, N.S.W.
34. Curracurrang, N.S.W.
35. Currarong, N.S.W.
36. Sassafras, N.S.W.
37. Durras North, N.S.W.
38. Bogong Cave, A.C.T.
39. Yankee Hat, A.C.T.
40. Burke's Cave, N.S.W.
41. Wilson's Prom. Middens, Vic.
42. Glenaire, Vic.
43. Mount William Quarry, Vic.
44. Lake Condah eel traps, Vic.
45. Mount William eel traps, Vic.
46. Toolondo eel traps, Vic.
47. Green Ant, Qld
48. Echidna Dreaming, Qld

Legend (from map):

▲ Sites containing backed blades
Approx. known northern limit of backed blades
○ Sites containing tula adzes
Approx. known tula adze distribution
■ Sites containing points
Approx. known distribution of stone points
✕ Other sites

points there were far more butts than tips, indicating that spears with the tips broken off were re-hafted in the shelter, where the broken butt was discarded. They are small enough to have been arrow tips, such as those found so widely in North America, Asia and other parts of the world, but there is no evidence that the bow and arrow ever reached Australia. It was certainly not in use in Australia in the eighteenth century when Captain Cook arrived, whereas stone-tipped spears were still in use then in north-western Australia. The bifacial points of the Kimberleys range from less than 3 centimetres to over 10 centimetres long; they are all spear points and museum examples exist of 3 centimetres long stone points hafted onto a spear handle, with only 2 centimetres projecting out of the gum hafting. Such tiny spear points would be less likely to shatter on impact than the longer variety.

Figure 15.2 *Stone projectile pirri point from Roonka, South Australia. This chert point was found in a grave.* (By courtesy of the South Australian Museum)

Many of the symmetrical, pressure-flaked Kimberley points with serrated edges are works of art. They were traded long distances, suggesting they were regarded more as status and ritual objects than as utilitarian spear points. Indeed, in historic times some magnificent specimens have been made from glass and porcelain, the porcelain coming from insulators on the overland telegraph line – which soon lacked a lot of its insulators. Such finely made Kimberley stone points were used a thousand kilometres away to circumcise boys in the desert. Other beautifully made, symmetrical points, such as the unifacially trimmed 'pirri' typical of South Australia, were confined to prehistoric times, and Aborigines, when consulted about their function, had no knowledge of it and deemed them to be made in the Dreamtime (figure 15.2).

Points are found over the centre of the continent, but they are absent from the west and east coasts. In contrast, from west to east of the continent south of the tropics there is a concentration of a different, distinctive new tool type – backed blades.

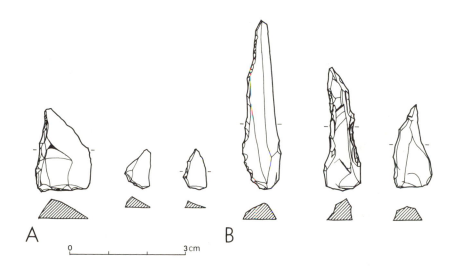

Figure 15.3 *Backed blades. A Geometric microliths of chert from the Australian Capital Territory. B Bondi points of chert from Sassafras (on left), and the Australian Capital Territory.*

BACKED BLADES

Backed blades are tiny blades, or 'flakelets', which have one edge blunted by steep retouch to form a back, resembling a miniature pen knife (figure 15.3). Many different forms of backed blades have been distinguished on the basis of small variations in shape. They are usually divided, however, into just two main varieties: Bondi points and geometric microliths. Bondi points are named after Bondi beach, where they were first discovered in 1899; they are slender, asymmetrical backed blades, tapering to a point, more than twice as long as they are wide. Geometric microliths are broader and are made in a wide range of geometric shapes, such as triangles and half-circles.

Both varieties of backed blade are usually 'microlithic', which means 'small stone' and usually refers to a tool of less than 3 centimetres in the longest dimension. They also appear to have similar functions. Their major function, it has been suggested, was as spear barbs, mounted in rows on the sides of the shafts of 'death spears'.[3] In historic times death spears were used in fighting and hunting and were lethal weapons which caused great loss of blood. When they penetrated the victim's body, often they could not be extracted except by being pushed right through (figure 15.4).

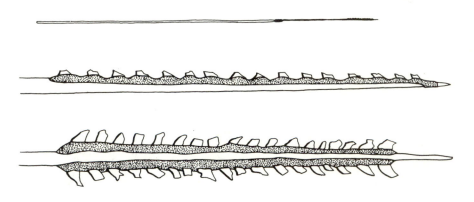

Figure 15.4 *Death spears barbed with quartz flakes set in gum. Top from the Rex Nan Kivell Collection, National Library, Canberra. Bottom from north Queensland.*

A few death spears survive in museums, and they have as many as forty stone barbs, generally set with gum into grooves on the sides of the shaft. The barbs are made of sharp, unbacked quartz flakes without secondary working. Archaeological evidence (from sites such as Sassafras and Currarong) suggests that about 2000 years ago backed blades gradually disappeared, while the use of quartz flakes increased. It seems probable that earlier versions of death spears were barbed with backed blades. This interpretation is supported by the huge number of backed blades found, which is consistent with their use in rows rather than as individual tools, and by two discoveries by Isabel McBryde.[4] In excavations at Graman she found backed blades still retaining traces of hafting gum on the thick, blunted back. And at Seelands, two-thirds of the excavated geometric microliths had one end broken off, a type of breakage consistent with their use as spear barbs.

Death spears were used right across the south of the continent in historic times, the same region in which backed blades are found in huge quantities, although the distributions of death spears and backed blades elsewhere in Australia do not exactly coincide. In the south of Australia, backed blades are very common. The excavation of Curracurrang rockshelter south of Sydney produced over a thousand, and, in the days before legislation made private collecting of Aboriginal artefacts illegal, one collector found 7000 around Botany Bay and another collected 20 000 from near Lake Torrens in South Australia.

Points and backed blades were usually hafted to form composite tools. The term 'composite' here refers to the fixing of small stone flakes and blades into a handle, generally by means of a groove, hafting gum or twine. Thus the small tool tradition is characterized by the introduction of composite tools, which are added to the existing toolkit. The use of handheld tools continues; there is technological evolution, not revolution.

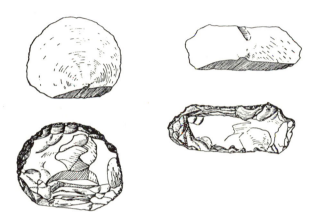

Figure 15.5 Adze stones. Left Inner (above) and outer surface of a tula adze of ribbon stone from Antony Lagoon, the Northern Territory (4.2 cm × 3.5 cm). Right Inner (above) and outer surface of a worn-out tula adze of quartzite from Mulka, South Australia (5 cm × 2 cm). (After Mitchell 1949)

ADZE FLAKES

Some existing tools became much more widely used at this time. In particular, the use of adze flakes increases. These may be an Australian invention. Small flaked stone adzes or adze flakes are wood-working 'chisels' (figure 15.5) and are not to be confused with the large ground and polished adzes found in Asia and the Pacific, which were never part of the Australian toolkit.

Adze flakes have continued in use to the present day in the Western Desert, where Aborigines use these chisel tips set in spinifex gum on the end of a stout handle or the spear-thrower, to shape hardwoods like mulga into shields, dishes, and the like. There are two sorts of adze flake: the 'tula' on which retouch and use-wear occur on the edge opposite the striking platform, and the 'burren adze', on which use is on the lateral edges. 'Tula' is the word used by Wongkonguru Aborigines of the Lake Eyre region of South Australia for this type of adze. The two forms of tula adze (figure 15.5) were originally thought to be two different tools, but then it was discovered that the smaller, step-flaked one was the worked-out 'slug' of the original tool, which gradually became smaller and smaller with constant resharpening. Where stone is in short supply, tools are resharpened again and again until they become too small to use and are then discarded.

Adze flakes appear in late Pleistocene horizons at two sites in Western Australia: at Puntutjarpa, about 10 000 years ago, and in a 12 000-year-old layer of Devil's Lair (one specimen). However, these are not the classic tula adzes, nor are they worn-out adze 'slugs'. In fact, they resemble small steep-edged scrapers. So there is as yet no good evidence for a Pleistocene antiquity for the distinctive wood-working adzes characteristic of the drier parts of Australia over the last few thousand years.

The typical tool of Aboriginal desert people, the tula adze is basically confined to the arid regions of central Australia with annual average rainfall of less than 500 millimetres, while the burren adze is more widely distributed and is found as far afield as Cape York and the east coast. It is generally thought that the adze flake was an Australian invention to solve the problem of working the extremely tough timbers of the arid centre of the continent.

TOOL DISTRIBUTION

After considerable uniformity in technology in ice age Australia, there is a bewildering diversity over the last 5000 years. New tools appear and others that were rare before suddenly become common. Thus ground-edge axes are found all over mainland Australia (but not Tasmania) during the last few thousand years, superseding pebble tools and horsehoof cores as the main chopping tool. Finely trimmed thumbnail scrapers occur in some Pleistocene industries but become much more widespread in the small tool phase.

There is great regional cultural diversity, but, apart from the association of the tula adze with desert regions, it is impossible to equate different tools with different environments and to explain the absence of a tool from an area on the grounds of environment. If particular tools were developed to cope with particular environments, why are backed blades so numerous on the coast of New South Wales but not on Queensland's? And why are they also found in great quantities in the arid salt desert of South Australia but not in the Tanami Desert of central Australia? And why are stone points so abundant in the Kimberleys and Arnhem Land, but not in the similar tropical environment of Cape York?

It is equally difficult to equate the use of these tools with culture areas, and their distribution bears no apparent relation to known major culture areas. Culture areas are regional groupings of interacting Aboriginal societies pos-sessing broadly similar languages, social organization and customs, material culture and art styles, lifeways and environment (figure 15.6). There is a general correlation between culture areas and major drainage basins, which has been explained on the grounds that a drainage basin is unified by its river system and bounded by its watershed; the water supply determines plant cover and hence available food and Aboriginal population density.[5]

Figure 15.6 *Major known cultural areas*
(N. Peterson)

ORIGIN OF THE NEW ELEMENTS

It has been widely believed that there were one or more migrations of new-comers into Australia, 4000 to 5000 years ago, who brought new tools together with the dingo, which first appeared on the continent at about the same time. Much of the speculation over the last two decades about such migrations has been based on very little evidence, and much of it has been found to be wrong. Since 1975 the dates of three key events have been revised: the time of the first appearance in Australia of backed blades, of points, and of the dingo. It is time to take a fresh look at the whole question of the origins of these new elements that appeared in Australia after the rising of the sea.

Until recently it was thought that the dingo was in Australia by 7500 years ago, the point industry by 7000, and backed blades by 6000, but it has now emerged that all these dates are too high. The dingo's arrival was dated from the presence of a few fragments of bone in the lower levels of the Mount Burr rockshelter in South Australia, sandwiched between layers dated to about 7500 to 8500 years ago. Later re-excavation of the site indicated that, in the jumble of rocks and cracks in the deposit, a few pieces of bone could well have fallen into an earlier level. Moreover, there were only a few fragments of dingo bone in the lower level, in contrast to an abundance of it in the higher, younger levels.

If the Mount Burr evidence is discounted, the earliest dates for dingo in Australia are 3230 ± 100 BP, for dingo bones associated with backed blades and unifacial pebble tools in the Wombah midden, on the north coast of New South Wales, and 3450 ± 95 BP for dingo remains in Madura Cave on the Nullarbor Plain in Western Australia. A date of 3170 ± 90 BP has been obtained for dingo at Fromm's Landing on the Murray River within 100 kilometres of Adelaide. This find also is associated with backed blades. It is not known how long it took the dingo to spread across the continent, but it may have been less than a century, since it took the fox, once introduced into Victoria, only sixty years to reach the Kimberley coast on the other side of the continent.

This leaves the point industry as the earliest of the new elements, but the earliest dates for these are now about 5000 instead of 7000 years ago. In several Arnhem Land sites there was a clear change in the sequence from a core tool and scraper industry in the lower sand to an upper shell midden containing remains of estuarine animal species and points. At first the change in industry was equated with the change in environment: the appearance of points at sites like Nawamoyn and Malangangerr was correlated with the base of the midden dated to 6500 to 7000 years. Further analysis of the data[6] has revealed that the first points do not appear until halfway up the middens, some 4000 to 5000 years ago. This agrees with their appearance in the Tyimede II site at about 5000 BP, and at Nauwalabila at a similar time. Points appear in a variety of other sites, from Queensland to South Australia, between 5000 and 4000 years .

Backed blades appear in Australia at about the same time as points, about 5000 years ago. More than 168 radiocarbon dates are available for occupation levels containing backed blades.[7] Dates earlier than 5000 years have been claimed for six of these backed blade industries, but close examination shows that none of the dates is absolutely reliable.[8]

The earliest reasonably reliable dates for backed blades in eastern Australia came from Burrill Lake: *after* 5320 ± 150 BP, and at Graman shelter I at 5450 ± 100 BP. Backed blades are found at a similar period in Western Australia, where at the Northcliffe open site a few were found 1 to 3 centimetres *above* a horizon dated to 6780 ± 120 BP.[9] But most Northcliffe backed blades are in a zone dating to about 3500 BP. Thus backed blades were certainly in use by 4000 years ago and possibly earlier.

Independent invention of backed blades in south-eastern Australia has been proposed on the grounds that the largest numbers and oldest dates come from there, and the dates tend to be younger further from Sydney, suggesting that they diffused from there. However, the concentration of backed blades in the south-east may simply reflect the greater number of sites excavated there. Almost 70 per cent of backed blade dates come from New South Wales, although that state represents less than one seventh of the area of Australia over which they are distributed. Another factor that argues against local invention of backed blades in south-east Australia is the lack of any prototypes from which these new tool types might have developed. Instead they are suddenly added to the flakes and core tools of the earlier industry. The nearest things to prototypes for backed blades in Australia are the small tools found in some late Pleistocene sites in Western Australia.

New items do appear in Australia relatively suddenly more than 4000 years ago, for which there are no obvious local prototypes. One of these new elements was the dingo, which must have come from overseas, and when we turn to Asia, we find not only possible original homelands of the dingo but also possible prototypes for backed blades and points.

ORIGIN OF THE DINGO

After studying the dingo for several years Professor Macintosh of Sydney University concluded that 'its ancestry and affinities remain enigmatic'.[10] Later an unpublished study by Klim Gollan suggested that the dingo resembles the Indian dog much more closely than any from South-East Asia.

The Indian pariah dog looks like a brother, or at least a cousin, of the dingo. In fact, the closest parallels to the dingo found were the skeletons of prehistoric dogs from India, such as those from Burzahom in Kashmir, and in particular the domesticated dogs from the Indus civilization city of Harappa, dating from 3500 to 4000 years ago.

Recently Dr Laurie Corbett of CSIRO Division of Wildlife and Ecology has completed eight years of examination of more than 100 canid skulls from Asia. His verdict is that the Australian dingo, far from being unique, is virtually indistinguishable from the wild dogs found throughout South and South-East Asia, which are all descended from the Indian wolf (*Canis lupus pallipes*).

When the dingo was brought to Australia it was probably semi-domesticated; it could not have been a really wild, wolf-like creature or it would hardly have been a fellow-passenger in a boat. The major role of dingoes seems to have been the use of their pups as pets by adults, as a release for the affection and nurturing behaviour which would normally be lavished on children. In an environment that could not support a large human population, and where babies who could not be fed had to be killed, a woman who had recently lost a child or who was barren or beyond the age of child-bearing would carry a dingo pup wrapped round her waist. At night the dogs also served as a blanket, and a very cold night in outback Australia is still called a 'five dog night'. In central Australia on cold desert nights Aborigines depended greatly on their dogs for warmth.[11]

Dingoes also have an important place in ritual and mythology. They are taken as pups from the wild, to which they would eventually return. Dingoes did not create the over-population problem that modern Aboriginal camps suffer since the acquisition of European hunting dogs, for these never return to the wild and the dog population continues to increase.[12]

The effect of the importation of the dingo was profound. It can scarcely be coincidence that the other main carnivores, thylacine and Tasmanian devil, became extinct on the mainland after the dingo's arrival but survived in Tasmania, which the dingo never reached. The thylacine would have been no match for the dingo, which has been known to kill even German shepherd dogs in pre-mating fights. They would also have been competing for the same prey, and this may well have been the main cause of the extinctions.

INVISIBLE ARRIVALS: LANGUAGE AND TECHNOLOGY

It has been suggested that the distribution of Aboriginal languages in Australia can best be explained by an influx of new people 4000 to 10 000 years ago, speaking a language termed by linguists 'proto-Australian', from which modern Aboriginal languages are descended. However, there is no sure way of telling whether proto-Australian was brought to Australia with the dingo about 4000 years ago or was spoken at Lake Mungo 30 000 years earlier.

About two hundred different languages were spoken in Aboriginal Australia at the time of European settlement. Although they were mutually unintelligible, almost all belonged to the same language family – Australian – in the same way that most of the languages of Europe and western Asia belong to the Indo-European family. Thus two languages could be as different from each other as Russian and English and still belong to the same language family. Within an Aboriginal language there would often be several different dialects, but these could be understood by other speakers of the language. This situation may be compared with that in Scandinavia, where there is one Scandinavian language, of which Danish, Swedish and Norwegian are mutually intelligible dialects.

All but two or three Aboriginal languages have now been shown to be descended from one ancestral stock: proto-Australian.[13] Australian languages have been classified in a variety of different ways, but it is agreed that the languages of southern Australia are very similar, whereas there is much more diversity in the extreme north. The languages of nine-tenths of the continent have been grouped together and termed Pama-Nyungan, after the words for 'man' at the north-eastern and south-western ends of the linguistic region.

Similarities between languages are assessed by comparing grammar, vocabulary and the sounds used. For example, although grammatically very different, the non-Pama-Nyungan languages of Arnhem Land and the Kimberley region are genetically related to Pama-Nyungan, with which they share similar verbs and sound systems. Both .derive from a single ancestral language (proto-Australian), but the non-Pama-Nyungan languages have developed in a different direction and undergone more radical changes. Only two languages show no links with other Australian languages: those of the Djingili of the Barkly Tableland and Tiwi of Bathurst and Melville Islands. Tasmanian languages are inadequately recorded, but there is no evidence that Tasmanian was not a language of the Australian family.

Languages outside Australia have been examined by a number of linguists, but little has emerged suggesting possible links with Australia. In Papua New Guinea there are several dozen language families with a total of eight or nine hundred languages (about 20 per cent of all the languages in the world), but none of these languages appear to be genetically related to the Australian languages.

The only suggested links with Australia that deserve to be taken seriously are the Dravidian languages of southern India. Similarities between Australian and Dravidian languages were noticed as far back as 1856 by Bishop Caldwell. There are remarkable superficial similarities especially in the sound system, but a thorough study suggests there are no genetic connections.

In fact, it is probably impossible ever to demonstrate a genetic connection between Australian and any other language family, since languages change at such a rate that after 3000 to 4000 years of separation genetic links are no longer visible. For example, over only the last 2000 years the original language of France, Gaulish, was replaced so completely by Vulgar Latin, the language of the invading Roman army and ancestor of modern French, that the existence of Gaulish would be unknown were it not for the records – written in Latin – of the conquest of Gaul.

In summary, almost all the two hundred or so modern Aboriginal languages are genetically related and are descended from a single ancestor, called proto-Australian. There is no way of telling whether proto-Australian was spoken by the earliest Australians or was introduced by later migrants, but it was probably spoken over a much longer time than proto-Indo-European. Thus, although proto-Australian could have been introduced with the dingo about 4000 years ago, it is more likely that it was the language of the original ice age colonists, and that the great diversity of modern Aboriginal languages developed as the colonists spread over the continent. If so, the development of Aboriginal languages would mirror that of tool types, as there is considerable uniformity over the continent in early times but great diversity later. And some of the differences noted in the languages of Arnhem Land and the Kimberley region may reflect influence on these tropical Australians from their Asian neighbours. Finally, no evidence exists of any connection between proto-Australian and any sister language in Asia, but the time involved means that languages that were originally similar could by now have changed out of all recognition.

One other item possibly brought into eastern Australia at the same time as the small tool tradition was the knowledge of the technology for converting *Macrozamia* nuts into edible food. The exploitation of this 'dangerous harvest' is described in the next chapter, but the know-how involved is so specialized that its apparently sudden appearance in Queensland about 4500 years ago has been ascribed to an outside origin rather than to Australian invention. However recent evidence from south-west Australia shows that Aborigines there had mastered *Macrozamia* leaching techniques by 13 200 years ago.

CONCLUSION

The dingo was imported into Australia some time between 8000 and 3500 years ago, most probably about 4000 years ago. The most likely provenance is South or South-East Asia. Domesticated or semi-domesticated dogs could well have been taken by traders in their canoes, for as long as 8000 years ago there was a well-developed trading network in the South-East Asian region. The presence of microliths in the Andaman Islands in the Bay of Bengal, 270 kilometres from the nearest land, implies that a marine network had developed also in the Indian Ocean. Thus contact between the Indian sub-continent and Australia could have been by way of a series of islands, such as the Andamans and Java.

The appearance of the dog and specialized small tools in Australia but the absence of Neolithic elements, such as pottery and food production, suggest that the main migrations were in pre-Neolithic times, from a society of hunter–gatherers rather than cultivators. The different distribution of backed blade and point industries in Australia can be neatly explained by two main migration routes: one through Australia's north in the region of Arnhem Land by people using stone projectile points, and the other via the north-west coast by people using backed blades. The latter would be a natural landfall for people coming from the Indian Ocean, so the Indian sub-continent may have been the original homeland of both Australian backed blades and the dingo. The point industries could derive from the same source, or could have filtered down from Japan and north-east Asia, where projectile points were widespread in late Pleistocene times.

Those who believe in an independent Australian origin for the specialized new tools have suggested that the small tools of Sulawesi and Java might be the result of migration from Australia, rather than the other way round. While the migrations are not necessarily just a one-way phenomenon, the idea of such exports from prehistoric Australia seems rather far-fetched in view of the extremely limited range of Aboriginal watercraft in historic times. Pacific voyagers in contrast had large outrigger sailing canoes and reached Tonga and Samoa by 5000 years ago.

The wide and apparently rapid spread of backed blades across Australia is best understood, according to some, as a fashion or 'transcontinental stylistic phenomenon'.[14] It should be pointed out, however, that both backed blades and points are parts of composite weapons of warfare or the hunt, that is death spears and stone-tipped spears. New weapons tend to spread faster than other artefacts, and it is probably no coincidence that the spear-thrower or woomera seems also to have made its first appearance in Australia about the same time as the new small tools. The spear-thrower, which increased the distance a spear could be thrown to more than 100 metres, was probably invented independently within Australia.

It is also probably no coincidence that these new weapons appear at the time the sea had risen to drown huge tracts of land. About 2 500 000 square kilometres of continental shelf around Australia were lost to the hunters, but the effects on the Sunda shelf were particularly dramatic. Here a peninsula the size of India was suddenly turned into the world's largest archipelago. The tremendous loss of territory, particularly if it happened fairly rapidly, may well have been what triggered migration and conflict, bringing new technology, new tools and ideas to Australia, and at least two dingoes. There is no evidence for a great influx of new people and the new elements were added to the traditional Australian way of life, changing but not radically transforming it.

CHAPTER SIXTEEN

HARVESTERS, ENGINEERS AND FIRE-STICK FARMERS

Traditional Aboriginal society was much more dynamic than is usually believed. Considerable change did occur, and over the last few thousand years the pace of development and innovation quickened. It is only within the last 5000 years that the highlands of eastern Australia have been occupied with any intensity. Before that, there is evidence of only a slight occupation in some of the highlands such as the Blue Mountains and the Carnarvon Ranges of southern central Queensland. The intensification of occupation in the last 5000 years comes after the beginning of the small tool tradition, which seems to mark the adoption of new food management techniques. These apparently led to an increase in population and an expansion into areas relatively poor in food resources.

The focus of this chapter is the Great Dividing Range, a chain of low mountains in eastern Australia running from north of the Tropic of Capricorn south to Victoria. Nowhere in this range do Aborigines still lead a hunter–gatherer way of life, so archaeological evidence and nineteenth century historical records are our only sources of information about traditional society. These records are uneven and usually reflect a time when Aboriginal life had already been drastically disrupted by European settlement. Smallpox had decimated the Aboriginal population; measles, flu, syphilis, and alcohol had taken their toll; hunting grounds had been usurped, game wiped out, waterholes poisoned, tribes massacred.[1] In these regions where traditional life was shattered so early, archaeological evidence becomes an all-important means of discovering the traditional ways of life, settlement patterns, and prehistory of the original inhabitants.

POISON

The most specialized and sophisticated of all the economic systems was the exploitation of *Macrozamia* nuts and other cycads, studied by John Beaton.[1] The technology is claimed to have arrived in Queensland 4500 years ago in nearly the same form in which it is applied today.[2] The main support for external origin is the considerable know-how required to process the poisonous nuts, but in Cheetup Shelter near Esperance, Moya Smith found that *Macrozamia* nuts were apparently being de-toxified in grass-tree-lined pits in the late Pleistocene.

Macrozamia is a species of cycad, a strange, palm or fern-like plant whose history goes back 200 million years. It produces unique, pineapple-like reproductive structures called 'stroboli'. These are large and brightly coloured, but extremely poisonous, as a number of explorers have found to their cost. They are also toxic to herds of livestock, causing what is described by stockmen in the outback as 'the zamia staggers'. Moreover, it has been discovered that cycads contain one of the most powerful cancer-causing substances in the world. 'There is no such thing as people who eat cycads and who are only just learning about how to prepare them.'

Removing the poison from cycad kernels was a lengthy, complicated procedure. Slightly different methods were used in different regions. One technique was to cut open the kernels and soak out the poison with water. Later, when the kernels were free of toxin, they were ground into a starchy, flour-like substance and baked into 'cycad bread'. Another approach was fermentation, in which the dissected kernels were placed in large containers or pits for several months. The material is safe to eat when the kernels have either frothed or grown mouldy.

The food value of cycads is exceptionally high: about 43 per cent is carbohydrate, and 5 per cent protein. And many species produce huge quantities of kernels, yielding more food per hectare than many cultivated crops. Aborigines also increased the size of the stands of cycads by a careful use of fire to clear competing vegetation. Indeed, such cycad stands are ecological artefacts. Regular burning also could increase kernel production by seven or eight times and make them all ripen at the same time. This meant that they could be used to support large gatherings of people on ceremonial occasions.

Cycads were certainly used in Arnhem Land to provide an adequate food supply for ceremonies, when hundreds of people were gathered in a camp for weeks or months at a time. Similarly, the main use of *Macrozamia* nuts in the Carnarvon Ranges was as a 'communion food', supporting large gatherings for ceremonial or ritual purposes. Whether a staple or 'communion' food, cycads are a highly nutritious, productive, predictable and easily harvested food, once the way to process them is known. And the whole process is not as time-consuming as one might think. The collecting and processing of cycad bread among the Anbara of Arnhem Land yielded about 1 kilogram, containing 1300 calories, per hour of work. This meant that one woman could feed herself adequately on just two hours work per day.

The exploitation of the cycad *Macrozamia* appears in south-central Queensland to be associated with the introduction of new small tools and the first intensive prehistoric settlement of this rugged region. Dozens of rockshelters have now been excavated in the Carnarvon Ranges by John Beaton and Mike Morwood, revealing intensive use of the region during the last 4000 years, but two 10 000-year-old rockshelter deposits, Native Well I and II, have also been found.[3] In the rainforests of north Queensland Nicky Horsfall has found toxic nuts used at 4000 BP in Jiyer Cave.

Intensive occupation associated with macrozamia nuts has been discovered in the Blue Mountains, in sites such as Noola and Capertee III.[4] As in the Carnarvon Ranges, earlier occupation does exist but it was slight, and possibly intermittent, whereas there was a widespread intensification in use of the Blue Mountains 3000 to 4000 years ago associated with the small tool tradition.[5]

Other parts of the Great Dividing Range were far less rich in food than the Carnarvon Ranges or Blue Mountains. For example, the northern tablelands of New South Wales around Armidale are a particularly harsh environment, and only one occupation site has been found at an elevation of over 1000 metres, in spite of intensive archaeological work in the area.[6] However, certain other types of site are relatively common in this bleak region: ceremonial sites and art sites. There are over a dozen bora grounds and stone arrangements and a handful of art sites. This high country may have been of religious importance, associated with the belief in a sky god – Daramulan or Baiami – which was widespread in eastern Australia. Elevated, remote sites were preferred for ceremonies, particularly ceremonies such as initiation of the young men, from which women and children were excluded. Whilst carrying out the rituals, the men could have existed on kangaroos (caught with long, fixed hunting nets made of kurrajong bark) and on the region's one abundant plant food, the daisy yam or mirr'n-yong (*Microseris scapigera*). These have large yellow daisy-like flowers and fat, sweet, milky tubers which were dug up and roasted. They have a coconut-like flavour but tend to be fibrous. Common throughout New South Wales and Victoria, the daisy yam was a major Aboriginal food. So extensive was the digging for these tubers that sometimes an area was left looking like a ploughed field, as Governor Hunter observed on the banks of the Hawkesbury River near Sydney in 1793. And, like *Macrozamia*, the range of the daisy yam could be extended by careful firing.

MOTHS

The daisy yam was also an important food in the south-eastern highlands, but here an outstanding resource enabled large gatherings to be held: the Bogong moth (*Agrotis infusa*). Each year these small brown moths migrate in their millions from their breeding grounds on the inland plains to spend the hot summer on the roof of Australia. On the highest peaks of the Snowy Mountains and the Victorian Alps they aestivate – the summer equivalent of hibernate – from November to February. What made them an outstanding food for Aborigines was their habit of swarming together into rock crevices, covering the wall like a carpet (colour plate 12). As many as 14 000 have been observed on one square metre of rock wall.[7]

The moths usually only leave their resting places to fly around at dawn or dusk, so they were easily gathered. Since each one rests on the one in front, simply scraping a stick along the bottom row makes them all fall down into a waiting container, but Aborigines also used a fine-mesh net (made from the fibre of the *Pimelea* shrub or *Kurrajong* tree) attached to two poles for easy introduction into narrow crevices. The moths seem to prefer the deepest, darkest places on the windward side of high granite tors, and sometimes they were so inaccessible that they had to be smoked out.

Before moths were gathered, a fire was prepared on a nearby rock, and then the embers were swept aside to leave a stone 'hot plate', on which the moths were grilled. Two minutes cooking sufficed. Then the moths were winnowed to remove the ashes and dust and the abdomens were eaten. Each is only about the size of a small peanut, but full of protein, with a taste resembling that of roast chestnuts. It was a rich diet, and Aborigines are reported to have come down from the mountains sleek and fat after several weeks or even months feasting on moths. The moths' high protein content was as valuable a source of energy to the highlanders of the mainland as were seals to the Tasmanians coping with an even colder climate.

Moth feasts were the occasion for great gatherings of different friendly tribes. They were summoned by messengers carrying message sticks to join in the feasting and festivities. An advance party went up to the peaks to check when the moths arrived, whilst the main gathering of several hundred Aborigines took place at the foot of the mountains, at places like Jindabyne and Blowering in the Tumut Valley. These seasonal congregations were the time for initiation ceremonies, corroborees, trade, marriage arrangements, and the settling of disputes, which sometimes involved pitched battles (the unsuccessful side lost its supply of moths for the season). Then, when the moths had arrived on the summits and the necessary rituals had been performed, a smoke signal created from wet bark was sent up and the parties wended their way upwards; each group apparently owned its own moth peaks.

What traces remain of this unique phenomenon in the archaeological record? The answer is regrettably few, but nevertheless enough to show that moth hunting has been going on for at least a thousand years. Only one stone tool was used in the exploitation of this food, and that was a smooth unmodified river stone used to grind up the cooked moths into a paste to carry them down to the valley. Such stones have been found in high level campsites at places such as Perisher Valley. They also occur as isolated finds high in the alpine zone, far above any natural source of river stones. The only logical explanation for anyone to carry river stones up mountains seemed that they had been used as moth pestles, but to prove it was more difficult. The stones were examined under ultra-violet light to see if they bore any traces of organic remains, which would fluoresce. They did fluoresce, particularly on the working ends. Grinding up moths with a stone of the same kind produced fluorescence in exactly the same way as the specimens from the archaeological sites. Further evidence came from a cave that is a moth aestivation site and also provided shelter for moth hunters. This Bogong Cave contained a similar moth pestle in an occupation deposit, and charcoal from the same layer gave a date of 1000 ± 60 BP.

Moth hunting is thus a specialized economic activity with an antiquity of at least a thousand years. When did it begin? The moth migrations are generally considered to be a means of escaping the oven-like heat of the breeding grounds in summer. This climatic pattern could have been established at any time after the end of the ice age, and is likely to have occurred more than 7000 years ago.

At the northern and southern extremities of the Snowy Mountains people were venturing on at least seasonal foraging trips in the Pleistocene, leaving slight traces of their passing around Lake George, at Birrigai and at Cloggs Cave in the Buchan Valley. But on present evidence the highlands proper seem to have been uninhabited until the small tool phase. If there was any earlier occupation it was certainly non-intensive, and probably only seasonal.

Ceremonial gatherings were a vital part of highland life. The moth hunters could have simply exploited the moths in their own territory, but instead they trekked from more than 100 kilometres away to meet. Large gatherings need large amounts of food, and the normal highland resources, such as roasted bracken roots, daisy yams and possums, might have been inadequate without the moths. Moths are relatively abundant, reliable and easily collected; indeed they are the easiest food to survive on if 'living off the land' in summer in the mountains, and they can be eaten by the kilo for breakfast, lunch and dinner with no ill effects. This unusual resource enabled men to carry out initiation and other ceremonies in seclusion, as some of their stone arrangements and bora grounds still silently testify on remote mountain peaks.

EELS

The same coincidence of new stone tool forms and intensive exploitation of a special food resource associated with large ceremonial gatherings is found not only in the highlands of Queensland and New South Wales but also among the swamps and plains of south-western Victoria. Here the special food was eels.

Eels were a major food source of the fast, coastward-flowing rivers in south-eastern Australia. Each year the large, fat, silver eels migrate upstream in spring to their inland feeding grounds and downstream in autumn to the sea and their breeding places far away in tropical waters. This eel (*Anguilla australis occidentalis*) is a temperate fresh-water species, which grows to a metre or more in length and to the thickness of a man's arm.

The fertile coastal plain of south-west Victoria is intersected by a network of small perennial rivers, swamps and wetlands. Rainfall occurs mainly in the autumn and winter and, before European settlement, used to turn vast stretches of land into marshes each year. There were thus extensive wetlands each autumn, the main eel fishing season, and elaborate canals and traps were constructed to catch the eels during their migrations.

Archaeological work by Harry Lourandos, Peter Coutts and others in the Western District of Victoria has revealed the existence of specialized, large-scale stone structures to exploit eels as a major seasonal food.[8] Extensive eel traps still exist at Lake Condah, Ettrick (also called the Mainsbridge Weir site), Toolondo and Mount William. The Lake Condah system has been mapped and studied in detail by the Victoria Archaeological Survey during a series of archaeological summer schools. The archaeologists found a large number of stone races, canals, traps and stone walls. The races were constructed by building walls from broken blocks of the black volcanic rock that litters the Lake Condah region. These walls were up to a metre in height and width and often more than 50 metres long. In some places, canals up to a metre in depth and as much as 300 metres in length were dug into basalt bedrock by removing loose and broken rock.

Traps were built across the stone races and canals; nets or eel pots were set in apertures in the stone walls, which were often constructed in a V-shape. The eel pots were made from strips of bark or plaited rushes with a willow hoop at the mouth (figure 16.1). The tapered shape allowed men standing behind the weirs to grab the eels as they emerged through the narrow end of the pot. The fishermen killed the eels by biting them on the back of the head. The same method of killing has been observed in Arnhem Land in recent times, but in this case women killed sea snakes by putting the heads in their mouths and biting.[10] When they were dead, the eels were threaded onto a stick to take back to camp.

The Aboriginal fishermen understood the hydrology of the lake perfectly. They designed and constructed an ingenious system for catching the maximum number of eels with minimum effort. Considerable organization of labour would have been required initially to excavate the canals, but no more than twenty people were needed to operate the traps once they were built. The sophisticated network was so cunningly designed that it took advantage of both rising and falling water. Traps were built at different levels and, as the lake rose or fell, different traps came into operation progressively. The archaeologists at Lake Condah, after a period of heavy rain, were treated to a demonstration of how the whole system operated.

In order to take full advantage of the fishing, people needed to live within a day or two's walk of the lake. This meant that some large campsites should exist in the area, and in January 1981 a field survey was conducted to try to find some.[11] Not only were campsites found, but also the remains of stone houses and whole villages!

The houses are U-shaped or semi-circular with low stone walls, probably originally about a metre high, with low ceilings of rushes and sheets of bark supported on a timber frame (figure 16.2). Most of the houses are only about 3

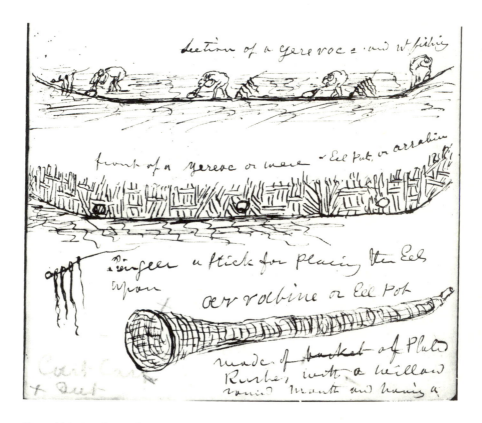

Figure 16.1 *An eel pot and trap sketched by G. A. Robinson in Western Victoria 1841, showing above the 'front of a yeroec or weir' with 'eel pot or* arrabine,' *set into the holes in the weir; centre 'lingeer or stick for placing eels upon'; and below 'arrabine or eel pot made of plaited rushes'.* (After Robinson 1841, by courtesy of the Mitchell Library, Sydney)

metres in diameter and probably housed just one family. There is a remarkable number of these stone houses around Lake Condah and Condah Swamp: in one paddock alone there are 146 houses. If most of them were occupied by one family, that suggests a population of about 700, in one village. Clearly, comments by early 'explorers' who came across 'villages' in south-eastern Australia should be taken more seriously than has hitherto been the case. The research of Elizabeth Williams on mound sites in Western Victoria supports this view.

Living in a small, snug, stone house in a large village, on an isthmus between two lakes teeming with waterfowl, cooking smoked eels on a hearth made of basalt rocks – this is a far cry from the traditional picture of the Aborigine as a lean and hungry nomad continually roaming the country, spear in hand in search of his next meal. The evidence from these villages and eel traps indicates that the population in south-western Victoria may have been partly or even wholly sedentary. At times when eels and fish were not available there were waterfowl, emus, plains turkeys, kangaroos, and plentiful vegetable

Figure 16.2 *Aboriginal stone houses, Victoria. More than 140 stone structures have been found in a village by Lake Condah. (Artist's impression by David White, the Age 29.1.81)*

foods, particularly the *Convolvulus* in winter and the tubers of the daisy yam in summer. The starchy rhizomes of bracken ferns may also have been an important food here as on the coast at Cape Otway, where, in the Seal Point midden, masses of pestles and mortars have been found. They were used for crushing up the bracken roots, which were eaten raw or roasted. Bracken is very common, spreads after bushfires, and is native to Australia; it is not a European import as has sometimes been said.

The age of the stone structures is not yet known, but some at least are certainly prehistoric for they contain both stone tools and debris from their manufacture. All sites that have been excavated so far in inland parts of the Western District have proved to be less than 3500 years old, and since both houses and traps at Lake Condah are generally well preserved, they may well belong to the fairly recent prehistoric past.

Even more remarkable than the complex eel harvesting at Lake Condah is the evidence of Aboriginal engineering near Mount William and Toolondo. At Toolondo an elaborate system of water control – a sort of prehistoric Snowy Mountains scheme – was developed. Artificial channels 400 metres long were dug out with digging sticks to join two swamps, 2.5 kilometres apart, in different drainage basins. They were separated by a low divide, which was cut through to allow water to flow in either direction. Eels were thus able to extend their range and increase in number, and the channels made it easy to catch them.

The system was also designed to cope with excess water during floods and to retain water in times of drought. It is estimated that over 3000 cubic metres of earth was dug out of the Toolondo complex, a remarkable feat implying a high degree of organization. The water control system at Mount William was described by George Augustus Robinson in 1841.

> At the confluence of this creek with the marsh observed an immense piece of ground – trenches and banks resembling the work of civilized man but which on inspection were found to be the work of the aboriginal natives – purpose consisted for catching eels – a specimen of art of the same extent I had not before seen . . . these trenches are hundreds of yards in length – I measured in one place in one continuous triple line for the distance 500 yards. The triple water course led to other ramified and extensive trenches of a more tortuous form – an area of at least 15 acres was thus traced out . . . These works must have been executed at great cost of labour . . . There must have been some thousands of yards of this trenching and banking.[12]

Robinson's detailed diaries provide one of the few sources of information on Aboriginal life in western Victoria. He tells us that the canals were dug with digging sticks, and that the eel fishermen at Mount William were camping on a group of oven mounds nearby. Such mounds, or mirr'n-yong heaps as they are often called, abound along the rivers and lakes of Victoria. Several have been excavated and all belong to the small tool phase, and indeed to the last 2000 years.[13] These kitchen middens reflect a semi-sedentary way of life – the nomads were becoming less nomadic as each century passed.

The hydraulic systems are indeed remarkable examples of resource management and stone age engineering, and, like the sophisticated and large-scale eel traps of Lake Condah and elsewhere, show that Aborigines were capable of ingenious manipulation of their environment, not necessarily to increase food production but to increase the regularity and reliability of food resources, making possible a semi-sedentary way of life and regular large tribal gatherings. Like moths and *Macrozamia*, eels were used as a 'communion food' to feed large numbers of people gathered together for ceremonies. They were also one of the very few food items that were traded in the exchange system (see chapter 18).

There is a close link between the holding of lengthy ceremonies and the management of food resources. As a society becomes more complex, it increases its demands on the economy; a more intensive social system is linked to more intensive food management.

Intensification of food management in south-western Victoria probably led to population increase, which in turn triggered more intensive occupation of the less favourable regions to the north: the Grampians and the arid 'Mallee', studied by Anne Ross. Aborigines probably expanded into the Grampians and Mallee proper only some 3500 years ago, mainly as a result of increased population density in south-west Victoria. There was some earlier occupation from about 12 000 to 7000 years ago on or near the River Murray, but not in the really arid areas of low sand dunes and dense mallee scrub.[14] This view is based on the belief that 'absence of evidence is evidence of absence'. Some would say that older sites are there waiting to be found, but a strong case has been made for late occupation of this harsh environment. This fits well with the pattern of occupation found in other unfavourable habitats.

Climatic change may also have played a part in changing Aboriginal settlement patterns and economy. There is some evidence for a cold, dry spell around 3500 to 3000 years ago. This may have been one factor leading to the development of artificial water management techniques for harvesting eels, a move into the wetter Grampian Mountains at that time, and later to population expansion into the Mallee once wetter conditions returned to this semi-arid region about 2500 to 1500 years ago.

In another semi-arid area in southern Australia – the Nullarbor Plain – human occupation seems to have been very slight until the last few thousand years. A great increase in Aboriginal population of the region about 4000 to 6000 years ago is suggested by a two to three-fold increase at that time in the density of artefacts in three excavated caves: Allen's, Madura and Norina.[15] This is accompanied by an apparent increase (reflected in the sites' pollen sequences) in pressure on the vegetation both through burning and cutting material for hut-building.

COASTAL FISHING

The middens of south-eastern Australia have yielded some fascinating evidence of diversity and change in both diet and technology of coastal fishing people during the last few thousand years.

Some middens reflect specialization, others a more generalized subsistence, such as the Currarong sites on the Beecroft Peninsula north of Jervis Bay, excavated by Ron Lampert.[16] Here the contents of midden deposits in four small rockshelters showed exploitation of the food resources of open beach, rock platform, estuary, wooded gullies and headland plateau. In the midden of Currarong Shelter I were remains of (in order of decreasing frequency) bandicoots, wallabies, potoroos, dingo (not necessarily food remains), fur seals and possum. Among the fish remains, snapper predominated, followed by bream, parrot fish and groper. Snapper is a bottom-dwelling reef fish which was probably caught from the headland using lines and shell fish-hooks, some of which were found in the site. Bream on the other hand is an estuarine fish that was probably caught by spearing with a multi-pronged fishing spear. These spears were armed with bone points, some of which were also present in the deposit (figure 16.3).

Further south on the New South Wales coast, the small sea cave of Durras North, which overlooks a large ocean beach, was excavated.[17] The deposit only spanned the last 500 years and revealed a number of surprises. There were almost no stone tools. The only numerous artefacts were fish-hooks (figure 16.4) and bone points, pointed at one or both ends and made out of bird bone. The deposit was full of bird bones, particularly of the muttonbird. These birds migrate down the coast each year and would have been caught when they collapsed exhausted at sea and were swept ashore. The muttonbird collectors

Figure 16.3 *Spear heads.* Left *Plain spear with single bone barb.* Centre *Fishing spear with multiple bone barbs.* Right *Three-piece spear-shaft, detachable head and stone spear point.*

also consumed fish, shellfish and *Macrozamia* nuts, and doubtless many other foods which were eaten away from the cave or have not survived in the midden. The southerly aspect of the beach at Durras makes it an ideal location for the collection of flotsam, and we can imagine these prehistoric beach-combers sitting in their cave in October and November – the best months for muttonbird casualties – looking out across the sand to the rolling surf which might bring them their dinner.

Just south of Sydney in the Royal National Park, several sandstone, rock-shelters overlook the beautiful deep lagoon and sandy beach of Wattamolla Cove. This is a favourite spot for picnickers and fishermen, who use metal fish-hooks, spears and scuba equipment to catch fish which Aborigines earlier caught with shell fish-hooks and vegetable lines or bone-barbed fishing spears. The public footpath to the beach runs through one of the rockshelter sites, which yielded a shallow shell midden, a large number of bones of reef fish, a few bones of muttonbird, seal and land mammals, together with seven bone points and eight crescentic fish-hooks.[18]

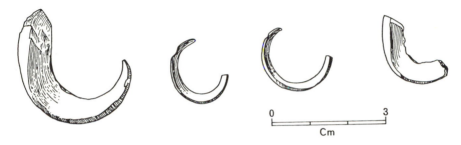

Figure 16.4 *Shell fish-hooks from Currarong, New South Wales* (After Lampert 1971)

The Wattamolla sites appear to have been specialized fishing sites: the men fished with spears and the women with hook and line. This division of labour according to technique is clearly documented in the Sydney district by the earliest European arrivals, such as Captain Cook, David Collins and John Hunter.[19] Both men and women, but more particularly women, used bark canoes for fishing, which were seldom seen without the smoke of a small fire curling up from them. The fire was kindled on a bed of seaweed and clay in the centre of the canoe, and fish and shellfish caught from the craft were often cooked and eaten in them. The fires thus served for cooking and warmth, and to provide light for fishing at night. This was a frequent practice, and if we could be transported back three hundred years in time we would see Sydney Harbour and Wattamolla Lagoon sprinkled at night with dozens of fishing canoes, each with its own twinkling light.

A specialized oyster-gathering site lies on the north coast of New South Wales, on the northern bank of the mouth of the Clarence River. This is Wombah midden, which consists almost entirely of oyster shells.[20] There were no fish-hooks and only a few bone points and stone tools, including ground-edge axes and pebble tools. Historical sources indicate that large numbers of Aborigines used to congregate in summer to crop the oyster beds on the north coast. It is interesting that on these occasions the traditional sexual division of labour broke down. Normally gathering shellfish was woman's work, but when shellfish was the main food enabling a large number of people to congregate together, both men and women did the collecting. Such seasonal abundance of particular food resources allowed large-scale social and ritual events to take place and ceremonies to be conducted in bora rings and other ceremonial grounds.

INTENSIFICATION

A remarkably consistent pattern has emerged from this overview of societies in south-eastern Australia during the last few thousand years. The major happenings seem to be the adoption of small composite tools, an increase in intensity of occupation (with more sites, artefacts and people), the spread of people into harsh environments with few or no earlier inhabitants, and the harvesting or management of special foods linked with the holding of ceremonies and extension of social networks. Within this overall pattern there is great regional diversity. Each region had its own distinctive way of life, material culture, and art style, although there was extensive social contact and exchange of ideas and goods.

In south-eastern Australia the small tool tradition characterized by specialized, composite small tools, such as backed blades, survived in a remarkably consistent form for 2000 years from their beginnings about 4000 years ago. Then, from about 2000 BP, changes gradually occurred. Some items, such as backed blades, dropped out of the toolkit and there was a proportional increase in others, such as ground-edge axes. Simple flakes, often of quartz, were used, without the earlier careful preparation of their working edges. There was also a greater use of bone and shell for tool-making. In fact, some young sites contain almost no stone tools at all.

Shell fish-hooks came into use some time during this period. Whether they were independently invented in Australia or were introduced from somewhere in Melanesia to the north we do not know, but they were being used in Australia during the last one thousand years. The presence of stone 'fish-hook files' in sites cannot be taken to indicate that fish-hooks were also present but have now decayed, because there is no good evidence that these smooth, polished stones ever served as files to manufacture fish-hooks.

It may be that the development of hook and line fishing and even of the multi-pronged fish-spear was a response to population pressure, enabling greater exploitation of marine resources. The use of hook and line made available a new range of deeper-water sea-fish unobtainable by spear fishing. If line-fishing were only done by women in the prehistoric as in the historic period, it could also imply a new and greater role for women in coastal societies. If this is so, environmental change led to population change which inspired technological change which caused economic and social change.

11. *Fly River turtle painting, Little Nourlangie Rock, Northern Territory. This colourful x-ray style painting depicts the Fly River turtle, until recently thought to be extinct in Arnhem Land.*   ▷

The general characteristics of this late phase of south-eastern prehistory seem to be the adoption of specialized fishing techniques, a greater use of bone and shell artefacts, a decrease in finely retouched tools and a corresponding increase in the use of untrimmed flakes. Most of these are made of quartz, the most common stone in Australia. This suggests that there were more people who were competing for the same resources and who were perhaps more restricted in their foraging area than in earlier days of an emptier continent.

FIRE-STICK FARMERS

One of the Aborigines' most important artefacts was one that is largely invisible to the archaeologist: fire. Much of the vegetation encountered by early white settlers in Australia was not natural but artificial: an Aboriginal artefact created by thousands of years of burning the countryside. Even before the colonists started ring-barking the trees, humans had had a great impact on the Australian environment,[21] as has been demonstrated by the research of Sylvia Hallam in Western Australia, Rhys Jones, Peter Latz, Dick Kimber and others.

There were many reasons for the extensive burning. It was used for signalling and also to make travel easier by clearing undergrowth along the route and killing snakes lurking in the bush. Aboriginal tracks were kept open by regular firing in the heavily timbered ranges of the Blue Mountains and in the dense tea-tree scrub of western Tasmania, and fire was also used to clear a path through the tropical grasslands of Arnhem Land. Throughout the continent burning was used as an aid to hunting; animals could be speared or clubbed as they broke cover to escape the flames.

Other uses of fire were for longer-term hunting strategies. After firing, the bush would regenerate, new grass would spring up and attract kangaroos and other herbivores, on which the hunters could prey. Likewise fire encouraged the regrowth of eucalypt trees and of edible plant foods, such as bracken roots, young leaves and shoots. The ashes acted like manure, and sweet, new green shoots would spring up after the first hard rain following the burn.

Extensive and regular burning had the long-term effect of altering and actually extending man's habitat. Rhys Jones has convincingly demonstrated that the sedgeland of the west coast of Tasmania is a human artefact, the result of the long use of fire, which gradually changed the original rainforest, dominated by the fire-sensitive beech, *Nothofagus*, through a phase of mixed eucalypts and rainforest to scrub and finally heath and sedgeland. Now that Aborigines are no longer burning in Tasmania, in some places rainforest is re-invading its old habitat. Likewise in highland north Tasmania, explorer Henry Hellyer found open grasslands among the rainforest in 1827, and he named them the Surrey and Hampshire Hills after the rolling grassy downs of England. These grasslands provided perfect pastures for sheep, but when

◁   12. **Above** *Moths at Mount Gingera, Australian Capital Territory. As many as 14 000 moths aestivate on one square metre of rock wall, each one resting on the moth in front of it* (By courtesy of I. Common)

13. **Below** *Fish traps at Brewarrina, New South Wales. These stone traps were constructed so that when high water levels receded, fish were unable to escape from the areas bounded by stones.* (National Parks and Wildlife Service of N.S.W.)

Aborigines were no longer present to maintain them with a regular fire regime, sour grass and scrub took over, gradually obliterating the open land so that sheep-grazing stopped around 1845, with considerable loss to the non-fire-stick farmers.

The changes brought about in Tasmania by Aboriginal use of the fire-stick had the effect of increasing the amount and diversity of food available. Tasmanian rainforest is not rich in plant and animal food, whereas the mixed heath and wet scrub and grasslands that replaced it under the Aboriginal fire regime provided an abundance of game and plant food such as two of the carbohydrate staples of temperate Australia: bracken, a vigorous colonizer of newly burnt forest, and the grass-tree, of which the starchy pith of the trunk was eaten.

In different parts of the continent different fire regimes were used, adapted to local needs. In Arnhem Land the Anbara practise a fire-management programme that maintains the existing vegetation. They spare fire-sensitive areas, such as jungle thickets, which contain many edible plants that do not readily regenerate after burning. Here there are strong ritual prohibitions against burning: jungles are the home of spirits who, if disturbed by fire, would send smoke into the eyes of the fire-lighters and make them blind. Moreover, fire-breaks are formed around such thickets: an area of about a kilometre broad is carefully burnt soon after the end of the wet season. Thus when the main burning is done between June and August in the dry season, the jungle-thickets are protected by a fire-break of already-burnt grasslands. The reasons given by the Anbara for burning throw an interesting light on Aboriginal attitudes to fire. Fire was seen as necessary to clean up the country, and they regarded un-burnt grassland as neglected. Every part of the grasslands, savanna and eucalypt woodland of their own territory would be burnt regularly, at least once every three or four years.

Such regular, light burning was the pattern all over Australia at the time of first European contact. The fires were of low intensity, which meant that they consumed the litter of leaves and branches on the forest floors but did not burn down the trees. Without such regular burning, forest litter accumulates at a fast rate. This litter accumulation leads to disastrous wild fires, such as that of 7 February 1967, which threatened Hobart.

It is ironic that the Australian parklands and open woodlands so admired by the early settlers should have been created by the Aborigines they regarded as ignorant nomads. Yet when Aborigines were driven off their land and the regular, light burning ceased, the old grass turned sour, scrub invaded the parkland, and the settlers' fine houses, fences and sheep became victims of occasional uncontrollable bush fires. It has taken over a century for the European settler to learn from such mistakes, and now a system of controlled, regular burning has been instituted in many National Parks. In the Kakadu National Park the burning is being done by local Aborigines.

Unlike modern conservationists, Aborigines never put out their fires. Camp fires were left burning, as were signal fires, including those lit in a sequence to indicate the direction of travel of humans or game such as kangaroos. Hunting fires were likewise left to burn themselves out, and Richard Gould reports 23 square kilometres of country being burnt in the process of catching three feral cats.[22] Indeed, Aborigines lit fires with such apparent abandon that they have been called 'peripatetic pyromaniacs'. Burning the country still continues in central and northern Australia, although instead of the fire-stick now lighted matches are tossed out of the back of trucks.

In the desert regions mosaic burning was usually carried out in winter, with parts, but not the whole, of an area being burnt. Much of the desert is clothed in clumps of prickly spinifex grass, which is of little economic value apart from the black, tarry gum it produces – a strong resinous adhesive used for fixing stone adzes to handles and other purposes. However, when large areas of spinifex are burnt, the burnt land is recolonized after rain by a variety of other desert plants more productive of food than spinifex. Gradually the country reverts to spinifex, but meanwhile there is likely to be an increased supply of edible plants such as the fruits of *Solanum* (wild tomatoes). These are the most important fruits of the desert people; they are up to the size of a nectarine, highly nutritious, full of vitamin C, and hang on bushes for months with excellent storage quality. Another food plant which loves to crawl up burnt trees is the 'wild banana', a vine with edible leaves, fruit and a yam-like root.

Aborigines in Arnhem Land have been observed to aim their fires in particular directions, and despite the apparently casual use of fire in the Western Desert, Gould 'never encountered an occasion when a fire actually invaded an area that was already producing wild food crops'.[23] It seems that, as well as increasing their future food supply, they also protected their present food resources. Fire is the most versatile and important tool of hunter–gatherers. It is used for warmth, light, cooking, hunting, signalling, track-making, and, whether intentionally or not, had the effect of improving the food supplies of prehistoric Australia.

The fire-stick was one of the few artefacts that was used all over prehistoric Australia at the time of contact with Europeans. The last thousand years had been a period of great regional diversity and complexity. There was no standard way of life but a series of remarkably different regional responses to varying environments, ranging from moth-hunting to sealing, from eel-trapping to cycad-harvesting. There was not only diversity, but also intensification in the use of resources. The pace of change was quickening – who knows where this initiative and creativity might not have led Aboriginal society, had not those ships of doom sailed into Sydney Harbour in 1788.

PART V

THE LAST TWO
THOUSAND YEARS

CHAPTER SEVENTEEN

THE QUESTION OF AGRICULTURE

It has long been remarked that Australia remained a nation of nomadic hunter–gatherers while most people in the rest of the world, including Papua New Guinea, became cultivators. Other traits of the Neolithic period such as the domestication of animals and the use of pottery likewise were never adopted in Australia. These traits never penetrated the fifth continent.

What is surprising, in view of the arrival of the dingo from the outside world, is that more new elements did not also reach Australia at that time. The pig was probably in New Guinea by 10 000 years ago, when a neck of land still linked New Guinea and Australia, and was certainly present by 6000 years ago, yet the pig was completely absent from prehistoric Australia. The pig was not native to New Guinea but must have been brought there from mainland South-East Asia or islands such as Java or Sulawesi, where it was indigenous.

The other major element found in New Guinea at an early date but absent from Australia was agriculture. Agriculture was being practised in New Guinea nine thousand years ago. The evidence comes from the Wahgi Valley near Mt Hagen in the central highlands.[1] In the late 1960s, when some tea planters drained a swamp, they discovered ancient wooden paddle-shaped spades, digging sticks and stone axes. These were associated with many water-control ditches, which were probably dug to aid the growing of taro, cultivated for its edible, starchy tuberous root. The oldest ditch, 2 metres wide by 1 metre deep and at least 450 metres long, was radiocarbon dated to about 9000 years ago. Taro, like the pig, is not native to New Guinea, so it must also have been introduced. Other evidence in New Guinea shows that by 5000 to 6000 years ago plant cultivation, based on both native and non-native species, forest clearance, relatively permanent village settlements, and complex water-management systems had already developed.

Possible reasons put forward to explain why Australian Aborigines did not become farmers have been lack of contact with agricultural groups, cultural conservatism, hostility to newcomers, lack of suitable plants and animals to domesticate, and deliberate choice.

CONTACT WITH CULTIVATORS

At the time of the drowning of the land bridge across Torres Strait, about 6500 years ago, subsistence throughout the region was based on hunting and gathering. Although agriculture developed early in New Guinea, it only became intensive in some regions, and wild food continued, until the present day, to make a large contribution to the diet in many areas.

In lowland Papua, north of the Torres Strait, there was a blend of limited agriculture with foraging (hunting and gathering). The system in the northern Torres Strait islands was similar, but further south, in the southern Torres Strait islands and Cape York Peninsula, subsistence was based on wild plant and animal food. These differences cannot be due simply to climatic differences, since across the thousand kilometres from Oriomo to Cooktown the climate is relatively uniform, with a markedly seasonal rainfall. Yet across this tract there is a gradient from the horticulturalists of New Guinea, with their pottery, pigs and fenced gardens, to the nomadic hunter–gatherers of Australia, with none of those things.

The Torres Strait islands form a set of stepping stones between Papua and Cape York and thus hold the key to discovering how much contact and what sort of contact there was between prehistoric Australia and the outside world. Fortunately, a considerable amount of research on Torres Strait has been done over the last decade.[2]

Agriculture was not practised on all the Torres Strait islands. The western islands are generally high islands, composed of old volcanic rocks, surrounded by shallow seas, reefs and sandbanks that provide a home for innumerable fish, shellfish, turtles, and dugong. The land provided a variety of plant food, particularly yams and the fruits of the mangrove, the same nutritious species that was used on Cape York. In this rich environment there was normally no need to engage in the labour of gardening. But in times of stress, when there was a shortage of turtles, gardens of yams were planted as a stand-by. There were dingoes on the islands but no pigs, another contrast with Papua New Guinea.

North of this Prince of Wales group of islands, agriculture was more firmly established. Yams were apparently the main root crop grown, and taro, sweet potato, banana and sugar cane were also important. The crops were usually grown in plots cleared by slash and burn. The wild vegetation was cleared from an area with the aid of fire and the seeds scattered over or planted in the disturbed ground.

The eastern islands in Torres Strait, which are small and low, with rich soils but less rich marine resources than their western neighbours, practised agriculture extensively. Agriculture is an intensification of food procurement and it is very possible that it began on the Torres Strait islands because of population pressure resulting from the enormous loss of land as the Sahul shelf was flooded by post-glacial rising seas, which crowded the previously wide-spread population onto islands. However, this is speculation: no archaeological evidence is available to indicate how long these islands have been inhabited. Stone tools, stone arrangements, middens and fish traps have been found on the islands, but no site has yet been excavated to provide an idea of length of occupation.[3]

On Cape York itself there are indications that shellfish were an important part of the diet, at least over the last thousand years. The existence of huge shell mounds on the west side of Cape York at Weipa has been known since 1901. Archaeological investigations have shown that the mounds were of human, not natural, origin.[4] Excavation of sections of two of the larger mounds revealed the presence of charcoal layers, bone and stone – all distinguishing marks of midden deposits. And the shells are predominantly of a single species: cockle shell (*Anadara granosa*).

There are about 500 shell mounds along the banks of the four rivers that flow into the bay where the modern bauxite mining town of Weipa stands. Thanks to their remoteness in the early days of European settlement, and more recently to the conservation policy of Comalco, this magnificent series is one of the few major groups of shell middens in Australia to be still almost intact.

The mounds generally occur in clusters. Most are only 1 to 2 metres high, but some reach a height of 9 metres and the tallest is no less than 13 metres high. It has been calculated that the largest mound has a volume of 9400 cubic metres, and that the 500 mounds contain 200 000 tonnes of shell, or about nine thousand million cockles! Radiocarbon dates from the base of the excavations show that the mounds began to accumulate about 1200 years ago. This means that at Weipa nine million cockles were collected each year, yielding about 27 tonnes of meat: enough to feed eighteen people for the whole year. The main artefacts found were a few ground, polished bone points, of the type bound to wooden handles for use as spear barbs. Broken pieces from stingray barbs, presumably used for a similar purpose, were also present in the middens. Several wallaby incisor teeth had been artificially split to form a cutting edge, forming a toothed scraper, probably used for sharpening spear tips.

One of the puzzles about the cockle shell mounds was that more than half the cockle shells appeared to be intact and unopened. This conundrum was solved by local Aborigines, who showed that heat is traditionally used to open the shells, and the meat is removed without having to break the shell, which then closes again. (The live shells are placed in a pile on the ground and a small fire of leaves and twigs is made above them, which creates enough heat to open the valves.)

The other puzzle about the middens of Cape York and Arnhem Land is why they were so much larger and more steep-sided than the middens of the southern half of the continent. The answer would seem to be the wet season of tropical Australia, which turns low-lying land into a swamp or floodplain. The tall, steep-sided mounds at Weipa are all on flattish, open ground or on isolated ridges clear of woodland, whereas on higher ground among the trees the mounds are lower. The reason for developing some mounds on water-logged open ground would seem to be the desire to be near the cockle beds and to escape the insect pests, which at times make life in the woodlands intoler-able. Shell mounds in fact make excellent living sites: they are dry, good heat insulators, comfortable to sleep on with the aid of a few sheets of bark, and they afford the chance of a sea breeze and a strategic look-out for defensive purposes.

A recent discovery has shown that the Weipa mounds are not unique on Cape York as previously thought, but that similar huge shell middens also exist on the east side of the cape, in the Princess Charlotte Bay–Bathurst Head area. The shell middens occur in clusters, as at Weipa, and consist mainly of cockle shells, and some are of similar dimensions. The research is still in progress, and no information is yet available of the antiquity of the mounds. In the same region dugong hunting sites, bone points, shell ornaments, and many rock paintings have been found. The subjects of the colourful rock art reflect the marine environment; they are mainly sharks, porpoises, turtles, trepang, starfish, dugong and canoes. Other unusual motifs are winged insects, probably moths or butterflies.

Torres Strait has often been seen as a clear-cut frontier between the sophisticated gardeners of New Guinea and the primitive hunter–gatherers of Australia, but even this brief look at the evidence shows that there is no frontier but a complex situation, with considerable variety within a similar type of economy extending right across the strait. Different islanders achieved different balances between wild food and cultivated food, and between a more nomadic or more sedentary type of existence, but none of them were the pig-keeping, pottery-using, gardening villagers who practised 'agriculture' in New Guinea. We know that Australian Aborigines had some contact with some of the Torres Strait islanders and with Macassan fishermen from Indo-nesia, but they may have seen little horticulture being carried out. So although there was contact with cultivators, there was probably not much prolonged contact.

CONSERVATISM

The argument that Aborigines were too conservative to adopt agriculture is hard to sustain in view of all the other elements in Aboriginal culture adopted from overseas. These include outrigger canoes, platform disposal of the dead, wooden sculpture, fish-hooks, complex netting techniques, and various art designs, myths and rituals.[5] The main influences into the Kimberley and Arnhem Land seem to have come from Indonesia, such as the meander-type art design found on pearl shell ornaments in the Kimberley, and the carved figures, opium-type smoking pipe and dugout canoe with sails of Arnhem Land. New Guinean influences can also be seen in Arnhem Land, for example, painted grave posts, wooden gongs, painted skulls, string figures, arrow-like reed spears, and bark mourning armlets and belts.

In Cape York there is undoubted Papua New Guinean influence on technology, ritual, art, mythology, language and physical characteristics.[6] The Cape York Aborigines possessed skin drums, bamboo smoking pipes, tobacco, and double outrigger canoes. And in physical characteristics New Guinean traits were marked at the north of the peninsula but declined steadily to the southward. There was certainly contact and marriage with outsiders and adoption of some of their ideas and technology, although this seems to have come about through trade and raids rather than by any settlement or voyaging down the Cape York coast by islanders.

Some material items were imported, others made locally in imitation of Papuan prototypes. The Cape Yorkers had some large double outrigger dugout canoes, up to 18 metres long, which had originally been made in the Fly River region of Papua New Guinea and had been acquired through trade or as 'cast-offs', but most of their canoes were similar but much smaller double or single outriggers. The Aborigines were not head-hunters, so they did not participate in the extensive trade in canoes organized in Torres Strait by the head-hunters.

THE BOW AND ARROW

Something that has long puzzled culture-historians is why the bow and arrow were never used in Australia. If mainland Australia, like Tasmania, had been completely isolated from the outside world since their invention, their absence would be explicable, but this is less easily explained when other items, such as outrigger canoes, were adopted by Aborigines. The bow and arrow were in use in every inhabited continent except Australia during the post-glacial period. It has usually been assumed to be a more efficient hunting and fighting weapon than the spear, but in the case of Australia, at least, this assumption would appear to be wrong. The bow and arrow were used in Papua and in the Torres Strait islands, and they were seen by Captain Cook on small islands immediately off Cape York, but they were not used by Australian Aborigines. It seems that not only Cape York Aborigines but also the islanders regarded the mainland spears and spear-throwers as superior weapons for fighting, hunting and fishing. The main items traded by Cape York Aborigines were spears, which were eagerly sought after in the western Torres Strait islands as far north as Mabuiag. Spear-throwers were also traded to the islands and were used in spear-fishing for dugong. The two main types of spear traded were the fishing spear with four bone barbs, and fighting spears with a bone lashed on to form both a barb and a point (see figure 16.3). Spears were probably Australia's first export goods.

A spear, particularly with its range and penetrating power increased by the extra leverage of a spear-thrower, was doubtless more effective than an arrow against the large marsupials found in Australia. Arrows were used to hunt the largest Papuan wallaby, *Macropus agilis*, in the trans-Fly region, but much larger animals exist in Cape York and other parts of Australia, with tougher hides, against which an arrow would have little effect.

It appears that the Australian Aborigines were selective, taking what was most useful or appealing from overseas, but rejecting other items. That they had, and have, a great capacity for change is apparent. Both in prehistoric and historic times people successfully adapted their technology and life-style to the changing environment. For example, when for the first time Tasmanian Aborigines encountered dogs, they rapidly acquired them and turned them into effective hunting dogs. It should also be pointed out that conservatism – or at least a very slow rate of change – is the normal state of affairs in human societies. Conservatism only seems exceptional to us because we live in a period of immense change and tend automatically to equate progress with change. Thus what should surprise us about prehistoric Aboriginal society is not how little change there was but how much.

HOSTILITY

It has been suggested that new elements, such as agriculture, did not penetrate prehistoric Australia because of hostility on the part of Aborigines to newcomers. The only way that an archaeological site can tell us about relations between two peoples is when traded items are present. In any case, Aboriginal relations with the outside world varied tremendously from region to region and from time to time.

This seems to be the case with relations between Aborigines and the Indonesian fishermen, who sailed their praus from Macassar to northern Australia each year in search of trepang, also called bêche-de-mer or sea-slug. The trepang industry had begun by AD 1700. It was largely controlled by Chinese merchants resident in Macassar, who exported the dried sea-slugs to China, where they were highly valued for making soup and as an aphrodisiac. Trepang fishing involved catching the animals by hand, nets or spearing, then boiling, gutting, re-cooking with mangrove bark to give flavour and colour, then drying and smoking. The end result according to naturalist Alfred Wallace looked like 'sausages which have been rolled in mud and then thrown up the chimney'.

This complex processing necessitated lengthy stays on shore and the setting-up of camps, stone fireplaces with huge, iron boiling-down cauldrons, smoke houses, and wells to obtain drinking water. Along the coast of Arnhem Land

and the Kimberleys traces still remain of Macassan visits, the last of which took place in 1907. The remains include broken pieces of pottery and glass, and tall green tamarind trees, sprung up from the seeds of the astringent tamarind fruit brought by prau from Indonesia. The Macassan camps were situated in positions that could be readily defended, such as small islands or promontories. Historical records from Indonesia testify to hostility from Aborigines and numerous massacres of prau crews. Yet at times relations were friendly, and the Aborigines even travelled on praus overseas to Macassar.[7] The Arnhemlanders adopted Macassan words as well as new items into their material culture, notably smoking pipes and small dugout sailing canoes. The Indonesian name for the canoes, 'lepa-lepa', became 'lippa-lippa' in Arnhem Land.

The trepang fishermen did not attempt permanent settlement and kept to the shore, never penetrating far beyond the mangroves fringing the coast. Foreign intruders who did try to traverse the interior in northern Australia often did not live to tell the tale. This hostility to foreigners may well have been one reason why farmers or even their ideas did not penetrate prehistoric Australia.

ANIMALS AND PLANTS

In assessing the suitablity of prehistoric Australia for agriculture, the question of the possible domestication of Australian mammals is easily answered: there were no native marsupials suitable for domestication. None of the animals that were domesticated in other countries existed in Australia in prehistoric times; there were no pigs, cows, sheep, goats or chickens in Australia then. However, other native birds, such as geese, pelicans or scrub turkeys, might have been domesticated by a people so inclined.

In northern Australia plants are gathered which are cultivated on the other side of Torres Strait. One such food plant found at a few places along the east coast of Cape York in prehistoric times was the coconut palm, which probably established itself naturally following chance dispersal of coconuts across the sea as flotsam. There is no evidence that Aborigines deliberately planted or tended coconuts before the arrival of Europeans.

The yam (*Dioscorea* species) was a staple in both areas, and also present were other tubers: taro (*Colocasia* species) and 'Polynesian arrowroot' (*Tacca* species). However, it is not just the presence of a food plant that is important; its relative abundance or scarcity and ease or otherwise of cultivation must also be considered. A large number of food plants that grow wild in Cape York, but which are domesticated in Asia, are adapted to regular rainfall and have a limited distribution in the infertile soils and seasonally dry climate of Cape York.[8] The plants that flourish in the steady rain of tropical New Guinea would need much more effort in northern Australia. The soils most favourable to agriculture in Cape York were occupied by rainforest. This could have been cleared by would-be farmers with the aid of fire, but motivation would have had to be strong to undertake such labour. Unlike the islanders, the mainland Aborigines could respond to food shortages by moving elsewhere, so the motivation to cultivate gardens was unlikely ever to be strong. The seasonally dry monsoon climate and poor soils of Cape York have been seen as the main barrier to the spread of Papuan species into Australia.[9]

The economy of one coastal group in northern Arnhem Land has been studied in depth by Betty Meehan and Rhys Jones.[10] In a year spent with the Anbara of the Gidjingali language group, they recorded every facet of the economy: what people ate, how many hours and how far they walked each day on the food quest, what artefacts were used for each activity, how often they moved camp, what refuse was left behind, and so on. This type of study, in which the researcher studies a living human society in the field to gather data that help archaeologists to understand the past, is known as 'living archaeology' or 'ethnoarchaeology'.

The important part played by Aboriginal women has been brought out by Meehan's work. In Aboriginal society there is a strong division of labour. The women generally gather plant food, shellfish and small animals, while the men hunt and fish the larger game. Women's contribution to the diet is less spectacular but more reliable, and they provide the basic regular food.

YAMS

These hunter–gatherers, on one of the world's richest coastlines, have two semi-agricultural practices. The first concerns yams, one of the principal starch-yielding staples of tropical Australia. For the Anbara the parsnip yam (*Dioscorea transversa*) was particularly important. When yams were dug out, the top of the tuber was left still attached to the tendril in the ground so that the yam would grow again.[11]

This same practice has been recorded from other parts of Arnhem Land and from Cape York. At Lockhart on the eastern coast of Cape York Peninsula the vines were marked as a sign of 'ownership'. Yams were also planted on offshore islands to extend their distribution and to ensure a 'reserve' supply. This is certainly plant tending and management, if not quite agriculture. True agriculture would have produced a higher yield per plant, but would have involved the labour of tilling the ground.

FRUIT TREES

The other semi-agricultural practice of the Anbara was the deliberate spitting-out of fruit tree seeds into the debris of fish remains and shells in refuse heaps at the edge of a camp. These midden soils with their compost of decaying organic matter and lime from shells provided an ideal environment for tree growth, so in a few years the campsite would be well supplied with fruit trees. Indeed, there is a consistent association between old campsites and trees with edible fruit. This meant that stands of native fruit trees can be used by archaeologists to discover prehistoric sites, in the same way that the presence of exotic trees often leads the colonial archaeologist to the ruins of a historic building.

MILLET HARVESTERS

Although prehistoric Australia was not endowed with the corn that formed the basis of agriculture in Mexico and Meso-America, or the wheat and barley of the Middle East, it does have one native cereal grain, which became the major food in parts of arid inland Australia. This was wild millet (*Panicum decompositum*). *Panicum* and one of the main grasses utilized, the *Setaria* species, are closely related members of the same plant families which in other parts of the world produced the domesticated common panicum (*Panicum miliaceum*) and Italian millet (*Setaria italica*).

Cereal gathering was predominantly an adaptation to the arid lands of the dry heart of Australia, in areas that received rainfall of 300 millimetres or less. In better-watered areas in the north and around the coasts, the fruits, nuts and tubers of plants provided the main vegetable food rather than seeds. The seed-collecting economy of Aborigines of the Darling Basin of western New South Wales has been studied in some detail by Harry Allen.[12]

Until the 1880s the semi-arid basin of the Darling River was inhabited by Aborigines of the Bagundji language group. The Bagundji or 'river people' lived on both sides of the large, slow-flowing Darling River, and practised a riverine economy based mainly on aquatic foods, such as fish, shellfish, ducks and bulrush roots, and on the collection of cereals. In spring and summer food was usually plentiful, but winter was the time of stress when the river was less productive of food. Then the people dispersed in smaller groups into the back country, where they collected wattle and flax seeds, lured emus into net traps by means of a decoy horn that imitated the cry of a female, and drove kangaroos into nets, using a team of beaters or a few men firing the grass. Pools of rainwater provided drinking water in winter, but in the scorching heat of summer these soon evaporated and the only water available away from the river was that stored in the roots of some plants, or carried in kangaroo-skin bags.

In summer the main vegetable food was the seeds of the native millet, which grows only in summer and seeds between December and March. One of the main problems with gathering wild cereals is that the seeds tend to ripen at different times, making it difficult to harvest large quantities of grain at any one time. The Bagundji cleverly overcame this problem by gathering the grass when the seed was full but the grass still green. The grass was then stacked in heaps and the seeds left to dry and ripen, until later they were threshed so that the seed all fell to the ground in one place.

This harvesting of grass seed was done on a large scale. When the explorer Sir Thomas Mitchell was travelling down the Darling River in 1835, he reported that 'the grass had been pulled, to a great extent, and piled in hayricks, so that the aspect of the desert was softened into the agreeable semblance of a hayfield . . . we found the ricks, or hay-cocks, extending for miles . . . the grass was of one kind, a species of *Panicum* . . . and not a spike of it was left in the soil, over the whole of the ground . . . The grass was beautifully green beneath the heaps and full of seed.'[13] Mitchell made his observations in July, and what he saw was a method of 'in field' storage of seeds which must have been harvested at least three months earlier.

The harvesting was done by pulling up the cereal grasses by the roots, pulling the stalks off, or just pulling the seed off into a bark dish, the usual method in central Australia. In one area, Cooper's Creek in south-west Queensland, a stone knife was used for reaping. Stone knives were also used for

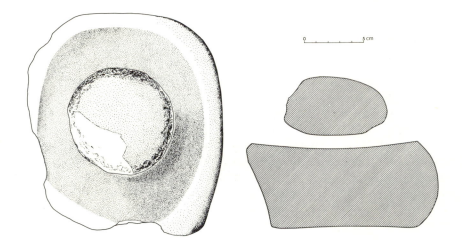

Figure 17.1 *A grindstone used to grind up vegetable food, from Lake George, New South Wales*

reaping in the early days of cereal growing in the Middle East, so this is important evidence of semi-agricultural practices in inland Australia. It also shows the archaeologists what to search for in their sites, for reaping grass stalks with stone knives produces a distinctive type of sheen on the edge of the tool, called 'use-polish'.

Seed-grinding stones are distinctive, as they are larger, flatter and smoother than stones used to grind up other plant foods, such as fruits and nuts (figure

17.1). In fact, seed-grinding stones should really be called millstones, since they are used for the milling of flour. Such millstones were found in some of the Darling basin sites. And analysis of the distribution of all grindstones from New South Wales in the Australian Museum in Sydney showed a correlation between the presence of grindstones and that of wild millet.

Archaeological evidence from the Darling basin shows a strong continuity in life-style but also some changes, such as the adoption of the specialized small tools about 2000 years ago. Thirty thousand years ago the Mungo people lived on fish, shellfish, small mammals, reptiles, birds and emu eggs. Fifteen thousand years ago the lakes dried up and the focus of occupation shifted to the rivers, but the diet remained essentially unchanged, except for the addition of grass seeds. Seed-grinding stones are associated with middens post-dating the final drying-up of the Willandra Lakes, and the same economy based on fish, shellfish, small mammals and cereals still existed in the nineteenth century.

Why did the cereal gatherers not become cereal cultivators? They had all the 'pre-adaptations' generally considered necessary: they ate a broad spectrum of wild foods, they had ground-stone technology, and storage facilities. The semi-arid river basins and humid Western Slopes of inland New South Wales offer similar environments to Mexico and Mesopotamia where agriculture did develop, although the last two have more varied terrain and probably suffer less disastrous droughts and floods than inland Australia.

AFFLUENCE

It may be that hunter–gatherers in Australia were so affluent that they had no need to increase the yield of food plants or to store food. This affluence may have been achieved by the establishment of an equilibrium, in which population was kept below the level the country could support, its carrying capacity. In other words, the available food could have fed far more mouths than actually had to be fed. There would thus have been no stimulus to increase the food supply by developing agriculture, unless some environmental or population stress were experienced.

This seems to be the most plausible explanation of the absence of agriculture from prehistoric Australia. The people had no need to increase the food supply, because they kept their own population in balance with their environment. The return from their highly efficient foraging was so great that expenditure of additional effort on cultivating crops was not worthwhile.

The Bagundji were in some form of equilibrium with their food supply; their relatively low population density was due largely to the incidence of droughts. During bad seasons new-born children were killed, but there is no evidence that droughts caused deaths in the rest of the population. Thus the number of mouths to feed was regulated by bad seasons, and little effort was needed to find enough food during normal or good seasons.

STORAGE OF FOOD

Agriculture implies the production of food surpluses, which are then stored. Some storage of grass seed was practised both in the Darling basin and central Australia. The seed was stored in skin bags or wrapped up in grass and coated with mud. In central Australia wooden dishes might be used, and one store of seed was found in which an estimated thousand kilograms of grain were held in seventeen huge wooden dishes, about 30 centimetres deep and 1.5 metres long.[14]

Storage of food was also practised elsewhere in Australia. The nuts of the Bunya Bunya pine were sometimes buried to be eaten later, and the nuts of the cycad palm were sliced, wrapped in paperbark, and placed in grass-lined trenches, which were then filled with earth. These trenches were as much as 6 metres long and were probably the largest Aboriginal larder so far recorded in Australia.[15]

The tubers of water-lilies and yams were occasionally stored in Cape York, and in Arnhem Land yams were placed in stacks ready for the lean winter months. These yams were probably protected from animal predators by the poison they contained, which could only be leached out by complex processing, as was the case with cycad nuts.

Long-term preservation of many foods, however, presented serious problems. Indeed, the difficulties of food storage in the Australian environment may be of prime importance in understanding why food surpluses were not produced. The combination of high temperatures and pronounced seasonality of rainfall made food storage difficult in tropical Australia, not only for Aborigines but also for early European settlers. Early explorers, even with the benefit of salting and smoking techniques unknown to Aborigines, often found that the game they killed went bad within a few hours.

In many of the food preservation techniques used in other parts of the world boiling was an essential part of the process, but Aborigines had no way of boiling food. On the Torres Strait islands, almost within sight of the tip of Cape York, large shells were used to boil up slices of turtle meat, which was then stuck on skewers and dried in the sun. This preserved meat provided food for canoe voyages lasting several weeks. In contrast, on Cape York shells were used as water containers but not for boiling; cooking was done in ground ovens or by broiling, grilling, or roasting.

Generally Aborigines made no attempt to store meat, fish or shellfish, but one remarkable exception has been found. Near Lake Victoria in western New South Wales a heap of fresh-water mussels buried in a sand dune was exposed by wind erosion. Close examination of the hoard of 360 shells revealed that they had been stacked in neat layers and were still alive when buried.[16] It seems that mussels can live for weeks or even months deep in moist sand, so the hoard acted as a 'living larder', like a tank in a gourmet restaurant containing live lobsters.

While grain and other plant food is much less prone to going bad, there are still many hazards, such as damage from water, insects, especially termites, birds, diseases, locusts, dingoes, and burrowing animals. Dingoes are particularly persistent. In parts of the Australian bush, graves of Aborigines and early settlers can be seen heaped with large stones to keep the dingoes off. Dingoes have been observed opening food tins with their teeth and extracting the contents with their long tongues.

The other main factor operating against food storage was the traditional nomadism of Australian Aborigines. Groups might stay for several months at the same camp in a rich environment, but no groups stayed in the same place all year round. Where food was less abundant, they would move camp more often. A few items, such as heavy grindstones, might be left behind, but hunter–gatherers carried all their basic equipment along with them. And of course babies and young children also had to be carried.

Comparison of the material culture of different regions has shown that the largest range of material goods is owned by those in rich environments where there is little nomadism. Thus the Bagundji of the Darling River had far more material possessions and more elaborate huts than Aborigines of the south-eastern highlands, who had to move camp much more often.

Another type of food storage was practised, which is quite invisible in the archaeological record but was probably of considerable importance in those parts of the continent less rich in food and where preservation of food in the extreme heat was a real problem. This type of food storage is the concept of a 'living larder' or refuge area. In the desert and semi-desert regions of central Australia there are a few favoured environments centred on permanent water in rock-holes or in soakages in otherwise dry river beds. Such places were not used for regular foraging, but were kept as last retreats in time of drought.[17] Examples of such 'game reserves' are Partjar in Clutterbuck Hills of Western Australia and the Finke River at Hermannsburg Mission, west of Alice Springs. In these refuge areas, Aborigines at times increased the amount of game by moving kangaroos and other animals into them.

In the Western Desert, Aborigines possess the technology to prepare and store many of their staple plant foods, but 'it is hard to imagine what advantage these people would gain from industriously gathering, processing and storing large amounts of plant staples that are often available in a sort of de facto storage in the wild caused by natural desiccation'.[18] In particular the quandong fruit remains available for long periods on the ground, in a sun-dried, desiccated condition, as long as the weather remains dry. This makes it an important food during drought years, and it is a highly nutritious fruit, with twice the vitamin C of an orange.

Some plant foods were stored in desert Australia, such as the fruits of *Solanum* and the wild fig, which keep well and were packed up into balls of ochre the size of a basketball and stored in trees. There are also more quandongs growing around old Aboriginal campsites than elsewhere; in some places, water has been diverted into small channels to water the plants. This would seem to be casual cultivation of the type also practised with fruit trees in northern Australia.

The idea of restraint in taking animal and other food is supported by the system of taboos, making certain foods forbidden fare for particular people in a tribe. Thus in the south-eastern highlands and on the central Murrumbidgee River the eating of emu flesh was forbidden till the age of manhood; as the explorer Charles Sturt commented, 'This evidently is a law of policy and necessity, for if the emus were allowed to be indiscriminately slaughtered, they would soon become extinct.'[19] Among the Walgalu tribe of the Tumut Valley it was forbidden to eat emu eggs, which must have been a conservation measure in this highland area, where emus can never have been plentiful and are now reduced to two small flocks at the northern and southern ends of the Kosciusko National Park.

The maintenance and increase of the food supply was also the subject of a great deal of ritual, involving complex and lengthy 'increase ceremonies'. These ceremonies ensure the continued fertility of both human and non-human populations by re-creating the founding drama to renew the life-force in living things. In central Australia, about 20 per cent of plants have special increase ceremonies with associated songs. Some are women's ceremonies, some men's, and some are joint. Such ceremonies serve to transmit to the next generation vital information about the location of water sources and food plants and the habits and movements of game. In a society without written record or books, information is transmitted by example and experience, and in stories, art, songs and ceremonies. This traditional life has been put on record recently by workers such as Dick Kimber, Dianne Bell, Peter Latz and Mike Smith.

THE AUSTRALIAN ECONOMIC SYSTEM

The main reason that agriculture, with its sedentary life style and increased material possessions, did not develop in Australia was probably affluence. In the tropical north the abundance of wild food meant that Aborigines had no need to adopt the more laborious gardening practised on some Torres Strait islands. Once this choice had been made in the north, where there would have been knowledge of the islanders' methods of food production, intensive cultivation techniques were unlikely to spread further south in the continent.

In the centre and south of the continent there were virtually no foods that could have been domesticated except the wild millet of the Darling River and Cooper's Creek basins, which was exploited intensively but not stored on a large scale or planted. The people of these inland riverine plains were, therefore, really the only people in temperate Australia who could have become cereal farmers. Their exploitation of wild millet has been called 'incipient agriculture', and it provided about 30 per cent of their diet, but they did not take the final steps of tilling the soil, planting seeds, and storing the surplus food produced. No doubt the labour involved in tilling and planting outweighed the possible advantages. 'The Bagundji found, after a long period of experimentation, that by hunting and gathering a wide range of foods and by using a sophisticated array of highly specialized techniques, their labours ensured a maximum return of food.'[20]

When food was difficult to obtain, the food quest simply required more time and effort rather than new strategies. There was also no pressure on the amount of land available, in strong contrast to the Middle East and the narrow neck of Mexico. Thus when times were hard, the people could simply move more often and further afield. In the toughest environment of all, the Western Desert, journeys of 400 to 500 kilometres were common, especially during droughts. In recent times it has been recorded that the people from Tikatika moved nine times in three months, foraging over an area of almost 2600 square kilometres.[21]

Australia is the world's driest and probably most capricious continent. Sometimes there is abundance, sometimes disaster, such as the interminable drought in the 1960s which brought the last desert people to seek water at the bore-holes of the white man. Conditions and rainfall are most unpredictable in the centre, but even in the lush tropics food sources available in profusion one year can be wiped out the next. This happened on the Arnhem Land coast where an influx of fresh water from unusually heavy monsoon rain wiped out whole beds of one shell species, which in the previous year had contributed 61 per cent of the total weight of shellfish eaten.[22] Such shortages were infrequent but unpredictable and severe. The Anbara can cope with such losses because they have a varied, broad-based economy, and do not rely on only one or two foods. In this situation it is wiser not to have all your eggs in one basket.

The typical Australian tribe's economy is flexible, with a wide variety of foods sought and advantage taken of seasonal abundance or chance events, such as the stranding of a whale. Such a broad-based system minimizes risks and overcomes shortages of any one type of food much better than can an agricultural community that relies on more restricted food sources. Aboriginal Australia was not vulnerable to famine through the failure of one crop.

The Aboriginal population was controlled by the food resources available, which in turn were related to water resources: the areas with the highest rainfall were generally richest in food. The number of mouths that could be fed was regulated by the food available at the leanest time of year. In temperate regions this was usually winter. The summer abundance of food was used, not to feed more people by collecting and storing surplus food, but as a time when there was more leisure for intellectual life. In a rich environment the food quest will only occupy an hour or two each day in the good season; in the poorest environment of the Western Desert it generally requires less than six or seven hours of work for a woman each day. Even during drought, only two or three hours of collecting by the women can provide a day's food for the whole group.[23]

Not only did Aboriginal men and women living a traditional life have more leisure than is available for the average farmer or office-worker, but they also generally ate better. The diet of those groups whose economy has been recorded in detail emerges as more balanced, varied and nutritious than that of many white people. The Anbara have an average intake of about 2400 kilocalories a day, of which 40 to 50 per cent comes from the flesh of fish, shellfish, crustaceans, and about fifty species of land animals and birds. Since the recommended energy intake for adults is about 2000 kilocalories, the Anbara are feeding well. The Anbara's economy is based on the eating of meat (used in the broad sense to include flesh of fish and shellfish also), but many plant and insect foods are also high in nutritional value. Mulga seeds contain more protein than peanut butter; yams can grow to the size of a man's head and are equivalent to sweet potatoes, and one witchetty grub yields the same amount of protein as a pork chop.

The quality of life and amount of leisure available in traditional Aboriginal communities were remarkably high. Those who are not convinced would probably have their doubts dispelled by comparing the physical and spiritual health of a group leading a traditional life, such as the Anbara, with the pitiful state of those living on tinned food and soft drinks in some government settlements.

Archaeological evidence has shown that the Australian economic system of a varied rather than specialized diet obtained by seasonal movement has great antiquity. The diet of people at Mungo 30 000 years ago is similar to that of the Bagundji last century, except for the addition of grass seeds. A similar, equally broad-based, diet seems to have existed 20 000 years ago at Devil's Lair and Miriwun in Western Australia. The same shellfish, seals, fish, birds, mammals, bracken roots and grass-tree pith were being eaten at Rocky Cape in Tasmania 8000 years ago and on the south-east Australian coast when Captain Cook arrived.

It seems that the basic adaptation to the Australian environment took place when the continent was first occupied, and, indeed, the environment was to a remarkable degree modified by its prehistoric occupants. Once the nomadic way of life had become firmly established, with its consequent need to travel light, it was unlikely that agriculture, pottery and sedentary life would be adopted. The 'naked savages' scorned by early white settlers were poor in material possessions but rich in spirit, leading a secure and healthy life ideally suited to their environment. Captain Cook perceived this as long ago as 1770. Emphasizing the dignity, simplicity and self-sufficiency of Aboriginal society, Cook wrote:

> From what I have said of the Natives of New-Holland they may appear to some to be the most wretched people upon Earth, but in reality they are far more happier than we Europeans. They live in a Tranquillity which is not disturb'd by the Inequality of Condition: The Earth and sea of their own accord furnishes them with all things necessary for life, they covet not Magnificent Houses, Household-stuff &c^a, they lie in a warm and fine Climate and enjoy a very wholesome Air, so that they have very little need of Clothing and this they seem to be fully sensible of, for many to whom we gave Cloth &c^a to, left it carelessly upon the Sea beach and in the woods as a thing they had no manner of use for. In short they seem'd to set no Value upon any thing we gave them, nor would they ever part with any thing of their own for any one article we could offer them; this in my opinion argues that they think themselves provided with all the necessarys of Life and that they have no superfluities.[24]

CHAPTER EIGHTEEN

THE LAST THOUSAND YEARS: TRADE, RELIGION AND ART

More than 50 000 Aboriginal archaeological sites have been formally recorded in Australia. The vast majority of these sites belong to the last thousand years. From this time span, thousands of shell middens lie around the coast, dozens of campsites and canoe trees line the banks of large rivers, while hundreds of rockshelters contain paintings, engravings and occupation deposits. In New South Wales alone more than 15 000 sites have been recorded, in Western Australia some 12 000, and between about 3000 and 6000 in each of Victoria, Queensland, South Australia, Tasmania and the Northern Territory, together with a few hundred sites in the Australian Capital Territory.

Many other archaeological sites are known to exist but have not yet been formally recorded. And thousands of natural landmarks are associated with mythology. These are sites of significance to Aborigines but they generally contain no material traces of Aboriginal culture. However, the life of the spirit is all-important in Aboriginal society, and these sites that lack tangible remains nevertheless usually hold as great or even greater significance for Aborigines than sites containing spectacular rock paintings.

A number of the archaeological sites from the last thousand years provide revealing evidence of Aboriginal religious life, ceremonial exchange and trading networks. They do not, of course, provide a complete account of the rich and complex Aboriginal social and religious life, much of which is not related to material culture.

TRADE

The exchange of artefacts and other goods among prehistoric societies is usually referred to as 'trade', but 'exchange' and 'distribution' are better terms, for the far-flung Aboriginal network of exchange systems was based on social and ritual needs as well as utilitarian requirements and the laws of supply and demand. The exchange might well be rooted in systems of reciprocal gift-giving, rather than a need for raw material or desire for exotic goods not available locally.

Not just artefacts were exchanged, but also raw materials, such as ochre and spinifex gum, myths, corroborees, dances and songs. There was little or no trade in food, but a roaring trade in native tobacco. The stems and leaves of the narcotic plant pituri, which grows in south-west Queensland and central Australia, were dried, broken into small pieces, packed in special net bags and traded as far as 800 to 900 kilometres from their source, over a region of 500 000 square kilometres. Pituri contains nicotine and is a psychotropic plant: it has a considerable effect on the mind. It induced voluptuous dreamy sensations according to Walter Roth, and was found highly intoxicating by W. J. Wills. Aborigines mixed it with alkaline wood ash, which reduced its hallucinogenic effect, but they used it as a tobacco, as a stimulant on long journeys, and for ceremonies.[1]

Pearl shell from the north-west of Western Australia travelled further perhaps than any other object.[2] The broad, gleaming, silvery-white shells of the Kimberleys, often incised with geometric patterns and perforated by a small hole, were seen worn as 'aprons' or pendants by Aborigines as far away as the Great Australian Bight, 1600 kilometres from their place of manufacture (figure 18.1). Likewise baler shells from Cape York were chipped, ground and perforated to make oval ornaments up to 10 centimetres long. These were exchanged by many transactions between neighbouring groups, along trade routes that carried them into the deserts of central Australia and even Western Australia, as well as down Cooper's Creek to Lake Eyre, the Flinders Ranges and eventually, the coast of South Australia. These shells were items of enormous significance and were used in both sorcery and the most sacred rituals.

Axe-stone was a more utilitarian item that was traded great distances. In south-eastern Australia axes have been shown to have been traded 600 to 700 kilometres from their source, and some even as much as 800 kilometres.[3]

Aboriginal quarry sites are not immediately obvious to the untrained eye, but on the south-eastern slopes of Mount William (near Lancefield in Victoria) evidence of intensive exploitation of rock outcrops and stone-working activity is found for over a kilometre along a ridge.[4] On the western side of the ridge, quarry waste and flaked stone have accumulated in heaps up to 50 metres long. About thirty distinct flaking floors are also visible. These are circular mounds about 20 metres in diameter made up of worked stone and waste flakes. On the eastern and northern sides of the ridge over 250 circular or oval pits have been quarried out to obtain stone from below ground surface. The stone is a volcanic greenstone, which has the hardness, toughness and fine grain needed to make heavy-duty stone axes with a ground edge.

Work at the quarry would have consisted of the stone being extracted and roughly trimmed into 'blanks': pieces of a convenient size and shape for making into axes. The final trimming of the axe and the grinding of the blade would have been done elsewhere. Very few finished axes or other stone tools have been found on Mount William, and it lacks the soft rock, such as sandstone, and water needed for the grinding process. Axes were finally hafted to wooden handles by means of resin from the grass-tree and sinew from kangaroo tails.

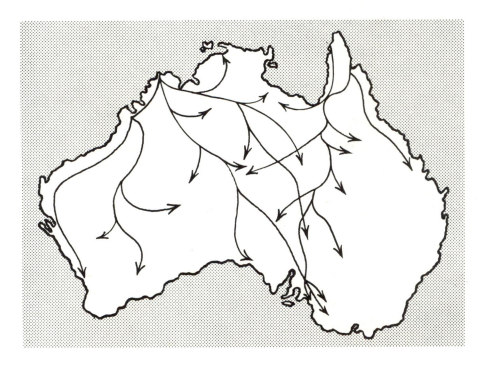

Figure 18.1 *Major trade routes for pearl and baler shells* (After UNESCO 1973, based on data from Mulvaney)

The use of the Mount William axe quarry is known through the work of early anthropologist A. W. Howitt, whose Aboriginal informant, Barak, witnessed its final operations. The last man responsible for working the outcrops was Billi-billeri, who died in 1846. Mount William was the centre of a vast exchange system. Tribes came from more than a hundred kilometres away to conduct negotiations for the exchange of goods. It is known that axe stone was traded for reed spear-shafts, from the Swan Hill district on the River Murray, some 300 kilometres away to the north-west. Mount William stone was also exchanged for sandstone from St Kilda, Melbourne, 16 kilometres to the south.

The 'rate of exchange' is unknown, except that in the 1840s the donor of one possum skin rug received three axe blanks. Since it would take much longer to make a possum skin rug, which involved obtaining, preparing and sewing together as many as seventy skins, than the two hours or so of work to turn an axe blank into the finished tool, this indicates the high value placed on axe stone.

The distribution of axes has been studied in detail by Isabel McBryde and geologist Alan Watchman.[5] The distinguishing characteristics of the stone from this and other quarries were identified by microscopic examination. Then thin sections – tiny slivers of stone – were sawn from ground-edge axes in museums and private collections. The specimens were then ground down to transparent thinness and examined under the microscope. In this way the axe could be matched with quarry and distribution maps drawn up for axes from the various quarries.

This painstaking study showed that axes from Mount William were very widely dispersed: more than half the axes were carried over a hundred kilometres away from their source quarry. Even greater distances were covered by axes from the Moore Creek quarry near Tamworth in New South Wales.[6] This is the largest quarry in the New England region. It is based on a greywacke deposit which runs for about 90 metres along a saddle-back ridge. Aborigines apparently levered the stone from a trough cut into the outcrop, and the concentration of broken rock, flakes and cores indicates the prolific quarrying undertaken there.

ABORIGINAL MINERS

Ochre pigments, used regularly for cosmetics, body and artefact decoration, and cave painting, were traded widely from the main ochre quarries. Expeditions were made from western Queensland all the way to the Yarrakina red ochre mine at Parachilna in the Flinders Ranges in South Australia to obtain the special sacred iridescent ochre mined there. Paint was made from ochre by crushing up lumps of the pigment-bearing rock into a powder, and mixing it with water, or sometimes with the fat of fish, emu, possum or goanna, or with orchid juice for a fixative.

There are several ochre mines in Australia. One near Mount Rowland in Tasmania was visited by George Augustus Robinson in 1834.[7] There Aboriginal women were the miners. They levered out the red iron ore by the hammer and chisel method, except that their hammer was simply a stone and their chisel a pointed stick. The women enthusiastically squeezed themselves down narrow crevices to get at the red ochre – one even became stuck and had to be pulled out by the legs! Everywhere there were signs of strenuous mining: heaps of stone, old workings and narrow holes. The ochre was packed into kangaroo-skin bags and carried off in heavy loads by the women.

The most remarkable Aboriginal mine in Australia is that of Wilgie Mia (or Wilgamia), north-west of Cue in the Murchison district of Western Australia (plate 25). This site was almost obliterated by European quarrying, but it is now a protected area. On the northern side of a hill, Nganakurakura, an immense open cut has been excavated, between 30 and 15 metres wide and 20 metres deep. The pit opens into a cavern from which numerous small caves and galleries branch off, formed as the miners followed the seams of red and yellow ochre.

Ochre was mined at Wilgie Mia by men battering at the rock with heavy stone mauls and prying the ochre out with fire-hardened wooden wedges up to half a metre long. Pole scaffolding was erected for working at different heights. The lumps of stone were carried out to the top of the northern slope, where they were broken up to get the ochre. The ochre was then pulverized with rounded stones, dampened with water, and worked into balls to be traded.

The cavity floor is stratified in places to a depth of 6 metres, and excavations have revealed stone implements and wooden wedges going back a thousand years in time.[8] The several thousand tonnes of rock that have been removed and broken up imply a considerable antiquity for mining, which was still going on in 1939.

Red ochre was the most highly prized pigment in prehistoric Australia, and pieces from deposits created by ancestral spirits were essential for use in rituals. Long expeditions were, therefore, made to these sites, or sometimes the special ochre was obtained by barter. Wilgie Mia is known as 'a place of fabulous wealth' to all Aborigines in the west, and it is told how the ochre was formed by the death of a great kangaroo, who was speared by the spirit being called Mondong. The kangaroo leapt in his death agony to Wilgie Mia, where the red ochre represents his blood, the yellow his liver, and the green his gall. The last leap took the kangaroo to another hill, called Little Wilgie, which marks his grave. This hill was apparently mined for ochre before Wilgie Mia, which would make it an extremely ancient mine.

Aborigines traditionally regarded the ochre mine with fear, except for the elders who were its custodians. Areas which it was unsafe for the uninitiated to enter were marked by piles of stones and no mining implements could be taken away. People leaving the site had to walk out backwards and sweep away their tracks, so that the spirit Mondong did not follow and kill them.

The ochre from Wilgie Mia was used in a huge area of Western Australia and is said to have been carried as far afield as Queensland. Not only is it an impressive example of the quarrying techniques of Aborigines, but the archaeological evidence from excavation at Wilgie Mia has also shown that large scale, highly organized exploitation of ochre in Australia goes back at least a thousand years and probably much further.

The major trade routes that criss-crossed the continent show that Aboriginal tribes were not isolated groups, but part of a complex social and economic network. Nearly all communities traded with their neighbours, and this exchange system served to pass on not only goods but also ideas. This is

Plate 25. *Ochre mining at Wilgie Mia, Western Australia. This photograph, taken in 1910, shows traditional mining methods.* (Courtesy of the Western Australian Museum)

important to remember when considering the spread of new artefact types. Change could come about through the diffusion of an idea as well as of the actual artefact. It could also come about very quickly. For example, a ceremonial dance or corroboree (the Molonga) appeared on the Great Australian Bight only twenty-five years after it was first 'exchanged' in north-west Queensland over 1600 kilometres to the north.[9] If the exchange had been of a stone tool, the archaeological record would seem to show the appearance of the same tool in the extreme north and south of the continent simultaneously.

RELIGION

In a country with natural wonders such as Uluru, where every major topographical feature was endowed with mythological significance, it was not part of Aboriginal culture to build monuments such as megalithic tombs or pyramids. Much of the prehistoric monumental architecture in other parts of the world is associated with religious worship, but Aboriginal religion takes a different form. Natural landmarks are the centres of religion and ceremony. The places where Aboriginal people gather for the great ceremonies are not marked by formal structures – the land is their cathedral.

In Aboriginal Australia concern for the dead is expressed not through buildings but through complex rituals, which may go on for weeks. The rituals are to safeguard the living from the spirit's anger, to avenge the deceased, and to ensure the safe return of the dead person's spirit by way of the sky, a waterhole or an offshore island to the spirit home or totemic centre. Totemism is the religious system in which people are identified with a particular animal, plant or natural feature, which, like themselves, in the Dreamtime was endowed with life essence by creation ancestors. These totems are used to distinguish groupings in society and can be influenced by ceremonies conducted by their human 'kinsmen', such as ceremonies to maintain the natural species. Some totemic increase sites are marked by arrangements, not of stones, but of bones. Thus, in the Northern Territory a striking star-shaped pile of crocodile bones was found on the floor of Sleisbeck rockshelter, and a group of emu skulls was found at Ingaladdi.[10] These are rare examples of evidence of ceremonial life surviving in the archaeological record.

Elaborate drawings in the sand or earth were part of the ritual in many ceremonies. On the ceremonial or bora grounds of New South Wales large, elaborate mythological figures as much as 10 metres long were often moulded in earth or clay in the centre of the bora ring (plate 26). Such sand or earth sculptures were not meant to last. The most usual form of bora ground was two circles surrounded by low earth banks, linked by a connecting path, which was also marked by earth banks. One of the bora rings was a 'public place', where women and children participated in the corroborees and preliminary ceremonies. At the climax of ceremonies like these, the young men to be initiated would be led away by tribal elders to the second, secret ring for the further rituals of initiation, which might involve tooth avulsion or circumcision.

The trunks of trees surrounding the ritual site were often carved, and ceremonial grounds are on record as being surrounded by from between six and a hundred and twenty trees carved with massive geometric designs. Carved trees, also called dendroglyphs, have designs carved into the wood, whereas a tree from which bark has simply been removed to make a container, shield, canoe, or other artefact is known as a scarred tree. Carved trees were associated particularly with burial or initiation sites; initiation trees tend to have carvings only in the bark, whereas the engravings on the burial trees are in the inner sapwood or heartwood.

Carved trees have a limited distribution in Australia: they are confined to eastern and central New South Wales and south-east Queensland, the region occupied largely by the Wiradjuri and Kamilaroi people. They are particularly vulnerable. In 1945 all the carved trees reported from New South Wales were catalogued: 131 sites were listed and contained between 700 and 1000 trees, but many of these trees have now died or disappeared in bush fires, as was found in a recent survey by David Bell.[11] Moreover, carvings on many still-living trees have been almost covered over by overgrowth of the bark.

The designs carved onto trees were usually geometric and linear patterns cut with a stone hatchet or, in the nineteenth century, with a metal axe. The motifs include circles, spirals and concentric lozenges, and diamonds. They resemble the patterns used to decorate wooden weapons and skin cloaks, patterns which were often said to indicate ownership. It may be, therefore, that the designs carved on trees beside a grave indicate the totem or kinship affiliations of the dead person.

Four carved trees still guard the grave of Yuranigh, guide to the explorer Sir Thomas Mitchell. When Yuranigh died near Molong in New South Wales in 1850, he was buried according to traditional custom, but Mitchell also had a tombstone erected over his grave expressing his appreciation of Yuranigh's fine qualities (This site is open to the public.)[12]

Bora grounds are also vulnerable sites, and many have disappeared under the plough or bulldozer, but a few still remain. They are almost the only Aboriginal sites to be visible on aerial photographs (plate 26).

Most Aboriginal ceremonies left no material traces behind. It took several months to carve and intricately decorate the huge grave posts used in the final rites of the Pukimani ceremony by the Tiwi of northern Australia. These were erected around the grave during the lengthy mourning ceremony in which

Plate 26. *Bora ground at Tucki Tucki, near Lismore, New South Wales, from the air* (National Parks and Wildlife Service N.S.W.)

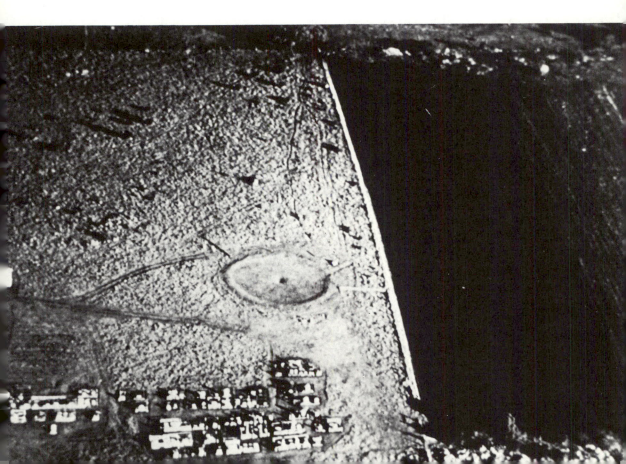

dancers wearing elaborate body decoration mimed events in the life of the deceased and drove the spirits away from the grave into the bush. Yet when the great collective mourning gathering was over, the magnificent poles were simply left in the ground. They were not repainted, maintained, or re-used but allowed to rot away naturally.

In 1972–73 the Gidjingali of Arnhem Land organized two major *Kunapipi* ceremonies, which brought together 200 to 300 people. Some 400 man-weeks were invested in carrying out these ceremonies, but Rhys Jones wrote that 'visiting the great camp of *Ngaladjebama* three months after the religious climax there, all we saw was the wind, whirling red dust over midden debris, and strips of paperbark rattling against bleached poles of collapsed hut structures. The investment had been made into the intellectual and not the material sphere of life.'[13]

The only prehistoric Aboriginal religious structures that have lasted well were made of stone. Stone arrangements are very difficult to date, but they probably have been part of Aboriginal culture for a long time. A wide range of types of arrangements, or alignments, of stones occur. There are circles, lines, 'corridors', single standing stones or piles of stones heaped up into a cairn (plate 27). The significance and mythology of stone arrangements is unfortunately generally unknown even to local Aborigines, for most of the sites have not been used for many decades or even centuries. In most cases all that is known is that the stones were used to tell a mythological story and represented either certain totemic beings or enclosed areas where special events took place. The only stone arrangement so far dated is that of the Bay of Fires in north-east Tasmania, where a new arrangement had been set on top of an earlier one covered with shell midden and charcoal, 750 years old. This gives at least a minimum antiquity for this type of prehistoric monument.

ART

Rock art sites are found in their thousands in Australia, especially in the north of the continent, and have been studied by many researchers such as Robert Bednarik, George Chaloupka, John Clegg, Ben Gunn, Darrell Lewis, Mike Morwood, Pat Vinnicombe and Grahame Walsh.[14] One of the reasons prehistorians are interested in rock art is that some of it is certainly prehistoric and thus opens a window into the past. Some engravings and hand stencils belong to the Pleistocene, as described in chapter 11, and some paintings may have a similar antiquity.

It was explorer George Grey who first recorded the huge *Wandjina* figures of Western Australia, paintings of such quality and aesthetic accomplishment that he could not believe they were the work of Aborigines. Indeed, for over a century Aboriginal culture was held in such low esteem that simple figurative paintings were considered to be primitive, child-like daubings and any-

Plate 27. *Namadgi stone arrangement, Australian Capital Territory, consists of a 50 metre long single line of stones, two stone 'corridors' and a number of circles, on top of a remote granite peak*

thing fine or spectacular was attributed to visiting Egyptians, Hindus, Greeks, Romans, the lost tribes of Israel or visitors from outer space. It is only in the last two decades that Aboriginal art has been recognized for what it is at its best: great art of world heritage quality.

The great diversity of recent Aboriginal culture is mirrored in the very different art styles found in different parts of the continent. These differences do not stem from the different types of rock surface available as 'canvas' but appear to reflect different culture areas. Tasmanian rock art is virtually all engravings, that of Victoria almost all paintings. Only two engraving sites have been found so far in Victoria, but some hundred painting sites have been identified, mainly in the Grampians. They are small figurative paintings and symbolic marks, such as rows of short strokes whose significance is unknown. These have been thought to be hunters' tallies of their success in.the chase, but there is no evidence to support this interpretation.

The most colourful galleries in New South Wales lie in the west in the Cobar region, where small, lively, red and white figures dance across the walls of dozens of shelters. In contrast, on the coast of New South Wales in the Hawkesbury sandstone paintings are larger and include more marine subjects, but the outstanding feature of the Sydney region is the engraved art. There are thousands of outline engravings, and the figures usually approximate life size. Subjects range from whales to lyre birds, from dingoes to sailing ships, from emus to what appears to be a lady in a crinoline dress. Engravings are also found in western New South Wales, but these tend to be pecked rather than outlined. These are dominated by tracks and circles, like the ancient petroglyphs of south and central Australia.

The art of the engravers reaches its height in the Pilbara region of Western Australia. There the development of this art medium can be seen in all its richness and variety. Ancient geometric figures, concentric circles, tracks and lines have weathered back to the same dark colour as the parent rock, a process that takes many thousands, even tens of thousands, of years, suggesting great antiquity. There are realistic, linear drawings of animals, often life size, and pecked-out human and animal figures, standing out a fresh cream-colour against the brown of the background rock. Although it is impossible to date these engravings, the fresher, lighter coloured ones are in general younger than those almost obliterated by cracks, heavy weathering and patination.

A particularly dramatic series of apparently recent motifs occurs among the engravings at Woodstock. This younger art is amazingly full of life and movement for such a difficult medium as rock engraving, executed with stone implements. Elegant figures are shown in bold silhouette and dramatic compositions – running, dancing, fighting, love-making. The many humans include strange anthropomorphs – human-type figures. These male figures have forked hands instead of fingers, gigantic genitals, protruding muzzles and long 'antennae' waving from their heads. The Woodstock engravings were not kept secret, for they are often placed on tiers high on pyramidal piles of huge boulders, where they look out, as if from the walls of a gigantic picture gallery, across the featureless sand plains. Gallery Hill contains one of the finest collections of these animated figures which occur in sites throughout the Western Australian Museum Reserve of Abydos–Woodstock, and at numerous other sites within the Pilbara region.[15]

Not only could these sites be seen by women and children as well as by men, but they may also have been the work of women, for they are invariably close to a waterhole and usually within a few metres of oval patches of rock worn smooth from seed-grinding. Often the upper millstone is still left on the milling floor, and debris consistent with grass seeds has been found in the cracks of some of the ground surfaces. Grinding of seeds to be mixed with water and made into dough was traditionally a woman's activity in Aboriginal Australia. There is a consistently close association between seed-grinding patches and engravings.[16] The virile Woodstock men seem likely to be women's art, in the same way that voluptuous female figures have been painted as 'love magic' by male Aboriginal artists elsewhere.

In visual splendour the rock paintings of the Kimberley, Northern Territory and Cape York rival those anywhere in the world. The Kimberley is famous for its huge colourful *Wandjina* figures, but these replaced an equally fine earlier tradition of animated small 'Bradshaw' figures, outstanding for their delicate draughtsmanship and bold, simple lines. Equal vigour and artistic excellence appears in the tiny *Mimi* figures of early Arnhem Land art. Impressionistic and dynamic, they still depict in remarkable detail lively scenes of prehistoric life.

Much better known is the later style of Arnhem Land, the elaborate x-ray rock art, in which the skeleton and internal organs of creatures are portrayed as well as external features.[17] This tradition is continued on bark paintings. Rock art is only one aspect of Aboriginal art, which can perhaps now be more readily appreciated through bark painting. Bark paintings are easier to relate to Western art, for they have a representational form with which we immediately feel familiar. And, even when decorated with what is to us an abstract pattern, this can still be assessed in terms of our own abstract art and its technical excellence and beauty of line and colour can be admired.

The rock art of Queensland is different again. The Cape York peninsula contains one of the most colourful and prolific bodies of rock art in the world. Enormous naturalistic figures of animals, birds, plants, humans and spirit figures adorn the walls of hundreds of rockshelters. Mythological ancestral beings are finely executed with careful decoration. Other paintings were used in magic or sorcery; one shows a pack rape, others depict men and women, upside down with distorted limbs and genitals, being struck by a spear or bitten by a snake. This use of art as an aid in death sorcery was still active in the nineteenth century, for one painting depicts a European clutching at the reins as he falls off his giant horse. However, sorcery was no match for the guns of the miners who flocked to the region in the Palmer River gold rush, and soon the rock painters were wiped out or forcibly moved away from their land.

Stencil art is found over most of Australia but is most highly developed as an art form in the Central Highlands of southern Queensland.[18] Here most of the paintings are stencils. The motifs of hands, feet, pendants, axes, clubs, boomerangs and other artefacts are arranged in decorative patterns, and stencilled with red, yellow and black pigment which stands out vividly against the white sandstone walls. Colourful and striking as art, these stencils are also a valuable record of local material culture, although they have been subjected to innumerable graffiti and other vandalism.

Paintings decay from natural weathering and few survive more than a few hundred years unless special processes are at work, such as the natural accumulation of a siliceous film over the surface or penetration and staining of the rock by the pigment. Traditionally, paintings were regularly retouched and repaired, or in regions such as the Kimberley they were often whitewashed over and completely re-painted. Since the disruption of Aboriginal society by European settlement this process has largely stopped, partly because Aboriginal art is owned by individuals and no one but the traditional owners may repaint the figures.

Rock painting now seems to have ceased in Arnhem Land: the last painting was done at Nourlangie Rock (in what is now the Kakadu National Park) in 1963. This fine work depicts in colourful orange and white a group of stylized male and female spirit figures, some x-ray fish and a 'Lightning Man', who has stone axes growing from his head, arms and knees ready to strike against the ground when angered, thereby making thunder, lightning and storms. Already the white pigment is beginning to flake off, but there are no rock painters to repaint and no scientific techniques yet available to preserve such paintings. Aborigines traditionally believe that if paintings are not being regularly repaired or replaced by the traditional owners, they should not be artificially conserved, but should be allowed to die a natural death. Non-Aborigines think differently – it seems tragic to us that this rich rock art should be vanishing.

Aboriginal art is a part of religious life and a vital accompaniment to ceremonies and rituals: it was never 'art for art's sake'. The aesthetic value has always been secondary to the religious or practical use of the decorated item. There were no professional artists in traditional Aboriginal society, although some individuals were recognized as particularly gifted.

The best and most significant art is a manifestation of spiritual beliefs. It conveys aspects of myth through symbolic representations of the great spirit beings, linking Aborigines to the Dreamtime. It is the tangible expression of the relevance and reality of myth and of Aboriginal unity with nature. Art is woven into the whole fabric of Aboriginal life: through art, music and dance the stories of the Dreamtime are re-enacted.

Even if we cannot understand the hidden messages of Aboriginal art, we can readily appreciate its beautiful patterns, vivid colours and elegant forms. Deceptively simple, the designs are often subtle, ingenious and sophisticated. Aboriginal art has a beauty, diversity and vitality all its own; at its best it is undoubtedly great art.

EPILOGUE

Prehistoric Aboriginal society was dynamic. Neither the land nor the people were unchanging, and it is the constant human adaptation to a changing environment which provides both the challenge and fascination of Australian prehistory. Much further research in many fields remains to be done before we will know even the outline of the full story, but what we know now from the archaeological record attests to a prehistoric culture of which contemporary Aborigines can be proud.

We will never know precisely when the first human footprint was made on an Australian beach, but it was certainly more than 40 000 and probably at least 50 000 years ago. At that time much of the world's water was frozen into ice sheets and the level of the sea was more than a hundred metres lower than it is today. This made the passage from Asia to Australia rather easier, but there was never a complete land bridge. The first humans to reach Australia must have crossed at least 50 kilometres of open sea. It may be that the craft used by the 'first boat people' were made of bamboo. Bamboo does not grow in Australia so the first migrants might have unknowingly sailed into a trap, with no possibility of return.

The earliest campsites in Australia are now underneath the sea, for in the Pleistocene the continental shelf was dry land so the coastline extended much further than it does today. New Guinea was linked to northern Australia by a wide plain, and it was possible to walk across what is now Bass Strait to Tasmania. The earliest occupation of the continent would have been off the present Kimberley coast or on what is now the Arafura Sea or Gulf of Carpentaria.

In fact the oldest campsites have been found in the far south-west and south-east corners of Australia. The earliest colonization was probably coastal, with people moving along the beaches and up river valleys, exploiting fish, shellfish and small land animals. Gradually they moved further inland, and certainly by 20 000 years ago people were inhabiting a wide variety of environments. They were scattered from the highlands of New Guinea to within sight of glaciers in south-west Tasmania; from the escarpments of tropical Arnhem Land to the arid Nullarbor Plain and the desert heart of Australia.

The first Australians were some of the earliest representatives of *Homo sapiens sapiens*. The most likely interpretation of the existing fossil evidence is that the earliest migrants were of large, robust build, with projecting faces and heavy brow ridges, similar to early *Homo sapiens* in Java. People with a different, much lighter, gracile build were living on the shores of Lake Mungo in New South Wales by 30 000 years ago, which indicates that a group of people of gracile form had entered Australia some time before then.

Some forty Pleistocene sites have now been discovered in Australia. These have revealed that these early hunter–gatherers used fire, ground up ochre pigments for decoration, wore ornaments, and honoured their dead. The rite of cremation goes back 25 000 years at Lake Mungo – the earliest evidence for cremation in the world. The people used stone and bone tools and more than 20 000 years ago were already mining flint – the finest tool-making material in Australia – from deep within Koonalda Cave in South Australia. In northern Australia by that time they had already mastered the technique of hafting handles to stone tools and of grinding the blades of axes to fine cutting edges, remarkably early technological skills which are only rivalled by similarly early developments in Japan.

Rock art began more than 20 000 years ago; the earliest dated art is of markings made on the soft limestone walls of dark chambers within Koonalda Cave on the Nullarbor Plain. These first, tentative finger designs developed into accomplished geometric style engravings found from Cape York to Tasmania and from the Pilbara to the Darling River basin. Later the art of figurative painting developed, and the relationship between the art of the engravers and painters is one of the fascinating, unsolved questions of Australian prehistory.

Another enigma is the impact of the earliest Australians on the giant marsupials which then roamed the continent. Did they become extinct because of the extreme aridity at the end of the Pleistocene, or fall victim to game hunters? The latter seems the more likely, but firm evidence and kill sites are still lacking.

At the same time as they were developing a rich culture, ice age Australians successfully adjusted to profound environmental and climatic changes and the loss of millions of square kilometres of their land in the rising of the seas. The economic achievements of Aborigines over the last few thousand years are remarkable. Their economy supported a healthy population in some of the harshest areas of the world's driest inhabited continent, areas where later explorers such as Burke and Wills died of thirst and malnutrition. It is ironic that such unsuccessful explorers were hailed as heroes, whereas the Aborigines who had successfully adapted to the rigours of the desert thousands of years before were considered to be primitive savages.

Hunter–gatherers have been described as the original affluent society, and an examination of archaeological and ethnographic evidence lends support to this view. Whether gathering Bogong moths or hunting seals, leaching poison out of cycads or re-planting yams, Aboriginal people evolved a series of successful, varied economies. These broadly based economic systems allowed them to exploit and to survive in a wide range of environments where European agriculture proved to be an abysmal failure. Extensive use was made of fire as a hunting tool, modifying the Australian vegetation so profoundly that contemporary flora has been called an Aboriginal artefact.

A far cry from the usual view of Aborigines as nomadic, hungry hunters is the picture of well-fed fishermen living in large villages beside their eel and fish traps, traps that were cunningly engineered to ensure an abundant and reliable food supply. And these masters of stone age economics had a healthier, more nutritious diet than have many Europeans today.

Testimony to the innovations that occurred over time is provided by the evidence of many sites. In the technological sphere there is the development of barbed spears, the spear-thrower, projectile points, ground-edge tools, and special stone adzes for working the iron-hard timbers of the desert. And by 10 000 years ago Aborigines had mastered the sophisticated aerodynamic principles of boomerangs. Far-flung trading networks were developed, and much time and energy devoted to ceremonial life.

It is in the creativity of the spirit, rather than in material goods, that Aboriginal society excelled. Society was so organized that there was ample leisure time. Prehistoric Australians had more leisure to devote to matters of the mind – art, ceremonial, music, dance and myth – than did all but a few Western artists until recent times. The achievements of early Australians are constantly underestimated by those Europeans who judge a society solely by its material possessions. The real richness of Aboriginal culture is thus only now beginning to be appreciated, as anthropologists reveal their incredibly complex social and religious systems and archaeologists uncover the distant past of this heritage.

The coming of the white man proved almost disastrous for Aboriginal society. Yet the present renaissance of traditional culture and life-style and renewing of the Dreamtime may help overcome this near-fatal impact, for the evidence of archaeology has demonstrated the extraordinary adaptability and creativity of these intellectual aristocrats of the prehistoric world.

APPENDIX: RADIOCARBON DATES REFERENCE LIST

Locality	Lab. no.	Age Years BP	Type of site
Pleistocene Sites			
Cranebrook, N.S.W.	Alpha-908	47 000 ± 5200	TL date: basal gravel
	Alpha-99	43 100 ± 4700	TL date: upper gravel
	ANU-4016	41 700 + 3000 − 2200	C14 date: on wood in basal gravel
	ANU-4017	40 500 + 2150 − 1700	C14 date on wood in basal gravel
Upper Swan Bridge, W.A.	SUA-1500	39 500 + 2300 − 1800	Open campsite (at 88−96 cm depth)
	SUA-1665	37 100 + 1600 − 1300	At 75−80 cm depth
Lake Outer Arumpo, N.S.W.	ANU–2586	35 600 + 1800 − 1500	Midden with mussel shell, ash and charcoal
Lake Mungo, N.S.W.	ANU-331	32 750 ± 1250	Shells and stone tools in Mungo unit
Lake Mungo, N.S.W.	ANU–1262	31 100 + 2250 − 1750	Hearth in Mungo unit
Lake Mungo, N.S.W.	ANU-680	30 780 ± 520	Palaeomagnetic excursion hearth, Mungo unit
Lake Mungo, N.S.W.	ANU-375B	26 250 ± 1120	Mungo I cremation site (minimum age)
Lake Tandou, N.S.W.	ANU-3000	26 900 ± 590	Earliest occupation (TNL 15)
Lake Tandou, N.S.W.	ANU-2371	24 050 ± 500	Frog kill site (TNL 34)
Keilor, Vic.	ANU-65	31 600 + 1100 − 1300	Extinct fauna; artefacts pre-date this level

Locality	Lab. no.	Age Years BP	Type of site
Bluff Cave, Tas.	Beta-25881	30 420 ± 690	Lowest occupation
	Beta-25877	11 630 ± 200	Youngest occupation
Cave ORS 7, Tas.	Beta-23404	30 840 ± 480	Oldest occupation
Kosipe, P.N.G.	ANU-190	26 450 ± 880	Artefacts and charcoal in open site
Devil's Lair, W.A.	SUA-585-6 SUA-546 }	32 800 ± 830	Mean pooled age of oldest occupation (limestone 'artefacts', extinct fauna)
Devil's Lair, W.A.	SUA-539	27 700 ± 700	Oldest definite occupation
Lake Menindee, N.S.W.	LJ-204 GaK-335 }	26 300 ± 1500 18 800 ± 800	Hearths, extinct fauna pre-date hearths
Lancefield Swamp, Vic.	SUA-685	26 000 ± 500	Extinct fauna, two artefacts
Puritjarra, N.T.	Beta-19901	21 950 ± 270	Lowest artefacts
Birrigai, A.C.T.	Beta-16886	21 000 ± 220	Lowest artefact
Newman Shelter, W.A.	SUA-1501	26 300 ± 500	Early occupation
Malangangerr, N.T.	ANU-77B GaK-629 GaK-628 }	22 900 ± 1000 22 700 ± 700 19 600 ± 550	Earliest occupation, ground axes
Nawamoyn, N.T.	ANU-51	21 450 ± 380	Ground axes
Nauwalabila (Lindner site), N.T.	SUA-237	19 975 ± 265	Earliest occupation pre-dates this
Lime Springs, N.S.W.	SUA-915	19 300 ± 500	Kartan tools and megafauna
Kalgan Hall, Albany, W.A.	ANU-2870	18 850 ± 370	Earliest occupation pre-dates this
Wallen Wallen Creek, Qld	SUA-2341	20 560 ± 250	Earliest occupation
Malakunanja II, N.T.	SUA-265	18 040 ± 300	Earliest occupation
Koonalda Cave, S.A.	ANU-244 ANU-245	23 700 ± 850 21 900 ± 540	Wall markings, flint quarry
Roonka, S.A.	ANU-406	18 150 ± 340	Hearths
Allen's Cave, S.A.	ANU-1042	18 860 + 2160 − 1700	Charcoal over 1 m above earliest occupation
Cave Bay Cave, Tas.	ANU-1498	22 750 ± 420	Earliest occupation
Kutikina Cave, Tas.	ANU-2785 ANU-2781	19 750 ± 840 14 840 ± 930	Oldest occupation Youngest occupation

Locality	Lab. no.	Age Years BP	Type of site
Beginners' Luck, Tas.	GaK-7081	20 650 ± 1790	Artefacts
Bone Cave, Tas.	Beta-26512	16 820 ± 110	Artefacts below this layer
Mt Newman, W.A.	SUA-1041	20 440 ± 360	Hearths, artefacts
Arumvale, W.A.	SUA-456	18 400 ± 540	Earliest occupation
Miriwun, W.A.	ANU-1008	17 980 + 1370 − 1170	Artefacts, tektites, ochre, grindstone
King's Table, N.S.W.	SUA-158	22 300 ± 1190	Earliest occupation?
Burrill Lake, N.S.W.	ANU-137	20 760 ± 800	Earliest occupation
Cloggs Cave, Vic.	ANU-1044	17 720 ± 840	Earliest occupation
Walkunder Arch Cave, Qld.	Beta-4325	19 520 ± 170	Artefacts
Kenniff Cave, Qld.	ANU-345	18 800 ± 480	Earliest occupation
Colless Creek, Qld.	ANU-2331	17 350 ± 420	Base of upper unit, artefacts well below this date, est. > 30 000 BP
Seton Cave, Kangaroo Is., S.A.	ANU-1221 ANU-925	16 100 ± 100 10 940 ± 160	Lowest occupation Top of occupation
Bass Point, N.S.W.	ANU-536	17 010 ± 650	Earliest occupation
Hawker Lagoon, S.A.	SUA-2131	14 770 ± 270	Kartan tools
Early Man, Qld.	ANU-1441	13 200 ± 170	Early engravings, occupation
Shaws Creek KII, N.S.W.	Beta-1209	12 980 ± 480	Earliest occupation
Lyre Bird Dell, N.S.W.	SUA-15	12 550 ± 145	Earliest occupation
Walls Cave, N.S.W.	GaK-3448	12 000 ± 350	Earliest occupation
Noola, N.S.W.	V-35	12 550 ± 185	Earliest occupation
Kow Swamp, Vic.	ANU-1236 ANU-869	13 000 ± 280 10 930 ± 125	Shells in K.S.5 grave Shells in grave fill
Wyrie Swamp, S.A.	ANU-1274	10 200 ± 150	Peat associated with wooden artefacts
Puntutjarpa, W.A.	I-5319	10 170 ± 230	Earliest occupation

Locality	Lab. no.	Age Years BP	Type of site
Native Well I,	ANU-2034	10 910 ± 140	Earliest occupation
Qld.	ANU-2001	6190 ± 100	Earliest grindstones
Native Well II,	ANU-2035	10 770 ± 140	Earliest occupation
Qld.			
Cheetup, W.A.	GX-6605	13 245 ± 315	*Macrozamia* treatment pit
Bridgewater South	Beta-3923	11 390 ± 310	Earliest occupation
Cave, Vic.			

Holocene Sites

Walga Rock,	Ly-1847	9950 ± 750	Earliest occupation
W.A.			
Koongine Cave,	Beta-14861	9710 ± 180	Earliest occupation
S.A.			
Warragarra, Tas.	Beta-4757	9760 ± 720	Earliest occupation
The Tombs, Qld.	NPL-64	9410 ± 100	Earliest occupation
Green Ant, Qld.	ARL-151	8660 ± 340	Earliest occupation
Echidna Shelter,	ARL-155	7280 ± 130	Earliest occupation
Qld.			
Green Gully, Vic.	NZ-676	6460 ± 190	Burial
Rocky Cape South,	GXO-266	8120 ± 165	Earliest occupation
Tas.			
Rocky Cape South,	V-89	5425 ± 135	Earliest occupation
Tas.			
Sisters Creek,	NSW-17	6050 ± 88	Earliest occupation
Tas.			
Curracurrang,	GaK-482	7450 ± 180	Earliest occupation
N.S.W.			
Capertee, N.S.W.	V-18	7360 ± 125	Earliest occupation
Seelands, N.S.W.	V-27	6445 ± 75	Earliest occupation
Ingaladdi, N.T.	ANU-60	6800 ± 270	Brackets rock engravings
	ANU-58	4920 ± 100	
Cape du Couedic,	CS-496	7450 ± 100	Brief occupation
S.A.			

Small Tool Tradition

Bushranger's	Beta-4852	5540 ± 100	Base of occupation
Cave, Qld			estimated at 6500–6000
			BP
Graman (B1),	GaK-806	5450 ± 100	Earliest backed blades
N.S.W.			

Locality	Lab. no.	Age Years BP	Type of site
Graman (A2), N.S.W.	ANU-1353	4960 ± 200	Backed blades established
Bobadeen, N.S.W.	ANU-287	5150 ± 170	Earliest backed blades
Burrill Lake, N.S.W.	ANU-335	5320 ± 150	Earliest backed blades are above this charcoal
Jiyer Cave, Qld	Beta-13174 SUA-2240	5130 ± 140 5110 ± 100	Earliest occupation of rainforest site
Seelands, N.S.W.	V-24	4040 ± 65	Earliest backed blades
Leichhardt, N.T.	SUA-244	5045 ± 125	Earliest points
Fromms Landing, S.A.	NZ-364	4800 ± 100	Earliest points and backed blades
Fromms Landing, S.A.	NPL-29	3170 ± 90	Dingo bones
Devon Downs, S.A.	L-2179	4250 ± 180	Climax of Pirri points
Northcliffe, W.A.	SUA-379	6780 ± 120	Date 3 cm below earliest backed blades
Tyimede II, N.T.	ANU-50	4770 ± 150	Earliest points
Nursery Swamp 2, A.C.T.	ANU-3033	3700 ± 110	Earliest occupation
Wombah, N.S.W.	GaK-568	3230 ± 100	Dingo bones, backed blades
Murra-el-elevyn Cave, W.A.	GaK-693	3280 ± 90	Thylacine bones
Madura Cave, W.A.	ANU-807	3450 ± 95	Dingo bones
Currarong, N.S.W.	ANU-243	1970 ± 80	Late backed blades
Sassafras I, N.S.W.	ANU-741	1690 ± 100	Late backed blades
Sassafras II, N.S.W.	ANU-744	2780 ± 120	Late backed blades
Weipa middens, Qld	I-1738 SUA-149	810 ± 105 1180 ± 80	Early stage of shell midden (Kwamter site)
Curracurrang, N.S.W.	GaK-898	1930 ± 80	Backed blades
Mt Cameron West, Tas.	ANU-339	1350 ± 200	Engravings made shortly before this date

Locality	Lab. no.	Age Years BP	Type of site
	ANU-337	840 ± 100	Top of midden covering engravings
Wattamolla, N.S.W.	ANU-177	840 ± 160	Earliest shell fish hooks, backed blades
Mazie Bay, Keppel Is., Qld	ANU-2489	1520 ± 50	Earliest shell fish hooks
Seal Point, Vic.	SUA-552	1420 ± 130	Base of midden
Durras North, N.S.W.	GaK-873	480 ± 80	Bone point industry
Glen Aire, Vic.	NZ-367	370 ± 45	Bone point industry
Bay of Fires, Tas.	ANU-2297	730 ± 100	Stone arrangement

NOTE: These radiocarbon dates have not been re-calibrated

NOTES

CHAPTER ONE DOCUMENTS OF STONE AND BONE

[1] H.H. Hale and N.B. Tindale, 'Notes on some human remains in the Lower Murray Valley, South Australia'. *Records of the South Australian Museum*, vol. 4, 1930, pp. 145–218. (Describes the excavation of Devon Downs rockshelter and Tartanga burial site.)

[2] For the history of Australian archaeology see D.J. Mulvaney, 'Blood from stones and bones'. *Search*, vol. 10, 1979, pp. 214–18; J.P. White, 'Archaeology in Australia and New Guinea'. *World Archaeology*, vol. 13(2), 1981. pp. 255–63.

[3] This definition and others in this chapter are based on B.M. Fagan, *People of the Earth. An Introduction to World Prehistory*. Boston, Little Brown & Co., 1980.

[4] Australian stone tools are described in F.D. McCarthy, *Australian Aboriginal stone implements*. Australian Museum, Sydney, 1976.

[5] For Australian archaeological techniques see G. Connah (ed.), *Australian Field Archaeology: a guide to techniques*, 1982.

[6] The excavation of Cloggs Cave is described in J.M. Flood, 'Pleistocene Man at Cloggs Cave – his tool kit and environment'. *Mankind*, vol. 9(3), 1974, pp. 175–88; *The Moth Hunters: Aboriginal Prehistory of the Australian Alps*, 1980.

CHAPTER TWO THE FIRST BOAT PEOPLE

[1] J. Isaacs, (ed.), *Australian Dreaming*. Sydney, Lansdowne Press, 1980, p. 5.

[2] J. Chappell and B.G. Thom, 'Sea level and coasts', in *Sunda and Sahul* (eds J. Allen et al.). 1977, pp. 275–92; J. Chappell, 'A revised sea-level record for the last 300 000 years from Papua New Guinea'. *Search*, vol. 14(3–4), 1983, pp. 99–101.

[3] For full discussion see G.G. Simpson, 'Too many lines: the limits of the Oriental and Australian zoogeographic regions'. *Proceedings of the American Philosophical Society*, vol. 121(2), 1977, pp. 107–20. For Asian discoveries in general see P. Bellwood, *Man's Conquest of the Pacific*. Sydney, Collins, 1978.

[4] R. Jones, 'The fifth continent: problems concerning the human colonization of Australia'. *Annual Reviews in Anthropology*, vol. 8, 1979, pp. 445–66; J.P. White and F.J. O'Connell, 'Australian prehistory: new aspects of antiquity'. *Science*, vol. 203, 1979, pp. 21–8.

[5] J.H. Calaby, 'Some biogeographical factors relevant to the Pleistocene movement of man in Australia', in *The Origin of the Australians* (eds R. Kirk and A. Thorne). 1976, pp. 23–8.

[6] J. Birdsell, 'The recalibration of a paradigm for the first peopling of Greater Australia', in *Sunda and Sahul*, op. cit., pp. 113–67.

[7] C.E. Dortch and B.G. Muir, 'Long range sightings of bush fires as possible incentive for Pleistocene voyagers to Greater Australia'. *W.A. Naturalist*, vol. 14(7), 1980, pp. 194–8.

[8] J.H. Calaby, op. cit.

[9] R. Jones, 'Tasmania: aquatic machines and offshore islands', in *Problems in economic and social anthropology* (eds G. de G. Sieveking *et al*). 1976, pp. 235–63; 'Man as an element of a continental fauna: the case of the sundering of the Bassian bridge', in *Sunda and Sahul*, op. cit., 1977, pp. 317–86; 'The Tasmanian paradox' in *Stone Tools as Cultural Markers* (ed. R.V.S. Wright). 1977, pp. 189–204.

[10] N.B. Tindale, 'Some population changes among the Kaiadilt of Bentinck Island, Queensland'. *Records of the S.A. Museum*, vol. 14(2), 1962, pp. 297–336.

[11] J. Golson, 'Land connections, sea barriers and the relationship of Australian and New Guinea prehistory', in *Bridge and Barrier: the natural and cultural history of Torres Strait* (ed. D. Walker). 1972, pp. 375–97.

[12] J. Chappell, 'Geology of coral terraces on Huon Peninsula, New Guinea: a study of Quaternary tectonic movements and sea level changes'. *Bulletin of the Geological Society of America*, vol. 85, 1974, pp. 553–70.

[13] L. Groube, J. Chappell, J. Muke and D. Price, 'A 40 000 year old human occupation site at Huon Peninsula, Papua New Guinea'. *Nature*, vol. 324, 1986, pp. 453–5.

[14] J.P. White *et al.*, 'Kosipe: a late Pleistocene site in the Papuan highlands'. *Proceedings of the Prehistoric Society*, vol. 36, 1970, pp. 152–70.

CHAPTER THREE LIFE AND DEATH AT LAKE MUNGO

[1] J.M. Bowler, G.S. Hope, J.N. Jennings, G. Singh and D. Walker, 'Late Quaternary climates of Australia and New Guinea'. *Quaternary Research*, vol. 6, 1976, pp. 359–94.

[2] J.M. Bowler, R. Jones, H.R. Allen and A.G. Thorne, 'Pleistocene human remains from Australia: a living site and human cremation from Lake Mungo'. *World Archaeology*, vol. 2, 1970, pp. 39–60; J.M. Bowler, A.G. Thorne and H. Polach, 'Pleistocene Man in Australia: Age and significance of the Mungo skeleton'. *Nature*, vol. 240, 1972, pp. 48–50.

[3] J.M. Bowler and A.G. Thorne, 'Human remains from Lake Mungo', in *The Origin of the Australians* (eds R.I. Kirk and A.G. Thorne) 1976, pp. 127–38.

[4] W. Shawcross, quoted in E. Stokes, 'Skeletons in the Sand'. *Geo*, vol. 3(3), 1981, pp. 27–49.

[5] M. Barbetti, 'Evidence of a geomagnetic excursion 30 000 BP'. *Nature*, vol. 239, 1972, pp. 327–30.

[6] D.J. Mulvaney, *Nomination of the Willandra Lakes Region for inclusion in the World Heritage List*. Canberra, Australian Heritage Commission, 1981.

[7] K. Kefous and J. Balme, unpublished.

CHAPTER FOUR THE ROBUST AND THE GRACILE

[1] N.W.G. Macintosh, 'Recent discoveries of early Australian Man'. *Annals of the Australian College of Dental Surgeons*, vol. 1, 1967, pp. 104–26; N.W.G. Macintosh and S.L. Larnach, 'The persistence of *Homo erectus* traits in Australian Aboriginal crania'. *Archaeology and Physical Anthropology in Oceania*, vol. 7(1), 1972, pp. 1–7.

[2] N.W.G. Macintosh, 'The Cohuna cranium: teeth and palate'. *Oceania*, vol. 23(2), 1952, pp. 95–105.

[3] E.D. Gill, 'Provenance and age of the Keilor cranium – oldest known human skeletal

remains in Australia'. *Current Anthropology*, vol. 7, 1966, p. 584; N.W.G. Macintosh and S.L. Larnach, 'Aboriginal affinities looked at in world context', in *The Origin of the Australians*, op. cit., 1976, pp. 113–26.

[4] A. Gallus, 'Excavations at Keilor'. *Artefact*, vol. 24, 1971, pp. 1–12; vol. 27, 1972, pp. 9–155; 'The Middle and Early Upper Pleistocene stone industries at the Dry Creek archaeological sites near Keilor, Australia'. *Artefact*, vol. 1(2), 1976, pp. 75–108.

[5] J.M. Bowler, 'Recent developments in reconstructing late Quaternary environments in Australia', in *The Origin of the Australians* (eds R.L. Kirk and A.G. Thorne). 1976, pp. 55–77.

[6] A.G. Thorne and P.G. Macumber, 'Discoveries of Late Pleistocene Man at Kow Swamp, Australia'. *Nature*, vol. 238, (5363), 1972, pp. 316–19; A.G. Thorne, 'The longest link: human evolution in Southeast Asia and the settlement of Australia', in *Indonesia: Australian Perspectives* (ed. J. Fox *et al*). Canberra, Australian National University, 1980, pp. 35–43.

[7] N.W.G. Macintosh, 'Analysis of an Aboriginal skeleton and a pierced tooth necklace from Lake Nitchie, Australia'. *Anthropologie*, vol. 9(1), 1971, pp. 49–62.

[8] L. Freedman and M. Lofgren, 'Human skeletal remains from Cossack, Western Australia'. *Journal of Human Evolution*, vol. 8(2), 1979, pp. 283–99.

[9] Quoted in P. Brown, 'Artificial cranial deformation: a component in the variation in Pleistocene Australian Aboriginal crania'. *Archaeology in Oceania*, vol. 16(3), 1981, pp. 156–67.

[10] A.G. Thorne, 'Separation or reconciliation? Biological clues to the development of Australian society', in *Sunda and Sahul*, op. cit., 1977, pp. 187–204; 'Mungo and Kow Swamp: morphological variation in Pleistocene Australians'. *Mankind*, vol. 8(2), 1977, pp. 85–9; 'Morphological contrasts in Pleistocene Australians', in *The Origin of the Australians*, op. cit., 1976, pp. 95–112.

[11] P. Brown, 'Pleistocene homogeneity and Holocene size reduction: the Australian human skeletal evidence'. *Archaeology in Oceania*, vol. 22(2), 1987, pp. 41–66; 'How the Earliest Australians arrived', in *Tracks Through Time: The Story of Human Evolution*. Australian Natural History, Supplement no. 2, 1988, pp. 52–7.

CHAPTER FIVE THE ORIGIN OF THE FIRST AUSTRALIANS

[1] A.G. Thorne, 'Regional continuity in Pleistocene human evolution: Asia and Australia'. Unpublished paper given in 'Bones, Molecules and Man Symposium', Australian National University, August, 1982; personal communication.

[2] R. Jones quoted in E. Stokes, 'Skeletons in the Sand'. *Geo*, vol. 3(3), 1981, pp. 27–49.

[3] A.A. Abbie, *The Original Australians*. Sydney, Reed, 1969; *Studies in Physical Anthropology*. (2 vols) Canberra, Australian Institute of Aboriginal Studies, 1975.

[4] J.B. Birdsell, 1977, op. cit.

[5] S.L. Larnach, 'The origin of the Australian Aboriginal'. *Archaeology and Physical Anthropology in Oceania*, vol. 9(3), 1974, pp. 206–13.

[6] A.G. Wallace and G.A. Doran, 'Early Man in Tasmania: new skeletal evidence', in *The Origin of the Australians*, op. cit., 1976, pp. 173–82.

[7] R.T. Simmons, 'The biological origin of Australian Aboriginals . . .', in *The Origin of the Australians*, op. cit., 1976, pp. 307–28.

[8] R.L. Kirk, 'Physiological, demographic and genetic adaptation of Australian Aboriginals', in *Ecological Biogeography of Australia* (ed. A. Keast), the Hague, W. Junk, 1981, pp. 1801–15; *Aboriginal Man Adapting*. Melbourne, O.U.P., 1983.

[9] J. Gribbin and J. Cherfas, *The Monkey Puzzle*. London, Bodley Head, 1982.

[10] ibid. pp. 247–58.

[11] ibid. pp. 253–8.

[12] A.G. Thorne, 'Regional continuity in Australian Pleistocene hominid evolution'. *American Journal of Physical Anthropology*, vol. 55, 1981, pp. 337–49.

[13] For detailed information on the Asian hominids see A.G. Thorne, 1980, op. cit.; T. Jacob, in *The Origin of the Australians*, op. cit., 1976, pp. 81–94; P. Bellwood, 1978, op. cit.

[14] A.G. Thorne, 1980, op. cit.

CHAPTER SIX THE PEOPLING OF AUSTRALIA

[1] J.B. Birdsell, 'Some population problems involving Pleistocene man'. *Cold Spring Harbor Symposia on Quantitative Biology*, vol. 22, 1957, pp. 47–69.

[2] S. Bowdler, 'The coastal colonization of Australia', in *Sunda and Sahul*, op. cit., 1977, pp. 205–46.

[3] D.R. Horton, 'Water and Woodland: the peopling of Australia'. *Australian Institute of Aboriginal Studies Newsletter*, vol. 16, 1981, pp. 21–7.

[4] N.B. Tindale, 'Prehistory of the Aborigines: some interesting considerations', in *Ecological Biogeography of Australia*, op. cit., 1981, pp. 1763–97.

[5] M.A. Smith, 'Pleistocene occupation in arid Central Australia'. *Nature*, vol. 328, 1987, pp. 710–11.

[6] J. Flood, B. David, J. Magee and B. English, 'Birrigai: a Pleistocene site in the south-eastern highlands'. *Archaeology in Oceania*, vol. 22, 1987, pp. 9–26.

[7] R.V.S. Wright, 'Prehistory in the Cape York Peninsula', in *Aboriginal Man and Environment in Australia* (eds D.J. Mulvaney and J. Golson). 1971, pp. 133–40.

[8] A. Rosenfeld, *Early man in North Queensland*. Canberra, Australian National University, 1982.

[9] J. Flood and N. Horsfall, 'Excavation of Green Ant and Echidna Shelters, Cape York Peninsula'. *Queensland Archaeological Research*, vol. 3, 1986, pp. 4–64.

[10] J.M. Flood, 'Rock art of the Koolburra Plateau, north Queensland.' *Rock Art Research*, vol. 4(2), 1987, pp. 91–126.

[11] J.M. Flood and P. Trezise, 'A boomerang from Cape York Peninsula'. *Australian Archaeology*, vol. 13, 1981, pp. 95–6.

[12] J.B. Campbell, 'New radiocarbon results for North Queensland prehistory'. *Australian Archaeology*, vol. 14, 1982, pp. 62–6.

[13] G. Singh, A.P. Kershaw and R.L. Clark, 'Quaternary vegetation and fire history in Australia', in *Fire and the Australian biota* (eds Gill, Groves and Noble). Canberra, Australian Academy of Science, 1981, pp. 23–54.

[14] P. Hiscock and P.J. Hughes, 'Backed blades in northern Australia: evidence from northwest Queensland'. *Australian Archaeology*, vol. 10, 1980, pp. 86–95; P.J. Hughes, 'Colless Creek rockshelter archaeological site', in *Proceedings of the Climanz Workshop* (eds J. Bowler, J. Chappell and J. Hope). Canberra, Australian Academy of Science, 1983.

CHAPTER SEVEN ARNHEM LAND AND THE WEST

[1] C. White, 'Early stone axes in Arnhem Land'. *Antiquity*, vol. 41, 1967, pp. 149–52; 'Man and environment in northwest Arnhem Land', in *Aboriginal Man and Environment in Australia* (eds D.J. Mulvaney and J. Golson). 1971, pp. 141–57; C. Schrire. 'Ethno-archaeological models and subsistence behaviour in Arnhem

Land', in *Models in Archaeology* (ed. D.L. Clarke). London, Methuen, 1972, pp. 653–70.

2 J. Kamminga and H.R. Allen, *Report of the Archaeological Survey, Alligator Rivers Environmental Fact-Finding Study*. Darwin, Australian Government, 1973.

3 J.P. White and J.F. O'Connell. 'Australian prehistory: new aspects of antiquity'. *Science*, vol. 203, 1979, pp. 21–8.

4 F.P. Dickson, *Australian Stone Hatchets*. London, Academic Press, 1981.

5 J. Kamminga and H.R. Allen, 1973, op. cit., pp. 45–52.

6 C.E. Dortch, 'Archaeological work in the Ord Reservoir area, east Kimberley'. *Australian Institute of Aboriginal Studies Newsletter*, vol. 3(4), 1972, pp. 13–18; 'Early and late stone industrial phases in Western Australia', in *Stone Tools as Cultural Markers* (ed. R.V.S. Wright). 1977, pp. 104–32.

7 S. Brown, *Towards a Prehistory of the Hamersley Plateau, North-west Australia*. Occasional Papers in Prehistory 6, Canberra, Australian National University, 1987.

8 K.H. Wyrwoll and C.E. Dortch, 'Stone artefacts and an associated Diprotodontid mandible from the Greenough River, Western Australia'. *Search*, vol. 9, 1978, pp. 411–13.

9 C.E. Dortch, 'Devil's Lair, an example of prolonged cave use in southwestern Australia'. *World Archaeology*, vol. 10(3), 1979, pp. 258–79; J. Balme, D. Merrilees and J.K. Porter, 'Late Quaternary mammal remains, spanning about 30 000 years, from excavations in Devil's Lair, W.A.' *Journal of the Royal Society of W.A.*, vol. 61, 1978, pp. 33–65; J. Balme, 'An apparent association of artifacts and extinct fauna at Devil's Lair, Western Australia'. *Artefact*, vol. 3(3), 1978, pp. 111–16; 'An analysis of charred bone from Devil's Lair, Western Australia'. *Archaeology in Oceania*, vol. 15, 1980, pp. 81–5.

10 C.E. Dortch, 'Australia's oldest known ornaments'. *Antiquity*, vol. 53, 1979, pp. 39–43.

11 C.E. Dortch, 'A possible pendant of marl from Devil's Lair, Western Australia'. *Records of the W.A. Museum*, vol. 8(3), 1980, pp. 401–3.

12 C.E. Dortch, 'Two engraved stone plaques of late Pleistocene age from Devil's Lair, Western Australia'. *Archaeology and Physical Anthropology in Oceania*, vol. 11(1), 1976, pp. 32–44.

13 Described in chapter 11.

14 *The West Australian*, 2 December 1981; *Perth Daily News*, 1 December 1981.

15 R.H. Pearce and M. Barbetti, 'A 38 000-year-old site at Upper Swan, W.A.' *Archaeology in Oceania*, vol. 16(3), 1981, pp. 173–8. Another new discovery in south-west W.A. is the open campsite of Kalgan Hall, which has an unbroken artefact sequence from the present to more than 18 000 BP (W.C. Ferguson, personal communication).

CHAPTER EIGHT THE EAST COAST IN THE PLEISTOCENE

1 D.J. Mulvaney and E.B. Joyce, 'Archaeological and Geomorphological Investigations on Mt Moffatt Station, Queensland, Australia'. *Proceedings of the Prehistoric Society*, vol. 31, 1965, pp. 147–212.

2 R.J. Lampert, *Burrill Lake and Currarong*. Terra Australis I. Canberra, Prehistory Department, Australian National University, 1971; 'Coastal Aborigines of south-eastern Australia', in *Aboriginal Man and Environment in Australia* (eds D.J. Mulvaney and J. Golson), 1971, pp. 14–32.

3 S. Bowdler, 'Hook, line and dillybag; an interpretation of an Australian coastal shell midden'. *Mankind*, vol. 10(4), 1976, pp. 248–58.

[4] R. Neal and E. Stock, 'Pleistocene occupation in the south-east Queensland coastal region'. *Nature*, vol. 323(6089), 1986, pp. 618–21.

[5] Gerald C. Nanson, Robert W. Young and Eugene D. Stockton, 'Chronology and palaeoenvironment of the Cranebrook Terrace (near Sydney) containing artefacts more than 40 000 years old', *Archaeology in Oceania* 22(2) (1987): 72–8.

[6] E.D. Stockton and W.N. Holland. 'Cultural sites and their environment in the Blue Mountains', *Archaeology and Physical Anthropology in Oceania* 9(1) (1974): 36–65.

[7] J.L. Kohen, E.D. Stockton and M.A.J. Williams, 'Shaws Creek KII rockshelter: a prehistoric ocupation site in the Blue Mountains piedmont, eastern New South Wales'. *Archaeology in Oceania* 19 (1984), 57–73.

[8] G. Singh, N.D. Opdyke, and J.M. Bowler, 'Late Cainozoic stratigraphy, palaeomagnetic chronology and vegetational history from Lake George, N.S.W.' *Journal of the Geological Society of Australia*, vol. 28(4), 1981, pp. 435–52; G. Singh, A.P. Kershaw and R. Clark, 'Quaternary vegetation and fire history in Australia', in *Fire and the Australian Biota* (eds A.M. Gill *et al.*). Canberra, Australian Academy of Science, 1981, pp. 23–54.

[9] J.M. Flood, 1980, op. cit.

[10] R. Wright, 'How old is Zone F at Lake George?'. *Archaeology in Oceania*, vol. 21, 1986, pp. 138–9.

CHAPTER NINE   AN ICE AGE WALK TO TASMANIA

[1] S. Bowdler, 'An account of an archaeological reconnaissance of Hunter's Isles, northwest Tasmania, 1973–4'. *Records of the Queen Victoria Museum, Launceston*, vol. 54, 1974, pp. 1–22; 1977, op. cit.

[2] *Sydney Morning Herald* and *The Age*, 21 January 1981 and 19 March 1981; *Canberra Times*, 17 February 1981; *The Australian*, 19 March 1981.

[3] R. Jones, 'The extreme climatic place?'. *Hemisphere*, vol. 26(1), 1981, pp. 54–9.

[4] K. Kiernan, R. Jones and D. Ranson, 'New evidence from Fraser Cave for glacial age man in southwest Tasmania'. *Nature*, vol. 301, 1983, pp. 28–32; R. Jones, 'Tasmania's Ice Age Hunters'. *Australian Geographic*, vol. 8, 1987, pp. 26–45.

[5] S. Harris, D. Ranson and S. Brown, 'Maxwell River Archaeological Survey 1986'. *Australian Archaeology*, vol. 27, 1988, pp. 89–97.

[6] R. Jones, R. Cosgrove, J. Allen, S. Cane, K. Kiernan, S. Webb, T. Loy, D. West, E. Stadler, 'An archaeological reconnaissance of karst caves within the Southern Forests region of Tasmania, September 1987'. *Australian Archaeology*, vol. 26, 1988, pp. 1–23.

[7] ibid., and T.H. Loy, 'Recent advances in blood residue analysis', in *Archaeometry: Further Australasian Studies* (eds W.R. Ambrose and J.M. Mummery), 1987, pp. 57–65.

[8] Jones, Cosgrove, Allen *et al.* op. cit.

[9] P.F. Murray, A. Goede and J.L. Bada, 'Pleistocene human occupation at Beginner's Luck Cave, Florentine Valley, Tasmania'. *Archaeology and Physical Anthropology in Oceania*, vol. 15(3), 1980, pp. 142–52.

[10] J. Allen, R. Cosgrove and S. Brown, 'New archaeological data from the Southern Forest region, Tasmania: a preliminary statement'. *Australian Archaeology*, vol. 27, 1988, pp. 75–88.

[11] R. Cosgrove, 'Thirty thousand years of human colonization in Tasmania – new Pleistocene dates'. *Science*, 1988, in press.

[12] W.M. Blom, 'Late Quaternary sediments and sea-levels in Bass Basin, southeastern Australia – A preliminary report'. *Search*, vol. 19(2), 1988, pp. 94–6; J.H. Cann,

A.P. Belperio, V.A. Gostin and C.V. Murray-Wallace, 'Sea-level history, 45 000 to 30 000 yr B.P., inferred from Benthic Foraminifera, Gulf St. Vincent, South Australia'. *Quaternary Research*, vol. 29, 1988, pp. 153–75.

CHAPTER TEN KARTA: ISLAND OF THE DEAD

[1] N.B. Tindale and B.G. Maegraith, 'Traces of an extinct Aboriginal population on Kangaroo Island'. *Records of the S.A. Museum*, vol. 4, 1931, pp. 275–89.
[2] H.M. Hale and N.B. Tindale, 'Notes on some human remains in the Lower Murray Valley, South Australia'. *Records of the S.A. Museum*, vol. 4, 1930, pp. 145–218.
[3] K.L. Parker, *Australian Legendary Tales*. Bodley Head, 1978.
[4] R.M.W. Dixon, *The Djirbal language of North Queensland*. Cambridge, Cambridge University Press, 1972.
[5] R.J. Lampert. *The Great Kartan Mystery*. Terra Australia 5, Canberra, Prehistory Department, Australian National University, 1981.
[6] J.H. Hope, R.J. Lampert, E. Edmonson, M.J. Smith and G.F. Van Tets. 'Late Pleistocene faunal remains from Seton rock shelter, Kangaroo Island, South Australia'. *Journal of Biogeography*, vol. 4, 1977, pp. 363–85.
[7] R.J. Lampert, 'The Great Kartan Mystery'. PhD thesis, Australian National University, 1979.
[8] R.J. Lampert, 'A preliminary report on some waisted blades found on Kangaroo Island, S.A.' *Australian Archaeology*, vol. 2, 1975, pp. 45–8.
[9] F.D. McCarthy, *Australian Aboriginal stone implements*. Sydney, Australian Museum, 1976.
[10] N.B. Tindale in *Ecological Biogeography of Australia* (ed. A. Keast). 1981, pp. 1772–3.
[11] H.M. Cooper, 'Large archaeological stone implements from Hallett Cove, South Australia'. *Transactions of the Royal Society of S.A.*, vol. 82, 1959, pp. 55–60.
[12] H.A. Martin, 'Palynology and historical ecology of some cave excavations in the Australian Nullarbor'. *Australian Journal of Botany*, vol. 21, 1973, pp. 283–316.
[13] R.V.S. Wright (ed.), *Archaeology of the Gallus Site, Koonalda Cave*. Canberra, Australian Institute of Aboriginal Studies, 1971.
[14] G.L. Pretty, 'The cultural chronology of the Roonka Flat: a preliminary consideration', in *Stone Tools as Cultural Markers* (ed. R.V.S. Wright). 1977, pp. 288–331.

CHAPTER ELEVEN ART AND TECHNOLOGY

[1] C.E. Dortch, 1976, op. cit.
[2] L. Maynard, 'Classification and terminology in Australian rock art', in *Form in Indigenous Art* (ed. P.J. Ucko). 1977, pp. 387–402.
[3] C.P. Mountford and R. Edwards, 'Rock engravings of Panarmitee Station . . .' *Transactions of the Royal Society of South Australia*, vol. 86, 1963, pp. 131–46.
[4] R. Edwards, 'Art and Aboriginal Prehistory', in *Aboriginal Man and Environment in Australia* (eds D.J. Mulvaney and J. Golson). 1971, pp. 356–67; W.C. Dix, 'Facial representations in Pilbara rock engravings', in *Form in Indigenous Art* (ed. P.J. Ucko). 1977, pp. 277–85; *Aboriginal Australia*. Catalogue by Australian Gallery Directors Council, Sydney, Australian Museum, 1981, p. 69.
[5] N.B. Tindale, in *Ecological Biogeography of Australia* (ed. A. Keast), 1981, pp. 1767–8.
[6] R. Jones, in *Heritage of Australia* (Australian Heritage Commission), 1981, pp.

786–90; P.C. Sims. 'Aboriginal petroglyphic sites in Tasmania', in *Form in Indigenous Art* (ed. P.J. Ucko). 1977, pp. 432–8.

[7] R. Jones, in *Sunda and Sahul*, 1977, op. cit., and personal communication.

[8] P.C. Sims, 1977, op. cit.

[9] H. Hale and N.B. Tindale, 1930, op. cit.

[10] D.J. Mulvaney, *The Prehistory of Australia*. Ringwood, Penguin, 1975.

[11] P.J. Trezise, *Quinkan Country*. Sydney, A.H. & A.W. Reed, 1969; *Rock art of south-east Cape York*. Canberra, Australian Institute of Aboriginal Studies, 1971.

[12] R. Edwards, *Australian Aboriginal Art. The Art of the Alligator Rivers Region, Northern Territory*. Canberra, Australian Institute of Aboriginal Studies, 1979.

[13] G. Chaloupka, 'Aspects of the chronology and schematization of the prehistoric sites on the Arnhem Land Plateau', in *Form in Indigenous Art* (ed. P.J. Ucko). 1977, pp. 243–59.

[14] D.J. Lewis, 'More striped designs in Arnhem Land rock paintings'. *Archaeology and Physical Anthropology in Oceania*, vol. 12(2), 1977, pp. 98–111.

[15] I.M. Crawford, *The Art of the Wandjina: Aboriginal Cave Paintings in Kimberley, Western Australia*. Melbourne, Oxford University Press, 1968.

[16] R.V.S. Wright, 1971, op. cit. A film was made of the site called *Flint Miners of the Nullarbor*; an earlier film entitled *Under the Nullarbor* was narrated by geomorphologist Joe Jennings and directed by Ian Dunlop, well-known for his superb films about Aborigines such as *Desert People*.

[17] S.J. Hallam, 'Roof markings in the "Orchestra Shell" Cave, Wanneroo, near Perth, Western Australia'. *Mankind*, vol. 8, 1971, pp. 90–103.

[18] D. Dragovich, 'Minimum age of some desert varnish near Broken Hill, New South Wales', *Search*, vol. 17, 1986, pp. 149–51.

[19] M.F. Nobbs and R.I. Dorn, 'Age determinations for rock varnish formation within petroglyphs: cation-ratio dating of 24 motifs from the Olary region, South Australia. *Rock Art Research*, vol. 5(2), 1988, pp.108–124; R.I. Dorn, M.F. Nobbs and T.A. Cahill, 'Cation-ratio dating of rock engravings from the Olary province of arid South Australia', *Antiquity*, vol. 62(237), 1988, pp.681–9.

[20] R. Luebbers, 'Ancient boomerangs discovered in South Australia'. *Nature*, vol. 5486(253), 1975, p. 39.

[21] J. Dodson, 'Late Quaternary palaeoecology of Wyrie Swamp, southeastern S.A.' *Quaternary Research*, vol. 8, 1977, pp. 97–114.

[22] S. Bulmer in *Stone Tools as Cultural Markers* (ed. R.V.S. Wright). 1977; B. Hayden, *Palaeolithic reflections: Lithic technology and ethnographic excavations among Australian Aborigines*. Canberra, Australian Institute of Aboriginal Studies, 1979; R. Jones, 1979, op. cit., pp. 455–7.

[23] G. Singh, 1981, op. cit.

CHAPTER TWELVE EXTINCTION OF THE GIANT MARSUPIALS

[1] C.W. Peck, *Australian Legends*. Lothian, 1933.

[2] D.R. Horton and R.V.S. Wright, 'Cuts on Lancefield bones . . .' *Archaeology in Oceania*, vol. 16(2), 1981, pp. 78–9.

[3] J.W.H. Lowry and D. Merrilees, 'Age of a desiccated carcass of a thylacine from Thylacine Hole, Nullarbor Region, W.A.' *Helictite*, vol. 7, 1969, pp. 15–16.

[4] D.R. Horton, 'The great megafaunal extinction debate – 1879–1979'. *Artefact*, vol. 4, 1979, pp. 11–25; 'A review of the extinction question: man, climate and megafauna'. *Archaeology and Physical Anthropology in Oceania*, vol. 15(2), 1980, pp. 86–97.

[5] D.J. Mulvaney, 1975, op. cit.

[6] R. Jones, 1968, op. cit.; D. Merrilees, 'Man the destroyer: later Quaternary changes in the Australian marsupial fauna'. *Journal of the Royal Society of W.A.*, vol. 51, 1968, pp. 1–24.

[7] M. Archer; I.M. Crawford and D. Merrilees, 'Incisions, breakages and charring, probably man-made, in fossil bones from Mammoth Cave, Western Australia'. *Alcheringa*, vol. 4(1–2), 1980, pp. 115–31.

[8] N.B. Tindale, 'Archaeological site at Lake Menindee, N.S.W.' *Records of the S.A. Museum*, vol. 11, 1955, pp. 269–98.

[9] L.G. Marshall, 'Fossil vertebrate faunas from the Lake Victoria region, southwest N.S.W.' *Memoirs of the National Museum of Victoria*, vol. 34, 1973, pp. 151–71.

[10] R. Gillespie, D.R. Horton, P. Ladd, P.G. Macumber, T.H. Rich, A. Thorne and R.V.S. Wright, 'Lancefield Swamp and the extinction of the Australian megafauna'. *Science*, vol. 200, 1978, pp. 1044–8.

[11] D.R. Horton, 'Lancefield: the problem of proof in bone analysis'. *Artefact*, vol. 1(3), 1976, pp. 129–43; D.R. Horton and R.V.S. Wright, 1981, op. cit., pp. 73–80.

[12] P.S. Martin, 'The discovery of America'. *Science*, vol. 17, 1973, pp. 969–74; P.S. Martin and H.E. Wright, *Pleistocene Extinctions*. Newhaven, Yale University Press, 1967.

[13] P.P. Gorecki, D.R. Horton, N. Stern, R.V.S. Wright, 'Coexistence of humans and megafauna in Australia: improved stratified evidence'. *Archaeology in Oceania*, vol. 19(3), 1984, pp. 117–19.

CHAPTER THIRTEEN TASMANIA: EIGHT THOUSAND YEARS OF ISOLATION

[1] R. Jones, 'A speculative archaeological sequence for northwest Tasmania'. *Records of the Queen Victoria Museum, Launceston*, vol. 25, 1966, pp. 1–12; 'Rocky Cape and the problem of the Tasmanians'. PhD thesis, Sydney University, 1971, unpublished.

[2] R. Jones, in *Holier Than Thou* (ed. Ian Johnson). Canberra, Prehistory Department, Australian National University, 1980, pp. 161–7.

[3] R. Jones, 1977, op. cit.

[4] G.A. Robinson, journals edited by N.J.B. Plomley, 1966; see also L. Ryan, *The Aboriginal Tasmanians*. Brisbane, University of Queensland Press, 1968.

[5] R. Jones, 'Why did the Tasmanians stop eating fish?' in *Explorations in Ethnoarchaeology* (ed. R. Gould), Santa Fé, University of New Mexico Press, 1978, pp. 11–47.

[6] S.M. Colley and R. Jones, 'New fish bone data from Rocky Cape, north west Tasmania'. *Archaeology in Oceania*, vol. 22(2), 1987, pp. 67–71. See also Jones, ibid., pp. 26–7.

[7] R. Jones, 1966, op. cit.

[8] A.G. Thorne, 'The racial affinities and origins of the Australian Aborigines', in *Aboriginal Man and Environment in Australia* (eds D.J. Mulvaney and J. Golson). 1971, pp. 316–25.

[9] A.G. Wallace and G.A. Doran, 'Early man in Tasmania', in *The Origin of the Australians* (eds R.L. Kirk and A.G. Thorne). 1976, pp. 173–82.

[10] H. Lourandos, 'Dispersal of activities – the east Tasmanian Aboriginal sites'. *Papers and Records of the Royal Society of Tasmania*, vol. 2, 1968, pp. 41–6; 'Stone tools, settlement, adaptation: a Tasmanian example', in *Stone Tools as Cultural Markers* (ed. R.V.S. Wright). 1977, pp. 219–24.

[11] R.L. Vanderwal, 'Prehistory and the archaeology of Louisa Bay', in *The South West Book*. Melbourne, Australian Conservation Foundation, 1978, pp. 12–22.

[12] H.R. Allen, 'Left out in the cold: why the Tasmanians stopped eating fish'. *The Artefact*, vol. 4, 1979, pp. 1–10.

[13] R. Jones, 'Tasmania: aquatic machines and offshore islands', in *Problems in economic and social anthropology* (eds G. de G. Sieveking, I.H. Longworth and K.E. Wilson). London, Duckworth, 1976, pp. 235–63; 1977, op. cit.

[14] J. Stockton, 'Preliminary note on an Aboriginal stone alignment and associated features'. *Proceedings of the Royal Society of Tasmania*, vol. 111, 1977, pp. 181–3; and R.L. Jones, personal communication.

[15] L. Ryan, *The Aboriginal Tasmanians*. Brisbane, University of Queensland Press, 1981.

CHAPTER FOURTEEN   RISING SEAS AND CHANGE

[1] C.P. Mountford and A. Roberts, *The Dawn of Time*. Adelaide, Rigby, 1969.

[2] J. Isaacs, 1980, op. cit., p. 108.

[3] ibid., pp. 26, 115–16.

[4] C.P. Mountford and A. Roberts, 1969, op. cit., p. 18.

[5] M.J. Rowland, 'The Keppel Islands – preliminary investigations'. *Australian Archaeology*, vol. 11, 1980, pp. 1–7.

[6] W.E. Roth, *North Queensland Ethnography Bulletin*, no. 14, 1910, p. 4.

[7] R. Jones, 1976, op. cit., p. 260.

[8] N.B. Tindale, *Aboriginal tribes of Australia*. Canberra, Australian National University Press, 1974; for criticisms see *Tribes and Boundaries in Australia* (ed. N. Peterson). Canberra, Australian Institute of Aboriginal Studies, 1976.

[9] J.B. Birdsell, 'Some environmental and cultural factors influencing the structuring of Australian Aboriginal populations'. *American Naturalist*, vol. 87, 1953; pp. 171–207; 1957, op. cit.

[10] R.J. Lampert and P.J. Hughes, 'Sea level change and Aboriginal coastal adaptations in southern N.S.W.' *Archaeology and Physical Anthropology of Oceania*, vol. 9(3), 1974, pp. 226–35.

[11] I. McBryde, *Aboriginal prehistory in New England*. Sydney, Sydney University Press, 1974; J.M. Flood, 1980, op. cit.; A. Ross, 'Holocene environments and prehistoric site patterning in the Victorian Mallee'. *Archaeology in Oceania*, vol. 16(3), 1981, pp. 145–55.

[12] J. Flood, B. David, J. Magee and B. English, 'Birrigai: a Pleistocene site in the south-eastern highlands'. *Archaeology in Oceania*, vol. 22, 1987, pp. 9–26; M.A. Smith, 'Pleistocene occupation in arid Central Australia'. *Nature*, vol. 328, 1987, pp. 710–11.

[13] E.D. Stockton and W. Holland, 'Cultural sites and their environment in the Blue Mountains'. *Archaeology and Physical Anthropology in Oceania*, vol. 9, 1974, pp. 36–65; I. Johnson (ed.), *Holier than Thou*, 1979.

[14] N.B. Tindale, 'Archaeological excavation of Noola rock shelter'. *Records of the S.A. Museum*, vol. 14, 1961, pp. 193–6.

[15] F.D. McCarthy, 'The Archaeology of the Capertee Valley, N.S.W.' *Records of the Australian Museum*, vol. 26, 1964, pp. 197–246.

CHAPTER FIFTEEN   ARRIVAL OF THE DINGO

[1] J.P. White and J.F. O'Connell, 1979, op. cit.

[2] J.M. Flood, 'A point assemblage from the Northern Territory'. *Archaeology and Physical Anthropology in Oceania*, vol. 5(1), 1970, pp. 27–52.

[3] R.J. Lampert, 1971, op. cit; J. Kamminga, 'A functional investigation of Australian microliths'. *Artefact*, vol. 5(1), 1980, pp. 1–18.

[4] I. McBryde, 1974, op. cit., pp. 264–5.

[5] N. Peterson, 1976, op. cit.

[6] C. White, 'Plateau and Plain: Prehistoric investigations in Arnhem Land'. Unpublished PhD thesis, Australian National University, 1967.

[7] R.H. Pearce, 'Spatial and temporal distribution of Australian backed blades'. *Mankind*, vol. 9, 1974, pp. 300–9; D.J. Mulvaney, personal communication.

[8] E.D. Stockton, 'Review of early Bondaian dates'. *Mankind*, vol. 11, 1977, pp. 48–51.

[9] C.E. Dortch, 1977, op. cit.

[10] N.W.G. Macintosh, 'The origin of the dingo: an enigma', in *The Wild Canids* (ed. M.W. Fox). 1975, pp. 87–106; L.K. Corbett, 'Morphological comparisons of Australian and Thai dingoes: a reappraisal of dingo status distribution and ancestry'. *Proceedings of the Ecological Society of Australia*, vol. 13, 1985, pp. 277–91.

[11] R. Gould, *Living Archaeology*, 1980.

[12] A. Hamilton, 'Aboriginal Man's best friend?' *Mankind*, vol. 8(4), 1972, p. 292.

[13] R.M.W. Dixon, *The Languages of Australia*, 1980.

[14] J.P. White and J.F. O'Connell, 1979, op. cit., p. 26.

CHAPTER SIXTEEN HARVESTERS, ENGINEERS AND FIRE-STICK FARMERS

[1] M. Smith, 'Late Pleistocene Zamia Exploitation in Southern Western Australia', *Archaeology in Oceania*, vol. 17(3), 1982, pp. 117–21.

[2] J.M. Beaton, 'Fire and Water: aspects of Australian Aboriginal management of cycads', *Archaeology in Oceania*, vol. 17(1), 1982, pp. 51–9.

[3] M.J. Morwood, 'Archaeology of the Central Queensland Highland: the Stone Component'. *Archaeology in Oceania*, vol. 16(1), 1981, pp. 1–52.

[4] N.B. Tindale, 1961, op. cit.; F.D. McCarthy, 1964, op. cit.

[5] I. Johnson, 1979, op. cit.

[6] I. McBryde, 1974, op. cit.; S. Bowdler, 1981, op. cit.

[7] See references in J.M. Flood, 1980, op. cit.

[8] H. Lourandos, 'Aboriginal settlement and land use in southwestern Victoria'. *The Artefact*, vol. 1(4), 1976, pp. 174–9; 'Aboriginal spatial organization and population: southwestern Victoria reconsidered'. *Archaeology and Physical Anthropology in Oceania*, vol. 12(3), 1977; 'Change or stability? Hydraulics, hunter-gatherers and population in temperate Australia'. *World Archaeology*, vol. 11(3), 1980, pp. 245–64.

[9] P.J.F. Coutts *et al.*, 'Aboriginal engineers of the Western District, Victoria'. *Records of the Victorian Archaeological Survey*, vol. 7, 1978.

[10] R. Jones, 'Hunters in the Australian coastal savanna', in *Human ecology in savanna environments* (ed. D.R. Harris). 1980, pp. 128–9.

[11] P.J.F. Coutts, personal communication; the *Age*, 29 January 1981, p. 11.

[12] Quoted in H. Lourandos, 1980, op. cit.

[13] P.J.F. Coutts *et al.*, 'The mound people of Western Victoria'. *Records of the Victorian Archaeological Survey*, vol. 1, 1976.

[14] A. Ross, 1981, op. cit.

[15] H.A. Martin, 1973, op. cit.

[16] R.J. Lampert, 1971, op. cit.

[17] R.J. Lampert, 'An excavation at Durras North, N.S.W.' *Archaeology and Physical Anthropology in Oceania*, vol. 1, 1966, pp. 83–118.

[18] J.V.S. Megaw (ed.), *The Recent Archaeology of the Sydney district. Excavations 1964–7*. Canberra, Australian Institute of Aboriginal Studies, 1974, pp. 1–12.

[19] See references in S. Bowdler, 1976, op. cit., and R. Lawrence, *Aboriginal Habitat and Economy*, 1968.

[20] I. McBryde, 1974, op. cit. pp. 284–92; *Coast and Estuary*, 1982, pp. 1–50.

[21] R. Jones, 'Fire-stick farming'. *Australian Natural History*, vol. 16, 1969, pp. 224–8; S. Hallam, *Fire and Hearth*, 1975; N.B. Tindale, 1959, op. cit.

[22] R. Gould, 1980, op. cit., p. 81.

[23] ibid., p. 82.

CHAPTER SEVENTEEN THE QUESTION OF AGRICULTURE

[1] J. Golson, 'No room at the top: agricultural intensification in the New Guinea highlands', in *Sunda and Sahul* (eds J. Allen, J. Golson and R. Jones). 1977, pp. 601–38.

[2] D. Walker (ed.), *Bridge and Barrier: the natural and cultural history of Torres Strait*. Canberra, Department of Biogeography and Geomorphology, Australian National University, 1972; J. Allen, J. Golson and R. Jones (eds), *Sunda and Sahul*, 1977; D. Moore, *Islanders and Aborigines at Cape York*, 1979.

[3] R.L. Vanderwal, 'The Torres Strait: prehistory and beyond'. *Occasional Papers of the Anthropology Museum, University of Queensland*, vol. 2, 1973, pp. 157–94.

[4] R.V.S. Wright, 1971, op. cit.; G.N. Bailey, 'Shell mounds, shell middens, and raised beaches in the Cape York Peninsula'. *Mankind*, vol. 11, 1977, pp. 132–43.

[5] F.D. McCarthy, 'Comparison of the Prehistory of Australia with that of Indo-China . . .' *Proceedings of 3rd Congress of Prehistorians, Far East*, Singapore, 1940, pp. 23–52.

[6] See articles by Moore, Wurm and Kirk in *Bridge and Barrier* (ed. D. Walker). 1972.

[7] See D.J. Mulvaney, 1975, op. cit. for a full account of the Macassans, and C. MacKnight, 'Macassans and Aborigines'. *Oceania*, vol. 42, 1972, pp. 283–321.

[8] J. Golson, 'Australian Aboriginal food plants . . .', in *Aboriginal Man and Environment in Australia* (eds D.J. Mulvaney and J. Golson). 1971, pp. 196–238; 1977, op. cit.

[9] N. Wace, in *Bridge and Barrier* (ed. D. Walker). 1972.

[10] R. Jones, 'The Neolithic, Palaeolithic and the hunting gardeners: man and land in the antipodes', in *Quaternary Studies: selected papers from IX INQUA Congress*, Bulletin 13, Royal Society of New Zealand, Wellington, 1975, pp. 21–34; 1977, op. cit.; B. Meehan, 'Man does not live by calories alone: the role of shellfish in a coastal cuisine', in *Sunda and Sahul*, op. cit., 1977, pp. 493–53; 'Hunters by the seashore'. *Journal of Human Evolution*, vol. 6(4), 1977, pp. 363–70.

[11] R. Jones, 1980, op. cit., p. 23.

[12] H.R. Allen, 'The Bagundji of the Darling basin: cereal gatherers in an uncertain environment'. *World Archaeology*, vol. 5, 1974, pp. 309–22.

[13] T.L. Mitchell, *Three Expeditions into the Interior of Eastern Australia*. London, Boone, vol. 1, 1839, pp. 238–9, 290–1.

[14] See references in H. Allen, 1974, op. cit.

[15] F.R. Irvine, 'Evidence of change in the vegetable diet of Australian Aborigines', in *Diprotodon to Detribalization* (eds A.R. Pilling and R.A. Waterman). 1970, p. 280.

[16] K.N.G. Simpson and R. Blackwood, 'An Aboriginal cache of fresh water mussels at Lake Victoria, N.S.W.' *Memoirs of the National Museum of Victoria*, vol. 34, 1973, pp. 217–18.

[17] R. Kimber, 'Beginnings of farming?', *Mankind*, vol. 10(3), 1976, pp. 142–50.

[18] R. Gould, 1980, op. cit., pp. 65–6.

[19] C. Sturt, *Two expeditions into the Interior of Southern Australia*. London, Smith Elder, vol. 1, 1833, pp. 54–5.

[20] H.R. Allen, 1974, op. cit., p. 313.

[21] R. Gould, 1980, op. cit., pp. 6–28, 68–9.

[22] B. Meehan, 1977, op. cit.

[23] R. Gould, 1980, p. 64.

[24] Beaglehole, J.C. (ed.), *The Journals of Captain James Cook on his Voyages of Discovery*. London, Hakluyt Society, 1955, 1967, p. 399.

CHAPTER EIGHTEEN THE LAST THOUSAND YEARS: TRADE, RELIGION AND ART

[1] G. Aiston, 'The Aboriginal narcotic pitcheri'. *Oceania*, vol. 7, 1937, pp. 372–7; P. Watson, *This Precious Foliage; A Study of the Aboriginal Psycho-active Drug Pituri*. Oceania Monograph no. 26, 1983, University of Sydney.

[2] D.J. Mulvaney, 'The chain of connection', in *Tribes and Boundaries in Australia* (ed. N. Peterson). 1976, pp. 72–94.

[3] I. McBryde, 'Wil-im-ee Moor-ring: or where do axes come from?' *Mankind*, vol. 11(3), 1978, pp. 354–82.

[4] P.J.F. Coutts and R. Miller, *The Mt William Archaeological Area*. Melbourne, Victorian Archaeological Survey, 1977.

[5] I. McBryde and A. Watchman, 'The distribution of greenstone axes in southeastern Australia: a preliminary report'. *Mankind*, vol. 10(3), 1976, pp. 163–74.

[6] R.A. Binns and I. McBryde, *A petrological analysis of ground-edge artefacts from northern New South Wales*. 1972.

[7] G.A. Robinson, op. cit., 1966 edn, pp. 600–601, 688, 903–5.

[8] Excavated by I.M. Crawford, Western Australian Museum (unpublished).

[9] D.J. Mulvaney, 1975, op. cit., p. 114.

[10] ibid., plate 78.

[11] F.D. McCarthy, 'Catalogue of the Aboriginal relics of New South Wales. Part III. Carved trees or dendroglyphs'. *Mankind*, vol. 3(7), 1945, pp. 199–206; D. Bell, 'Aboriginal carved trees in New South Wales – a Survey Report'. National Parks and Wildlife Service of New South Wales (unpublished), 1981.

[12] The book *Heritage of Australia* by the Australian Heritage Commission (Macmillan, 1981) includes descriptions and photographs of Yuranigh's grave and many other significant Aboriginal sites.

[13] R. Jones, 'The Tasmanian paradox', in *Stone Tools as Cultural Markers*, op. cit., 1977, pp. 191–204.

[14] See, for example, R.M. Berndt and E.S. Phillips, *The Australian Aboriginal Heritage*. 1973; F.D. McCarthy, *Australian Aboriginal Rock Art*. 1979.

[15] B.J. Wright, *Rock Art of the Pilbara Region: North-West Australia*. Canberra, Australian Institute of Aboriginal Studies, 1968.

[16] L. Maynard, personal communication.

[17] R. Edwards, 1979, op. cit.; G. Chaloupka, 1977, op. cit.

[18] M.C. Quinell, 'Schematisation and naturalism in the rock art of south central Queensland', in *Form in Indigenous Art* (ed. P.J. Ucko). 1977, pp. 414–17; M.J. Morwood, 'Time, Space and Prehistoric Art: a Principal Components Analysis'. *Archaeology and Physical Anthropology in Oceania*, vol. 15(2), 1980, pp. 98–109.

GLOSSARY

absolute//relative age	An absolute date applies to a specific time in calendar or radiocarbon years, whereas a relative age only indicates whether an item is younger or older than other items.
adze	Stone tool used as a wood-working 'chisel', usually mounted in a handle.
agriculture/domestication	Practice of cultivating the soil and bringing animals under human control.
anthropology	Study of the human species.
anthropomorph	Attribution of human form to a non-human figure.
archaeology	Study of the material traces of the human past.
archaic//modern	Early or primitive in contrast to late or recent characteristics.
artefact	Any object made by human agency (also spelt artifact).
assemblage	Set of artefacts found in close association with each other.
awl	A small pointed bone tool used for puncturing skin, hides etc.
axe/hatchet	A stone chopping tool, usually with a ground cutting edge.
axe-blank	A stone shaped to the form of an axe but not sharpened, flaked or ground.
axe-grinding grooves	Grooves left in friable stone, such as sandstone, by rubbing an axe to produce a ground cutting edge.
backed blade	A blade with one margin deliberately blunted to form a penknife-like back.

bifacially trimmed	An artefact worked on both faces.
bipoint	A bone artefact fashioned to a point at both ends.
blade	A parallel-sided flake, at least twice as long as it is wide.
Bondi point	An asymmetric, small triangular blade with a thick, trimmed back.
bora ground	A ceremonial ground usually consisting of two earth-banked rings linked by a pathway.
bulb of percussion	The rounded swelling left on the inner face of a flake or blade directly below the point of impact on the striking platform.
canoe tree	A tree scarred by removal of a large sheet of bark to make a canoe.
carrying capacity of land	The number of people an area of land can support.
chert	A fine-grained crystalline aggregate of silica, with excellent fracturing properties, producing good cutting edges on stone tools. Similar to flint, agate, chalcedony and jasper.
chipping/flaking floor	A workshop area covered in stone debris from the manufacture of stone tools.
chopper/chopping tool	A large heavy core tool used for chopping.
composite tool	An artefact consisting of two or more parts, such as small tools hafted onto a handle.
conchoidal fracture	Shell-like, curved surface with ripple marks formed in certain types of rock fracture.
core	A lump or nodule of stone from which flakes have been removed.
core tool	A core bearing trimming or use-wear indicating its use as an implement.
culture	(a) The distinctive and complex system of technology, social organization and ideology developed by a group of human beings to adapt to their environment.
	(b) An archaeological 'culture' is an assemblage of artefacts which recurs consistently with a limited distribution in space and time.

Dreamtime	The time when Ancestral Beings – some human and some animal – travelled the country creating the form of the landscape. The era of creation.
dugout	A canoe made of a hollowed-out log.
elouera	Triangular-sectioned stone backed blade, resembling an orange segment in shape.
ethnoarchaeology/living archaeology	The study by archaeologists of the economy and material cultue of living human societies to illuminate the past.
ethnography	Writings about local indigenous people.
experimental archaeology	The replication by archaeologists of past artefacts and activities in order to gain a greater understanding of the past.
fire-stick	A smouldering stick carried by Aboriginal groups when travelling.
flake	A piece of stone detached by striking a core with another stone.
fluorine analysis	Fluorine analysis allows archaeologists to determine the *relative* age of buried bones. These progressively absorb fluorine from the groundwater, so the fluorine content within bones increases with age. The fluorine content of bones from an archaeological site can be measured and compared, giving an idea of the relative age of the bones.
geometric microlith	A microlith of triangular, trapezoidal or other geometric shape, with an abruptly trimmed thick margin.
geomorphology	Study of the superficial form of the earth's surface.
gracile//robust	Lightly built and thin-boned in contrast to strongly built, thick-boned human.
grinding	Simple manual abrasion, as in rubbing an axe on sandstone to produce a ground cutting edge.
grindstone	Millstone for grinding up ochre, seeds, fruits or other foodstuffs.
ground-edge tool	Tool with a sharp cutting edge at one end produced by grinding rather than flaking.

hafting	The process of mounting an artefact in a handle or onto another artefact, for example, hafted axe, a stone point hafted onto a spear.
hammer-dressing	See pecking.
hammerstone	A lump of stone or river pebble used in fashioning small stone tools or pounding up foodstuffs.
hearth	The site of a campfire represented by ash, charcoal, discoloration, and possibly hearth stones around it.
Holocene	Recent geological time period, covering the last 10 000 years.
hominids	Both extinct and modern forms of man.
horsehoof core	High-backed, steep-edged stone core, typical of the old Australian core tool and scraper tradition.
ice age	Period of cold climate and a series of glaciations, spanning the Pleistocene period.
industry	An assemblage of artefacts including the same tool types so consistently as to suggest that it is the product of a single society.
in situ	Undisturbed in its original position.
interglacial	A warm interlude between two glaciations.
Kartan	A large tool industry characterized by horsehoof cores, hammerstones, pebble tools and scrapers.
lunette	A crescent-shaped dune of sand or clay found on the lee side of some Pleistocene lakes.
macropods	The animal family Macropodidae, meaning long-feet and including herbivorous marsupials such as kangaroos and wallabies.
material culture	The tangible objects produced by a society.
megafauna	Large extinct animals and birds, especially large variants of present kangaroos and wombats.

microlith	A small stone artefact, less than 3 centimetres in its maximum dimension.
midden	Prehistoric refuse heap, usually composed of shells.
Neolithic	The period in which food production commenced.
ochre	Consolidated earth, made up of clay and hydrated oxide of iron, used to make red or yellow pigment.
open campsite	A surface scatter of stone and/or other artefacts lying exposed on the surface of the land.
outrigger	A log or similar spar fixed parallel to a canoe to stabilize it.
oven	A shallow depression in the ground, containing ash and charcoal and lined with stones or lumps of baked clay. Ovens were used for roasting large animals.
palaeontology	Study of the fossil remains of animals.
palaeomagnetism	Study of fossil remnant magnetism acquired by ancient materials, such as baked earth and clay from prehistoric fireplaces.
pebble tool	Chopping tool made by flaking one or both faces of a large river 'pebble' or cobble.
pecking/hammer-dressing	The production of small pits or indentations on the surface of a rock by striking it with a hammerstone.
physical anthropology	Study of the physical nature of mankind, especially human fossil remains.
pirri point	Small, stone point, finely trimmed on one surface, generally used as a spear tip.
Pleistocene	Glacial epoch preceding the Holocene, extending back from 10 000 to about two million years ago.
pollen analysis/palynology	Study of pollen, especially ancient pollen, in connection with plant geography and vegetation history.
population density	The number of people in a region, usually expressed as an average people/land ratio, for example, 1 person to 20 square kilometres.

post-cranial bones	The human skeleton except for the cranium (skull).
prau	Malay-type boat with a distinctive large triangular sail and canoe-like outrigger, used by Macassans.
prehistory	The story of human development before the time of written records.
pressure-flaking	Shaping a stone by pressing off small thin flakes with a bone or wooden tool.
projectile point	Stone point mounted on a spear.
quartz	Common white stone with naturally sharp edges but generally poor fracturing properties, varying from clear and crystalline to milky or reddish in colour.
quartzite	A very hard, homogeneous, medium- to coarse-grained stone with good fracturing properties. Red, brown, grey, buff or yellow.
Quaternary	The period embracing both the Pleistocene and Holocene.
radiocarbon dating	The method of dating organic fossil remains based on their content of the radioactive isotope carbon 14 (C-14) (See chapter 1).
retouch (secondary)	Flaking or trimming of a stone artefact after detachment from a core, usually by trimming or re-sharpening the edges.
rockshelter	A naturally formed hollow or overhang in a more or less vertical rock face.
rolled artefact	Smoothed by water, sand and gravel action in a creek or river bed or on a river terrace or beach.
sclerophyll forest	Eucalypt-dominated forest.
scraper	Stone tool made on a flake, with one or more working edges, generally used for chiselling, cutting, gouging or planing wood.
secondary working	See retouch.
site (archaeological)	A place where past human activity is identifiable.

stratigraphy/stratification   Layering of sediments and/or occupational debris. A well-stratified occupation site has clear boundaries or breaks between successive horizons (layers) of occupational material.

striking platform   The area on a stone core on which a blow is struck to detach a flake. The detached flake bears on its butt end part of the original striking platform.

talus slope   The slope at the foot of a cliff or below a rockshelter, often covered with scree (rock debris).

toolkit   A set of artefacts.

totemism   System of relationships that provides spiritual linkages between people and the natural and physical universe.

tribe   Major Aboriginal social and kinship group, possessing a common language, identity, culture and territory.

type/diagnostic artefact   Artefact with a wide distribution in space but a restricted one in time, useful for correlating cultural sequences over large areas and for cross-dating.

unifacially trimmed   An artefact worked on only one face.

unipoint   Bone point worked at one end only.

use-polish/wear   Glaze or wear produced on the working edge of a tool from use.

x-ray art   A colourful and stylized art style of northern Australia showing internal anatomical details of animals, birds, fish and occasionally humans.

FURTHER READING

ALLEN, J., GOLSON, J. and JONES, R. (eds) *Sunda and Sahul, Prehistoric Studies in South East Asia, Melanesia and Australia.* London, Academic Press, 1977.

AUSTRALIAN HERITAGE COMMISSION. *The Heritage of Australia.* Melbourne, Macmillan, 1981.

AUSTRALIAN NATIONAL ADVISORY COMMITTEE FOR UNESCO. *Australian Aboriginal Culture.* Canberra, Australian Government Publishing Service, 1973.

BERNDT, R.M. and C.H. *The World of the First Australians. Aboriginal traditional life: past and present.* Aboriginal Studies Press, 1988; Canberra.

BERNDT, R.M. and PHILLIPS, E.S. *The Australian Aboriginal Heritage.* Sydney, Ure Smith, 1973.

BLAINEY, G. *Triumph of the Nomads. A History of Ancient Australia.* Melbourne, Sun Books, 1975.

BOWDLER, S. (ed.) *Coastal Archaeology in Eastern Australia.* Canberra, Department of Prehistory, Australian National University, 1982.

CONNAH, G. (ed.) *Australian Field Archaeology: a guide to techniques.* Canberra, Australian Institute of Aboriginal Studies, 1982.

DICKSON, F.P. *Australian Stone Hatchets.* London, Academic Press, 1982.

DIXON, R.M.W. *The Languages of Australia.* Melbourne, Cambridge University Press, 1980.

EDWARDS, R. *Aboriginal Bark Canoes of the Murray Valley.* Adelaide, Rigby, 1972.

— *Australian Aboriginal Art. The Art of the Alligator Rivers Region, Northern Territory.* Canberra, Australian Institute of Aboriginal Studies, 1979.

ELKIN, A.P. *The Australian Aborigines. How to Understand Them.* Sydney, Angus and Robertson, 1964.

FLOOD, J.M. *The Moth Hunters: Aboriginal Prehistory of the Australian Alps.* Canberra, Australian Institute of Aboriginal Studies, 1980.

— *The Riches of Ancient Australia.* Brisbane, University of Queensland Press, 1990.

GIBBS, R.M. *The Aborigines*. Hawthorn, Longman, 1974.

GOULD, R.A. *Living Archaeology*. New York, Cambridge University Press, 1980.

HAIGH, C. and GOLDSTEIN, W. (eds) *The Aborigines of New South Wales*. Sydney, N.S.W. National Parks and Wildlife Service, 1980.

HALLAM, S.J. *Fire and Hearth*. Canberra, Australian Institute of Aboriginal Studies, 1975.

HAYDEN, B. *Palaeolithic Reflections: Lithic Technology and Ethnographic Excavations among Australian Aborigines*. Canberra, Australian Institute of Aboriginal Studies, 1979.

HENDERSON, K.R. (ed.) *From Earlier Fleets: An Aboriginal Anthology*. Hemisphere, 1978.

ISAACS, J. (ed.) *Australian Dreaming. 40 000 Years of Aboriginal History*. Sydney, Lansdowne Press, 1980.

JONES, R. (ed.) *Archaeological Research in Kakadu National Park*. Canberra, Australian National Parks and Wildlife Service, Special Publication 13, 1985.

KIRK, R.L. and THORNE, A.G. (eds) *The Origin of the Australians*. Canberra, Australian Institute of Aboriginal Studies, 1976.

LAWRENCE, R. *Aboriginal Habitat and Economy*. Canberra, Geography Department, Australian National University, 1968.

MADDOCK, K. *The Australian Aborigines*. Ringwood, Penguin, 1982 (2nd edn).

MCBRYDE, I. *Aboriginal Prehistory of New England*. Sydney, Sydney University Press, 1974.

— *Coast and Estuary. Archaeological investigations on the north coast of New South Wales. Wombah and Schnapper Point*. Canberra, Australian Institute of Aboriginal Studies, 1982.

MCCARTHY, F.D. *Australian Aboriginal Stone Implements*. Sydney, Australian Museum, 1979.

MASSOLA, A. *The Aborigines of South-eastern Australia as they were*. Richmond, Heinemann, 1971.

MEEHAN, B. *Shell Bed to Shell Midden*. Canberra, Australian Institute of Aboriginal Studies, 1982.

MEEHAN, B. and R. JONES (eds), *Archaeology with Ethnography: an Australian Perspective*. Canberra, Department of Prehistory, Australian National University, 1988.

MITCHELL, S.R. *Stone-Age Craftsmen*. Melbourne, Tait Book Co., 1949.

MOORE, D.R. *Islanders and Aborigines at Cape York*. Canberra, Australian Institute of Aboriginal Studies, 1979.

MULVANEY, D.J. *The Prehistory of Australia*. Ringwood, Penguin, 1975.

MULVANEY, D.J. and GOLSON, J. (eds) *Aboriginal Man and Environment in Australia*. Canberra, Australian National University Press, 1971.

MULVANEY, D.J. and WHITE, J.P. (eds) *Australians: a Historical Library. Australians to 1788.* Sydney, Fairfax, Syme and Weldon Associates, 1987.

PETERSON, N. (ed.) *Tribes and Boundaries in Australia.* Canberra, Australian Institute of Aboriginal Studies, 1976.

ROBERTS, A. and MOUNTFORD, C.P. *The Dreamtime.* 1965; *The Dawn of Time.* 1969; *The First Sunrise.* 1971. Adelaide, Rigby.

RYAN, L. *The Aboriginal Tasmanians.* Brisbane, University of Queensland Press, 1981.

SMITH, M. (ed.) *Archaeology at ANZAAS 1983.* Perth, Anthropology Department, Western Australian Museum, 1983.

THORNE, A. and RAYMOND, R. *Man on the Rim.* Sydney, Angus and Robertson, 1989.

TINDALE, N.B. *Aboriginal Tribes of Australia.* Australian National University Press, 1974.

UCKO, P.J. (ed.) *Form in Indigenous Art.* Canberra, Australian Institute of Aboriginal Studies, 1977.

WALKER, D. (ed.) *Bridge and Barrier: the Natural and Cultural History of Torres Strait.* Canberra, Department of Biogeography and Geomorphology, Australian National University, 1972.

WARD, G.K. (ed.) *Archaeology at ANZAAS Canberra.* Canberra, Canberra Archaeological Society, Department of Prehistory and Anthropology, Australian National University, 1985.

WHITE, J.P. *Before the White Man. Aboriginal Life in Prehistoric Australia.* Sydney, Reader's Digest, 1974.

WHITE, J.P. and O'CONNELL, J. *A Prehistory of Australia, New Guinea and Sahul.* London, Academic Press, 1982.

WRIGHT, R.V.S. (ed.) *Stone Tools as Cultural Markers: Change, Evolution and Complexity.* Canberra, Australian Institute of Aboriginal Studies, 1977.

INDEX

Tindale, N.B. 79, 121-2, 127, 269, 271, 274, 290
Titan's Shelter, Tas. 163
Tiwi people 207, 253
tobacco (pituri) 233, 247
Toolondo eel traps, Vic. 197, 215, 218
Torres Strait 29, 64, 230, 232-3, 235, 240, 242
totem/totemism 251-3, 287
trade/exchange 198, 213, 218, 233-4, 246-7, 248, 249, 261
Trefoil Island, Tas. 181
trepang (bêche de mer, sea-slug) 232, 234-5
Trezise, P. 81, 137, 275
tribe 191-3, 213, 287
Truganini 188
tubers see vegetable food
Tumut Valley, N.S.W. 213, 242
turtles 230, 232
Tyimede Shelters, N.T. 197, 204, 266

Ubirr, N.T. 141
Uluru 251
unifacial flaking 17, 130, 196, 287
Upper Swan River site see Swan River
use-wear see stone tools

Vanderwal, R. 184
vegetable food/resources 175, 179, 193, 223, 235-44
    bracken roots 175, 214, 217, 223, 224, 244
    bulrush roots 237
    bunya bunya nuts 240
    coconuts 235
    convolvulus 217
    daisy yams (Microseris scapigera) 212, 214, 217
    figs 241
    flax 237
    fruit trees 236-7
    grass seeds 50, 52, 78, 154, 237-8, 240, 244, 256
    grass-tree pith 175, 224, 244
    kurrajong seeds 212, 213
    Macrozamia nuts (cycads) 208, 210-12, 218, 240, 261
    mangrove fruits 230
    millet (Panicum decompositum) 179, 237-9, 242
    mulga 244
    pandanus 83
    Pimelio 213
    quandong fruit 241
    Solanum fruit 225, 241
    spinifex 201, 225
    tubers 30, 175, 237, 240
    wattle seeds 237

western 214-9
yams 30, 143, 145, 179, 230, 235-6, 240, 244, 261
vegetation history 102, 103, 104-5, 223-5
Victoria 21-3, 64, 65, 162, 178, 194, 210, 212, 246, 255
villages 180-1, 215-16, 217
Vinnicombe, P. 254
volcanoes 37, 123

Wahgi Valley, P.N.G. 229
waisted artefacts 39, 64, 65, 126, 127, 130, 153
Walgalu tribe 242
Walkunder Arch Cave, Qld 32, 82-3, 264
wallabies 25, 27, 51, 81, 83, 88, 90, 113-15, 119, 120, 140, 159, 168, 178, 179, 220, 231, 234
Wallace, A. R. 33, 234
Wallacia 34
Wallen Wallen Creek, Qld 98-9
Walsh, G. 142, 155, 254
Wandjina spirits 29, 142, 155, 254-5
Wargata Mina, Tas. 116-7
Watchman, A. 249, 280
watercraft 35, 36, 37, 39, 122, 124, 125, 184, 186, 187, 191, 208, 221, 232, 240, 259
    dugout canoes 233, 235, 283
    outrigger canoes 208, 232-3, 285
    swimming logs 191, 192
Wattamolla Cove, N.S.W. 221, 267
Webb, S. 66, 118
Weipa middens, Qld 197, 231-2, 266
Wellington Caves, N.S.W. 159
Wepowie Creek, S.A. 126
West Point midden, Tas. 69, 180-2
Western Australia 29, 36, 71, 87-94, 149, 163, 193, 204, 205, 241, 244, 246, 251
Western Australian Museum 87, 162, 251, 256
whales 256
White, C. 86, 271, 278
White, J. P. 9, 268, 269, 290
Wildman River, N.T. 84
Wilgie Mia ochre mine, W.A. 197, 249-50, 251
Willandra Lakes, N.S.W. 32, 41, 42, 43, 46, 50-2, 74, 78, 83, 154, 165-6, 195, 239
    Willandra Lakes hominid 50, 67-8, 74, 158
Wilson's Promontory middens, Vic. 197
Wiradjuri people 252
witchetty grubs 244
Wombah midden, N.S.W. 164, 197, 221, 266
wombats 25, 51, 109, 161
women's role 44-5, 52, 181-2, 221-2, 236, 244, 249, 256